THE
DC-3
50 YEARS OF LEGENDARY FLIGHT

THE
DC-3
50 YEARS OF LEGENDARY FLIGHT
PETER M. BOWERS

AERO
A division of TAB BOOKS
Blue Ridge Summit, PA 17214

Other TAB books by the Author

No. 2384   *Unconventional Aircraft*
No. 2424   *A Complete Guide to Aviation Photography—2nd Edition*

FIRST EDITION
FOURTH PRINTING

© 1986 by TAB BOOKS
TAB BOOKS is a division of McGraw-Hill, Inc.

Library of Congress Cataloging-in-Publication Data

Bowers, Peter M.
    The DC-3 : 50 years of legendary flight.

    Includes index.
    1. Douglas DC-3 (Transport plane)   I. Title.
TL686.D65B69   1986   387.7'3343   86-1899
ISBN 0-8306-8194-9 (pbk.)

TAB BOOKS offers software for sale. For information and a catalog, please
contact TAB Software Department, Blue Ridge Summit, PA 17294-0850.

Questions regarding the content of this book should be addressed to:

    Reader Inquiry Branch
    TAB BOOKS
    Blue Ridge Summit, PA 17294-0214

Contents

Acknowledgments

I wish to acknowledge the following people who helped directly in the preparation of this book:

Hideya Ando
Harold Andrews
Robert E. Beechler
Peter Berry
Dustin W. Carter
Don Downie
Harry Gann,
   McDonnell Douglas
W.J. Kantzer, FAA
Gary Killion, FAA
Kent Kistler
William T. Larkins
Harvey Lippencott,
   United Technologies

David W. Menard
Clarence Miller
Kenneth M. Molson
James A. Morrow
Arthur Pearcy
Alain Pelletier
Milo Peltzer
Victor D. Seely
Jay Spenser, NASM
Jim Sullivan
Mary Sutlovich, FAA
Nick Wantiez, FAA
Gordon S. Williams

About the Photographs

Most of the DC-3 photographs used in this book have been collected by me over a period of 45 years, with a few being sought out in 1985 specifically to fill gaps in DC-3 history for this book.

Sources vary greatly. Some have been obtained from Douglas, the U.S. armed forces, or DC-3 operators. When such photos are used, they are credited to Douglas in spite of the present firm name of McDonnell Douglas, or USAF for U.S. Air Force in spite of previous identity as U.S. Army Air Corps (to 1941) or U.S. Army Air Forces (to 1947).

Many of the photos are printed from original negatives in my files. When the negative has been obtained from another collector who was the photographer, the printed photo is credited to him. I apologize to those photographers who may find their photos miscredited. Original negatives often pass through several hands, so determining the actual photographer several decades after the fact is not always possible. Prints obtained from other collectors but not taken by them are credited "courtesy of . . . "

The DC-3 drawing that appears at chapter headings is from the letterhead of Arthur Pearcy, eminent DC-3 historian and a contributor to this book. The other drawings, except Appendix Figs. A-2 and A-3, which were provided by Harry Gann of Douglas, are by Clarence Miller of Seattle, Washington.

Front Cover

Top: C-47-DL 41-18385 and others tow Waco CG-4A gliders on a training mission in the United States early in 1943. Note how easily the white nylon tow lines can be seen. (courtesy Douglas Aircraft Co.)

Center Left: The first American turbine-powered DC-3 to use other than Rolls-Royce "Dart" engines is the DC-3 Turbo Express. It was developed by the U.S. Aircraft Corporation using Canadian Pratt & Whitney PT-6A engines. (courtesy The Western Flyer)

Center Right: This 1939 American Airlines photograph shows the airline's markings. Note the color on the trailing edges of the wings and tail. The American Airlines' house pennant is visible above the copilot's side of the cockpit. (courtesy American Airlines)

Bottom Left: Aero Virgin Islands acquired DC-3C N100SD, formerly C-47A-20-DK 42-92291, in September, 1979. Note the elongated rear cabin window and the rare change from P&W Twin Wasp to Wright Cyclone engines. (photograph by Arthur P. Dowd)

Bottom Right: Because the orange "Day-Glo" coloring adopted for increased visibility faded badly, it was replaced by regular nonfluorescent orange in the late 1960s, as shown on this C-117D. Note the use of the last three digits of Navy serial 50782 on the nose and four digits on the tail. (Peter M. Bowers collection)

Introduction

This book was written to commemorate the 50th anniversary of the introduction of the world's most successful airplane design, the Douglas DC-3. Its first flight was made on December 17, 1935, 32 years to the day after the Wright Brothers opened the age of powered flight at Kitty Hawk in 1903. The last of 10,655 DC-3s was delivered in May 1946.

At the end of a full half-century, the DC-3 is still in civil and military service worldwide. There are some airplanes still flying today that are a few years older than the DC-3, but they are mostly treasured antiques flown for nostalgia, not day-to-day workhorses earning their keep in significant numbers. At this writing, there are 612 DC-3s (to apply the single designation to all variants) on the U.S. civil register, and Douglas estimates that between 1500 and 2000 are active throughout the world.

The 50-year story of the DC-3 is not one that can be told as a simple month-by-month chronology. There are many separate DC-3 stories, some running consecutively, some in parallel, and many overlapping. This book treats each story separately.

To avoid needless repetition, some information appearing in one part of the book is referred to from other parts. As a further simplification, the U.S. government regulatory agency concerned with aircraft licensing, at various times the Bureau of Air Commerce, the Civil Aeronautics Authority, and currently the Federal Aviation Administration (FAA), is referred to simply as *FAA* regardless of the time period under discussion.

Although World War II was responsible for the unprecedented production of the military version of the DC-3, the U.S. Army C-47 (which the British named "Dakota"), the DC-3 had already become the world's most numerous civil transport before that war broke out. The DC-3/C-47 went on to perform truly legendary feats of airlift during the war and resumed its prewar role as the world's most widely used airliner for several years afterward. Subsequent wars saw the C-47 reprising its World War II roles and taking on unexpected new ones.

Although there have been many attempts to replace the DC-3, none have fully succeeded. Its unique balance of capacity, performance, and operating cost permit it to perform certain commercial roles that no other design can match. This book should confirm for the reader the statement that has been true for many years:

"The only replacement for a DC-3 is another DC-3."

Chapter 1

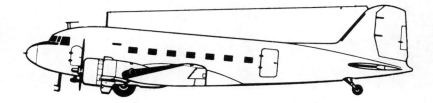

Transport Evolution
and Revolution

Soon after the end of World War I in November 1918, the European nations, former belligerents and neutrals alike, began to develop a network of airlines that covered the continent. At first the aircraft used were surplus military models quickly stripped of their arms and refitted with passenger seats. The larger models that could accommodate the passengers entirely within the fuselage instead of in open cockpits soon took on the appearance of railroad coaches, with rows of seats along each side separated by a narrow aisle; each single or double seat had its own window.

Air travel caught on quickly, and the war-surplus designs were soon replaced by dedicated civil designs that were faster, more comfortable, and more economical. Oddly, defeated Germany, which had severe restrictions placed on its aeronautical activity by the Allied Control Commission, became one of the most innovative designers and a major producer of transport planes.

In the United States there were no airlines on the European pattern until mid-1926. Several far-sighted individuals and firms sought to establish and operate inter-city airlines, also starting with converted war-surplus models (Fig. 1-1). Some actually served the public, but all failed. This was due to a peculiar circumstance.

RESTRICTIVE GOVERNMENT POLICIES

The U.S. Post Office Department was carrying the air mail in a fleet of its own airplanes. The struggling industry had tried to develop designed-for-the-purpose mailplanes for the Post Office, but that organization had standardized on a quickie conversion of the plentiful wartime De Havilland 4 (DH-4, Fig. 1-2) observation plane, a 1916 British design mass-produced in the U.S. in 1918. The Post Office felt justified in its use of the DH-4; the new designs offered were only marginally better, and besides, "the price was right" for the DH-4. An unlimited supply of new airframes and engines was available from Army stores by simple transfer. The private operators quickly found that they could not operate profitably on passenger revenue alone. The European lines were prospering from the combina-

1

Fig. 1-1. The first multi-engine airliners in the U.S. were converted war-surplus flying boats such as this Curtiss F-5L. To make more cabin room, the pilots' cockpit was moved from near the nose to the between-wings position shown. (courtesy Stephen J. Hudek)

tion of passenger and mail revenue, plus other forms of government subsidy.

The European airline business was big enough to boost an established aircraft manufacturing industry that was already in significant production of improved military models to replace obsolete war-

time models for nations that were still concerned about maintaining their military might.

No parallel existed in the States. The "War to End War" was over and the government and civil population alike were anxious to return to peaceful pursuits. The established aircraft manufacturers all

Fig. 1-2. Essential revenue from the carriage of air mail was unavailable to the fledgling airlines of 1919-25 because the Post Office Department was carrying the mail in its own airplanes, converted wartime observation biplanes like this De Havilland Four (DH-4). (photo by H.A. Erikson)

brought out new civil designs in 1919 and 1920 but found no customers; those who wanted to fly for pleasure could buy war-surplus planes of comparable performance at one-tenth the cost (or less) of new production. Some firms adapted their wartime twin-engine types to airliners, and even set up their own airlines, only to see them fail. It was quickly apparent that with no profits in passenger-only airlines, there was no justification to expend the major cost and time required to design and produce a bona fide airliner for an American market—there simply was no market.

Many of the aircraft builders that had prospered during the war hung on for a year or so and then closed their doors—some forever, thanks to other government policies. U.S. airpower during the war had been built on European designs manufactured in the U.S. No U.S.-designed airplanes other than a few Navy flying boats saw service in Europe before the Armistice.

Although the government now had thousands of obsolescent wartime models on hand, it was not interested in replacing them with new up-to-date designs. Since there was no civil market and the armed forces were not buying in other than small experimental and test quantities for the most part, still more firms shut down when their new high-performance prototypes were rejected by the service.

A final deterrent to airplane and powerplant development in the U.S. was the government's policy of owning the design rights to those airplanes that it did buy. As an example, the small Ordnance Engineering Company (Orenco) of Baldwin, L.I., sold four of its Model D fighter prototypes to the Army Air Service on a wartime contract. After the finished planes were tested in 1919, the Army decided that it wanted 50 production articles. However, it did not place the order with Orenco. Since it had bought the prototypes, the Army also owned the design. Seeking the best buy for its procurement money, the Army put the 50-plane order up for competitive bidding from the entire industry. Giant Curtiss, with far better production facilities, was able to submit the low bid; Orenco closed down shortly after.

A CHANGE OF POLICY

Not until 1925 did the government wake up to the effect its policies were having on the virtually nonexistent industry. Legislation known as the Kelly Act was passed that would get the government out of the air mail business by turning the existing routes over to private contractors over a period of a year and a half. This act sowed the seeds of an eventual airline network on the European pattern.

Other legislation also gave the stagnant aircraft industry a boost. A five-year plan was established to re-equip the Army Air Service (Army Air Corps after July 1, 1926) and the Navy's air arm with new up-to-date models (actually, some rebuilt World War I observation planes were still in service in 1932). Even more important to design incentive was the fact that the designing firm now retained its rights for new military models.

However, long before the industry was able to develop and produce bonafide passenger planes, it got a small boost from the Post Office Department. Recognizing that the venerable DH-4 was no longer suited to the job of mail carrier, the Post Office set up a fly-off design competition to be held in August 1925 for a new mailplane with better performance and greater capacity. The several entries all looked pretty much alike because of the tight specification to which they were designed and the fact that the wartime Liberty engine, a 400-hp water-cooled V-12 designed in 1917, was the required powerplant. So there was no real advance in aircraft design as a result of the contest. Douglas won with a minor variation of its current Army O-2 observation plane and received an order for 50, designated M-2.

A SLOW START

The transfer of the airmail routes from the Post Office to private contractors, which began in April 1926, was not completed until September 1927, but there was no immediate "Airline Industry" as a result. The contracts were for air mail only—the government was not concerned with passengers. Since most of the airplanes used by the new contractors were either DH-4s or Douglas M-2s taken over from the Post Office, or were other small single-engine planes designed to carry a small mail load (200 to 400 pounds) and the pilot, there was no room for passengers anyhow. Some operators using larger models such as the M-2 occasionally allowed a paying passenger to ride on top of the sacks in mid-1926 and early 1927.

The first true mail-and-passenger plane was the Boeing 40A (Fig. 1-3), a redesign of Boeing's 1925 Post Office contest entry updated with modern construction and a much more efficient 420-hp Pratt & Whitney Wasp air-cooled engine. Boeing developed this model early in 1927 when the company decided to bid on the San Francisco-Chicago mail route, which the Post Office was to relinquish on July 1, 1927. Boeing saved so much weight by the switch to an air-cooled engine that it was able to design in a two-passenger cabin and still carry the required mail load. Boeing confounded the competition by submitting what seemed to be an impossibly low bid and won the route. The ability of the 40A to supplement mail revenue with passenger revenue, thanks to the air-cooled engine, was Boeing's secret weapon in this case.

THE TRUE AIRLINER EMERGES

By late 1923 the majority of cheap war-surplus models used for instruction and charter work by the unregulated U.S. civil aircraft operators was beginning to wear out and open up a limited market for replacements. This demand resulted in the formation of some new small and venturesome companies and the rejuvination of some older ones. Business was fairly brisk by mid-1926.

However, since the industry had no airliners on hand or under development in 1926, it was necessary to import established European designs for passenger work. The foundation had been laid for this early in 1925 when Henry Ford, the automobile tycoon, was sold on the need for a healthy U.S. aircraft industry by his business associates and his son Edsel. Since such an industry could survive only if there was a public demand for its products, Ford reasoned that the first step was to overcome the public's inherent fear of flying. To accomplish this, he set up the first of an annual series of "Ford Reliability Tours" in which civil aircraft were flown on a tight schedule over a long course covering several major U.S. cities. Start and finish was at Ford's own airport at Dearborn,

Fig. 1-3. The first U.S. civil airplane to successfully combine mail and passenger revenue was the Boeing 40A of 1927. Note the new air-cooled radial engine but the old-fashioned open cockpit located behind the wings. (Boeing photo)

Fig. 1-4. The first Fokker trimotor, the F-VII/3M, was converted from a single-engine F-VIIA for the 1925 Ford Reliability Tour and set the pattern for nearly a decade of multi-engine airliner development. Ford bought the Fokker after the tour and loaned it to Richard E. Byrd for his North Pole flight of 1926. (Ford Motor Co. photo)

Michigan. The 1925 tour started on September 28 and finished 1775 miles later on October 4. It should be emphasized that this was not a race to determine the *fastest* plane; it was a demonstration of the *reliability* of modern commercial aircraft.

The sensation of the 1925 tour was the Dutch-built Fokker F-VIIA/3M (Fig. 1-4), a trimotor conversion of the eight passenger single-engine Fokker F-VIIA airliner. "Tony" Fokker had taken the word "reliability" to heart. Realizing that the least reliable part of contemporary single-engine airplanes was the engine, he replaced the single 450-hp engine in the nose of his standard F-VIIA with a 200-hp American Wright Whirlwind air-cooled radial engine and added two more Whirlwinds between the wheels and the high wing. This adaptation standardized the airliners of the world for the following eight years. (As proof of Fokker's good thinking, the single-engine F-VIIA that accompanied the new trimotor on its flight from the American Fokker plant in New Jersey to Dearborn for the tour was forced down en route—by engine failure.)

Following the success of the Boeing 40A, the contract mail carriers quickly moved up to new trimotors with their increased revenue potential. Principal models were improved American-built Fokker F-10s (the few F-VIIs of 1926-27 had all

been imports) and the Ford 4-AT and 5-AT models (Fig. 1-5), which had been adapted, like the original Fokker trimotor, from a single-engine design of William B. Stout that essentially married German Junkers all-metal construction to the Fokker F-VII outline. Ford bought the Stout Metal Airplane Company and used some of its single-engined products to set up his own company airline between Detroit and Chicago in April 1925. After the spectacular debut of the Fokker trimotor, other Ford employees developed the single-engine Ford-Stout "Air Pullman" model into the famous "Tin Goose" trimotor.

Other new multi-engine models soon appeared to supplement the Fokkers and Fords, but they were not true competitors in either quantity or quality. The Curtiss Condor (Fig. 1-6) was a twin-engine 18-passenger design adapted quickly from the contemporary B-2 Army bomber. It met such limited response that only six were built. Its major claim to fame is that it was the only U.S. airliner certificated with liquid-cooled engines.

The boxy 12-18 passenger Boeing 80 and 80A (Fig. 1-7) were trimotors that seemed to be a step backward in being biplanes in the opening years of the monoplane age, but there was method in Boeing's apparent madness. The Boeing route from San Francisco to Chicago crossed two high and rugged mountain ranges. Airports were small and at

Fig. 1-5. The Ford Trimotor—the "Tin Goose"—was inspired by the Fokker trimotor but was far more durable because of the adoption of German Junkers all-metal construction. This is the 5-AT model with 420 hp P&W Wasp engines and in-wing baggage compartments. (Boeing Air Transport photo)

high elevation. The Fords and Fokkers, designed primarily for operation from large airports at sea level, could not operate from such fields. Boeing deliberately used the inherent characteristics of the biplane's slower landing speed and greater payload for its power to obtain better high-altitude and short field capability for the mountains and increased fuel capacity and range for the greater western distance. The 80s were designed for that single route and operation and no other, in a prime example of design "tradeoff" to obtain certain desired characteristics at the sacrifice of others—namely range and altitude capability at the expense of speed.

DAWN OF A NEW ERA

By 1930 the U.S. airline industry had developed into a healthy network, with trimotors on the main (or *trunk*) routes and smaller single-engine models

Fig. 1-6. The original Curtiss Condor transport was a quick adaptation of the B-2 Army bomber airframe to an 18-passenger airliner in 1929. Only six were sold. (Curtiss-Wright photo)

Fig. 1-7. As a biplane in the emerging age of monoplanes, the Boeing 80 and 80A (shown) were not steps backward but were designed specifically as airliners that capitalized on inherent biplane characteristics for a route over high mountains. (photo by Gordon S. Williams)

on the short inter-city routes that fed the trunks. In spite of better powerplants and later aerodynamics, the aircraft industry in the U.S. and abroad was very conservative and its designs reflected some major design features that dated back to World War I. There were still plenty of biplanes around, and the new crop of monoplanes that served the short routes were mostly high-wing

Fig. 1-8. In the late 1920s single-engine mail/passenger monoplanes such as this Travel Air 5000 began to replace biplanes like the Boeing 40A, carrying equal or greater loads with only half the horsepower. (Beech Aircraft photo)

Fig. 1-9. As the monoplane replaced the biplane, the next step was aerodynamic cleanup of the monoplane. This Lockheed Vega deleted the struts, streamlined the fuselage, and added streamlined fairings to the wheels and radial engine. (Lockheed photo)

strut-braced designs such as the Ryans, Stinsons, and Travel Airs (Fig. 1-8). Some innovative designers, such as John K. Northrop at Lockheed, introduced greatly improved performance for a given power and weight through close attention to streamlining. The Lockheed Vega of 1927 (Fig. 1-9) eliminated the struts by use of a Fokker-like cantilever wing and used a sleek oval cross-section for its laminated wood veneer fuselage.

Many new features had been developed, and

Fig. 1-10. The Boeing Monomail of 1930 took monoplane refinement a step further by retracting the landing gear, but also took a backward step by readopting the old open cockpit. (photo by Gordon S. Williams)

8

some were actually put into production. Not until 1930 did a design appear that incorporated enough of these new features in one airplane to deserve the title "new."

This was the Boeing Model 200, named Monomail (Fig. 1-10). It was thoroughly modern in utilizing all-metal structure, a cantilever wing in a low position so that the landing gear could retract into it, and a cowling around the high-drag radial engine. However, old thinking and pilot pressure resulted in an open cockpit located far aft on the fuselage; after all, it had been in that position on mailplanes since 1918 and the pilots wanted it there. They were resisting enclosed cockpits, too; they felt they had to be out in the open so they could "feel the wind."

Unfortunately, the "Monomail" was not a commercial success; its aerodynamics got ahead of the prevailing state-of-the-art in propeller design. If the fixed-pitch propeller was set for fast takeoff performance, the cruising speed suffered. If it was set for best cruise, the takeoff suffered, especially at high-elevation airports. By the time suitable controllable-pitch propellers were developed, the Monomails (only two were built) had been replaced by other models.

When the Monomails didn't come up to expectations, Boeing applied the same design concepts to a new twin-engine bomber for the Army. The Boeing Model 215 (Fig. 1-11) was faster than con-

temporary Army pursuit planes. The Army bought the two prototypes as B-9 and ordered five service test models in 1932, but the expected big production order went to Martin, which had developed an even more advanced model, the B-10.

COMES THE REVOLUTION

Undaunted, Boeing applied the Monomail/B-9 design concept to a new twin-engine 10-passenger transport, the Model 247 (Fig. 1-12), and hit paydirt. United Air Lines (formerly The Boeing Air Transport System and then affiliated with the aircraft manufacturer through United Aircraft and Transport Corporation), which Boeing had helped set up in 1929, saw the great potential of this design. Although carrying four fewer passengers than the Ford, it was 70 mph faster and would obviously make the Ford and the other old trimotors obsolete overnight—and give the first airline to get it a huge advantage over the competition. To ensure this advantage, United made airline financial history by ordering an unprecedented 60 247s right off the drawing boards. Ironically, this historic act was to contribute to the early demise of the 247 as a trunk airliner.

The first 247 flew on February 8, 1933, and was in service with the airline in March. This is a prime example of the far simpler certification procedures that prevailed at the time. Since it was also

Fig. 1-11. Boeing extended the Monomail concept to a twin-engine Army bomber, the YIB-9, that turned out to be faster than contemporary pursuit planes, but was beaten out for production orders by the still more advanced Martin B-10. (Boeing photo)

Fig. 1-12. Boeing applied the YIB-9 bomber concept to a 10-passenger transport, the Model 247, and revolutionized the airline business. This is the prototype, photographed on February 8, 1933, the day before its first flight. (Boeing photo)

part of United Aircraft, Boeing naturally used other United products in the 247 as it did in its other models, notable the 550-hp Pratt & Whitney "Wasp" engine and Hamilton Standard propellers. The tie-in between Boeing and United Air Lines through United Aircraft was to have nationwide repercussions later.

The Douglas design that emerged to challenge the new Boeing is discussed in the next chapter, but another seemingly retrograde design that followed the 247 is mentioned here because of its eventual influence on the DC-3.

In 1932 Curtiss-Wright reopened its subsidiary plant in St. Louis, Missouri, which had been closed early in the great depression, to build a new twin-engine Condor transport (Fig. 1-13). This was a uni-

Fig. 1-13. The Curtiss Condor II of 1933 was a transition model between the "old" airliners represented by the Fords and Fokkers and the "new" spearheaded by the Boeing 247. The Condor, with features of both eras, pioneered flying sleeper service. (A.U. Schmidt photo.)

que combination of the old and the new. It was a biplane—clearly an anachronism in 1933—but it incorporated a retractable landing gear and cowled engines, a heritage of the 247. There was no detail similarity at all between it and the 1928 bomber conversion.

The main feature of the still-boxy Condor II was its wide fuselage, which could accommodate 15 day passengers plus a cabin attendant, or 12 sleeper berths. It was the first designed-for-the-purpose sleeper plane, drawing its inspiration and detail from the railroad industry. For night routes with sleeping passengers, high speed did not offer a competitive advantage. However, with two 720-hp. Wright Cyclone engines, the Condor II cruised along at 167 mph compared to the 155 of the early Boeing 247 with 550-hp Wasp engines, but could not match the 189 mph of the improved 247D. Still, progress in other areas limited the Condor IIs career to only three years.

Chapter 2

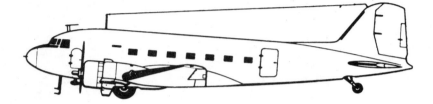

Birth of the DCs

The firm that will hereafter be referred to simply as "Douglas" in this book has had several names. It was established by 28-year-old Donald Wills Douglas after he resigned his position as Chief Engineer of the Glenn L. Martin Company of Cleveland, Ohio. While there he had designed the first of the famous Martin Bomber line. He moved to Southern California without even the proverbial shoestring upon which to found his own business.

DOUGLAS IN BUSINESS

Through a friend, he was introduced to wealthy Los Angeles sportsman David R. Davis. Davis had an ambition to make the first nonstop flight across the North American continent and needed a man with Douglas's talents to design and build a suitable airplane. As a result of their meeting and subsequent discussions, the Davis-Douglas Company was established in the back room of a Los Angeles barbershop on July 22, 1920. Its capital was $40,000 provided by Davis.

Here Douglas designed a large single-engine bi-

plane that was eventually named the Cloudster. Construction was undertaken in the rented loft of a planing mill and final assembly took place in the Goodyear airship hangar at what is now South Park and Florence Avenues in Los Angeles. As intended, the Cloudster could carry a great load of fuel and is reputed to be the first airplane in the world capable of carrying a useful load greater than its own empty weight (Fig. 2-1).

The Cloudster took off on its west-east record attempt from the Army's March Field on June 27, 1921, but was forced down with minor damage at Fort Bliss, Texas, by engine failure. By the time it was repaired and flown back to California, Davis had lost interest in the company and withdrew, leaving Douglas with the Cloudster.

Even before the Cloudster flew, Donald Douglas was at work on the design of a follow-on that he hoped would interest the Navy as a torpedo plane. The Navy was sufficiently impressed by later performance figures from the Cloudster to order three experimental prototypes. However, with Davis no longer providing the bankroll, Douglas had

Fig. 2-1. The start of it all—the Douglas Cloudster of 1921. This is the original long-distance configuration, with two-seat side-by-side open cockpit. Ryan later converted it to a passenger plane with a 10-seat cabin and the pilot's cockpit moved ahead of the wing. (Douglas photo)

to find other backing. He then formed a new firm, The Douglas Company, in July 1921. The DTs—one two-seat DT-1 and two three-seat DT-2s—were built in the Goodyear hangar and won Douglas an 18-plane order for production DT-2s (D for Douglas, T for Torpedo plane, -2 for second configuration, in Naval aircraft designations). With a need for more suitable production facilities, Douglas now moved into an abandoned movie studio in Santa Monica, a northern suburb of Los Angeles.

SUPPLYING THE MILITARY

The next significant customer was the U.S. Army Air Service, which hoped to accomplish the first flight around the world. It thought that a two-seat variant of the DT-2, operating alternately on floats and wheels, could do the job, and ordered five DWCs (Army abbreviation for Douglas World Cruiser) in 1923 (Fig. 2-2). Between March 17 and September 28, 1924, two of the four starters completed the 28,945-mile flight.

Fig. 2-2. Douglas prospered by selling torpedo plane developments of the Cloudster to the U.S. Navy, but gained worldwide fame after the around-the-world flight of two U.S. Army DWCs in 1924. (USAF photo)

Fig. 2-3. Douglas became a major supplier to the U.S. Army with the O-2 observation plane series and then sold 50 minor variants to the Post Office as mailplanes. This is one of 40 M-4s (M-for-Mailplane). (Douglas photo)

After winning an Army observation plane contest in 1924 with its XO-2, essentially a scaled-down DWC, Douglas became a major supplier to the U.S. Army. Douglas also won a 1925 Post Office fly-off design contest with the M-1, a modified O-2, and sold 10 M-3s and 40 M-4s (Fig. 2-3) to the Post Office. The basic O-2 was progressively refined to the O-2K variant, and there were re-engined Army derivatives through O-5, O-7, O-8, O-9, O-25, O-29, O-32, and O-38, (Fig. 2-4), plus BT-2 basic trainers for a total of 885 by the time Army biplane production ended in 1933. The Navy DT business carried on to a total of 26, not counting the 44 built under license by L. W. F. and Dayton-Wright.

Douglas got into the production of twin-engine aircraft indirectly. The U.S. Navy was still designing some of its own aircraft, building prototypes at the Naval Aircraft Factory in Philadelphia, and then putting the desired production models up for industry-wide competitive bidding. Through this channel, Douglas won an order for three XT2D-1 (second T-model for the Navy from Douglas) and

Fig. 2-4. The basic O-2 was refined to the final O-38 series through a variety of intermediate O-types. This is an O-38E, one of the last Douglas biplanes delivered in 1933. (Fred Bamberger photo)

Fig. 2-5. The first twin-engine model built by Douglas was the T2D-1 torpedo plane of 1927. The prototype had been designed and built by the U.S. Navy as the XTN-1. (U.S. Navy photo)

nine production T2D-1s (Fig. 2-5). These marked no great advance in design, but did give Douglas valuable construction experience.

While the T2D-1 work was under way, Douglas won other twin-engine orders from the Navy in December 1927, and built 25 PD-1 (Patrol, Douglas; Fig. 2-6) flying boats that the Navy had gradually refined from the wartime F-5L boats to the PN-12 version. The PDs were followed by 18 P2D-1s, which were duplicates of the T2D-1s designated for patrol rather than torpedo missions.

Douglas was now a major manufacturer, having reorganized as The Douglas Aircraft Company in November 1928, and moved into a brand-new

Fig. 2-6. Douglas got further multi-engine experience and familiarization with aluminum hull construction when it built production versions of the U.S. Navy's PN-12 as the Douglas PD-1 in 1928. (U.S. Navy photo)

plant on Santa Monica's established airport, Clover Field, in 1929.

THE COMMERCIAL MARKET

Not counting the Cloudster, which was eventually sold to Ryan Airlines, or the mail planes derived from Army models, Douglas was exclusively a producer of military models into 1930. A couple of civil sport prototypes found no buyers. However, with the experience of the PDs and the T2D/P2Ds behind it, the firm developed a new twin on its own, the Dolphin amphibian (Fig. 2-7). This proved to be one of history's most unfortunately timed airplanes. First flown in July 1930, the Dolphin was a rugged and versatile six to eight passenger model that found no commercial customers as a result of the Great Depression that started in October 1929. The Army and Navy proved to be the major customers for the Dolphins; only 12 of the 58 built into 1934 went to civil customers.

The stage was being set for the appearance of the soon-to-be-famous DC line (for Douglas Commercial), but the DCs were not evolutionary developments of the earlier Douglas military models. Rather, they drew their main structural features from a Douglas subsidiary, the Northrop Corporation.

John K. Northrop had worked for Douglas from 1923 into 1926, when he joined Lockheed as Chief Engineer and designed the famous Vega. In 1928 he left Lockheed and formed his own company, the Avion Corporation, to experiment with new methods of metal construction. His company was soon taken into the giant United Aircraft and Transport Trust and renamed Northrop Aircraft Corporation. Its single production model was the Alpha (Fig. 2-8), a mail and passenger plane quite similar to the Boeing Monomail except for fixed landing gear. Seventeen were built, with three going to the U.S. Army as YC-19s.

When United Aircraft merged Northrop with Stearman and moved the California plant to Wichita, Kansas, in September 1931, John Northrop resigned. He then formed a new company, the Northrop Corporation, and developed new models based on the Alpha, notably the Gamma mailplane and the Delta mail/passenger model (Fig. 2-9). The new firm was financed by Douglas, which held 51 percent of the stock, and moved into new facilities on Mines Field, the Los Angeles municipal airport, at Inglewood, California.

ENTER THE DC-1

Even though Douglas now had Northrop's advanced structural details "in house," the DC-1 still did not appear as a design built on speculation and then offered to potential customers as had been the case with the Dolphin. Rather, it was designed as

Fig. 2-7. The first twin-engine model designed by Douglas was the Dolphin of 1930. An amphibian, the wheels retracted simply to get them out of the water, not to reduce aerodynamic drag, a performance-improving feature that was to come later. (photo by A.U. Schmidt)

Fig. 2-8. Some of the basic design details of the famous Douglas DC line were first introduced on the Northrop Alpha of 1930, which improved on the design concept of the all-metal Boeing Monomail except for using fixed instead of retractable landing gear. (Van Rossem photo)

a result of the panic created in the airline industry by United Air Lines' 60-plane order for Boeing 247s. The other lines wouldn't be able to get 247s for nearly two years and could see a major loss of business to United's revolutionary new airliner.

The 247 hadn't flown yet, but enough of its details (plus those of the similar B-9) were known to the industry to trigger some serious thinking about the need for a competitive design. Jack Frye, Vice President/Operations of Transcontinental and Western Air (TWA), wrote to Douglas and other

leading manufacturers on August 2, 1932, with specifications for a new trimotored airliner that should meet or beat the Boeing. This had to carry 12 passengers for 1080 miles nonstop at a cruising speed of 150 mph with engines of 500-550 hp.

However, there were even more difficult performance requirements. The engines had to be supercharged to reach a service ceiling of 21,000 feet, it had to maintain 10,000 feet on any two engines, and be able to take off from any TWA route airport including Albuquerque, New Mexico

Fig. 2-9. Douglas acquired John K. Northrop's designing skills and concepts when it held 51 percent of the stock in the new company that Northrop founded in 1931. This is the Northrop Delta mail and passenger transport that saw limited airline service in 1932-33. Note the trademark Northrop landing gear fairings. (photo by A.U. Schmidt)

(elevation 4954 feet) with one engine out.

The Douglas design team—consisting of Harry E. Wetzel, Vice-President and General Manager; J.H. Kindelberger, Chief Engineer; Arthur E. Raymond, Assistant Chief Engineer; and Fred W. Herman, Project Engineer, assisted by Lee Atwood, Ed Burton, and Fred Stineman—went to work immediately. In ten days they had a presentation for a new airliner, the 12-passenger DC-1, ready for TWA's evaluation. This drew heavily on known details of the 247 and, with the advantage of hindsight, overcame some of the undesirable features and shortcomings of the unfinished Boeing.

In outline, the DC-1 was a low-wing cantilever monoplane with two cowled engines and retractable landing gear. Douglas had departed from TWA's suggestions and proposed two 700-hp engines instead of three smaller ones. The DC-1 had two big advantages over the 247 besides more passengers. A higher cabin, with the floor entirely above the center section, allowed even tall passengers to stand erect. (A major disadvantage of the 247 was that the wing spars ran through the cabin and the passengers, already stooped, had to step over the rear spar.) Another DC-1 advantage was the inclusion of wing flaps, something new to the industry and not yet used by Boeing. The DC-1 followed Boeing's pioneering use of elevator trim tabs rather than a movable stabilizer for longitudinal trim. Rudder trim for engine-out conditions was also by cockpit-controlled tab.

The structure drew heavily on proven Northrop detail, with three full-depth aluminum web spars for the wings and aluminum web ribs. The outer wing panels, with three degrees of dihedral, attached to the flat center section immediately outboard of the nacelles by means of bolts through full chordwise flanges. This detail was to remain a Northrop and Douglas feature for many years and would be adopted by other manufacturers. A distinctive feature of the wing was the straight-chord center section with straight trailing edges on the outer panels but 15 degrees of sweepback on the leading edges. The DC-1 was all-metal, except for fabric covering on the movable control surfaces, and used the new 29ST aluminum alloy instead of the previously standard 17ST.

SELLING THE DC-1

Raymond and Wetzel took the DC-1 proposal to TWA's headquarters in New York City and began a marathon round of detailed discussion. The airline liked the layout and passenger accommodations of the DC-1 and was pleased with the "Northrop" structure; the line had been using Northrop Alphas for several years and appreciated their integrity and ease of maintenance. However, it was deeply concerned about the requirement for takeoff from any TWA airport with one engine out. One out of three was only a 33 percent power loss; one out of two was a 50 percent loss, and no existing twin could get away with that. Douglas slide rules were finally able to overcome TWA apprehensions, and the airline accepted the twin-engine configuration.

Although Douglas had based its DC-1 performance calculations on a 700-hp engine, it had not picked a specific make or model. Two were then available, the 1690-cubic-inch Pratt & Whitney Hornet in the 650 to 700-hp range, and the 1820-cubic-inch Wright Cyclone in the same range. Both were nine-cylinder air-cooled radials of the same size and weight and were actually interchangeable. Both engine manufacturers were in on the TWA/Douglas negotiations in an intensive battle for a potentially lucrative market. Wright finally won, and the engines selected for the DC-1 were SGR-1820F Cyclones that delivered 690 hp for takeoff at 1900 rpm. The S in the identification stood for supercharged, the G for geared (8:5 reduction from crankshaft speed to propeller speed), and the R identified the radial type of engine. The 1820 was the displacement in cubic inches. At a dry weight of 920 pounds, this latest Cyclone in a series that had started in 1928 was reported to have the lowest specific weight of any production air-cooled radial in the U.S. at the time.

On September 20, 1932, TWA gave Douglas a contract for one DC-1 prototype at a price of $125,000. While this would by no means cover Douglas' costs of developing a single airplane, the contract included an option for the purchase of as many as 60 production articles, less engines, for $58,000 apiece. Amortization of development costs over this many units would assure Douglas of a profit on the contract. As it was, TWA did not buy that many, but Douglas sales of the production model DC-2 to other airlines and the military brought the total to 193 and resulted in a very profitable product line that was to become a deterrent to later development of the DC-3.

Back in Santa Monica, work got underway on the DC-1 airframe. In its initial configuration, the DC-1 (Fig. 2-10) was fitted with fixed-pitch three-blade propellers like the Boeing and had distinctive wing-like connections between the fuselage and the entire nacelles ahead of the center section called "winglets." These functioned as aerodynamic slots to improve airflow in the wing/fuselage area, but were found to be unnecessary and were soon eliminated.

The main wheels retracted forward, but still projected slightly out of the nacelles like those on the Boeing (the Boeing wheels retracted aft). Significantly, no mechanical downlocks were used on the DC-1. Small clamshell doors on each side of the nacelles closed the gaps between the wheels and the nacelles (Fig. 2-11). The nonretractable tailwheel was enclosed in a fairing of a style which,

when used on main landing wheels, was called "pants."

Fuel was carried in two main tanks each of 180 U.S.-gallon capacity in the wing center section plus two auxiliary tanks of 75 gallons each, also in the center section. One 20-gallon oil tank was in each nacelle. The steel tube engine mounts, along with the enclosing cowling, were removable and were interchangeable from side to side.

FLYING THE DC-1

The first flight, on July 1, 1933—less than ten months after the signing of the contract and just under five months after the initial flight of the Boeing 247 that had inspired it—nearly ended in tragedy. Following takeoff, both engines tended to cut out as the plane assumed climb attitude. Test pilot and Douglas Vice President/Sales Carl Cover managed to get the faltering DC-1 back on Clover Field safely. The trouble was traced to improper installation of a new type of carburetor by the engine manufacturer and was quickly remedied.

As was usual in the transition from proposal

Fig. 2-10. The Douglas DC-1 was designed to fill TWA's need for a new transport to meet or beat the performance of the revolutionary Boeing 247. The DC-1 successfully combined improvements on the 247 design concept with proven Northrop structural details. Note the tiny aerodynamic winglets between engine nacelles and fuselage, soon removed. (Douglas photo)

Fig. 2-11. The DC-1 during a public demonstration at Grand Central Air Terminal, Glendale, Calif., showing the original fixed-pitch propellers and the wheel well doors. Although the DC-1 was eventually certified to carry revenue passengers, most of its flying was done on an ''Experimental'' license. (Douglas photo)

figures to the flyable article, the DC-1 gained some weight. This necessitated a change to new controllable-pitch propellers to attain the performance guarantees. TWA was soon satisfied, and exercised its option on the contract for 20 production articles with enough minor changes to justify a new model number—DC-2.

Testing continued to eliminate the inevitable bugs that appear in any new design, especially one pushing the state of the art in both airframe and powerplant, as the DC-1 was doing. After the DC-1 passed the critical one-engine-out-on takeoff test at Winslow, Arizona (elevation 4878 feet) and made it across an 8000-foot-high pass to Albuquerque, TWA accepted ownership on September 13, 1933. However, the plane remained at the factory for continued testing and the installation of an airline interior. TWA did not take actual possession until December.

Pratt & Whitney, meanwhile, was still pushing to get its engines into the DC-1. The Cyclones were removed and 700-hp R-1690SD-G Hornets were tried briefly in October 1933. With these engines, the airplane was redesignated DC-1A. This configuration was short-lived, however, and the

Cyclones were soon reinstalled.

CERTIFICATION

Before a commercial airplane can be licensed for revenue passenger operation it has to undergo extensive engineering analysis, performance testing, and sometimes static testing, conducted by or under the supervision of the FAA. Upon completion of this testing, the airplane is awarded an Approved Type Certificate, or ATC. All subsequent duplicates built during the duration of the production period of the certificate can be issued ''Standard'' licenses for unlimited commercial operation.

The DC-1 was not awarded a full ATC. Rather, it was issued the lesser Category-2, or ''Memo certificate,'' 2-460 on November 8, 1933. Memo certificates are issued on an individual airplane basis to planes that do not meet full ATC requirements but are still permitted to carry revenue passengers. During some of its route testing, the DC-1 carried passengers for TWA on a standard license as NC223Y instead of X223Y. The X-license was restored for subsequent experimental test work.

An oddity of the 2-460 certification is that it

covered the DC-1 in both the original Cyclone-powered version and the Hornet DC-1A version. Normally, separate certificates are required for different engines and sometimes for minor variations of the same engine.

FURTHER TESTING

During TWA's use of the DC-1, an earlier design shortcoming was overcome. Because of its details, it was not thought that the landing gear needed a mechanical downlock. After two embarrassing cases of gear retraction on the ground during public demonstrations of the airplane (December 18, 1933, and February 11, 1934), mechanical locks were installed. Previously, the DC-1 had made a wheels-up landing on an early factory test flight, but this was due to a crew communications problem, not the landing gear itself.

The DC-1 took much of the glory away from Boeing's 247. On February 19, 1934, piloted by Jack Frye of TWA and Eddie Rickenbacker of Eastern Air Lines, the DC-1 carried the last load of mail flown by the airlines prior to the scandalous air mail contract cancellations of that month. The DC-1 made it from Glendale, California, to Newark, New Jersey with only two stops in 13 hours 2 minutes elapsed time, setting a new coast-to-coast record in the process. During subsequent demonstrations, this fact was proclaimed in large letters on each side of the fuselage.

In 1935 TWA lent the DC-1 to the National Aeronautic Association (NAA) for official attempts to set new world's records for airplanes in its weight category. The engines were now 875-hp F-25 Cyclones. Fuel capacity was increased to 2100 gallons by adding fuselage tanks, which resulted in most of the fuselage windows being eliminated. Gross weight increased to 28,500 pounds. The modifications were made at the factory, and when the DC-1 was flown to the East Coast for the record attempts it broke its previous record with a nonstop flight of 11 hours 5 minutes (Fig. 2-12). Among the several weight/speed/distance records set was one for a payload of 2205 pounds (1000 kg) for 3107 miles (5000 km), at a speed of 161 mph (272 km/h).

In January 1936, TWA sold the DC-1 to Howard Hughes, who installed still more fuel tanks for a nonstop range of 6000 miles in anticipation

Fig. 2-12. Following certification, the DC-1 reverted to "Experimental" status for further research and development. Note blanked-off cabin windows and final tail configuration used on the DC-1. Fuselage placard reads:

TRANSCONTINENTAL RECORD
LOS ANGELES — NEW YORK
11 HR. 5 MIN APRIL 30, 1935
HOLDER OF 8 INTERNATIONAL AND 11 NATIONAL RECORDS
FOR SPEED — WEIGHT — DISTANCE

(photo by A.U. Schmidt)

Table 2-1. Douglas DC-1 and Boeing 247 Compared to 1932 TWA Specification.

	TWA Specification (1932)	DC-1 (1934)	Boeing 247 (1933)
Powerplant	3 × 500-550 hp	2 × Wright SGR-1820F-3 Cyclone, 710 hp @ 1900 rpm @ 7000 ft.	2 × P&W R-1340-S1D1 Wasp, 550 hp @ 2200 rpm @ 5000 ft.
Accommodation	2 crew, 12 passengers	3 crew, 12 passengers	3 crew, 10 passengers
Span		85 ft. 0 in.	74 ft. 0 in.
Length		60 ft. 0 in.	51 ft. 4 in.
Wing Area		942 sq. ft.	836 sq. ft.
Empty Weight		11,780 lb.	8400 lb.
Gross Weight	14,200 lb.	17,500 lb.	12,650 lb.
Wing Loading		18.6 lb./sq. ft.	15.13 lb./sq. ft.
Power Loading		12.3 lb/hp	11.5 lb/hp
High Speed	185 mph	210 mph	182 mph
Cruising Speed	150 mph	190 mph @ 8000 ft.	155 mph @ 5000 ft.
Landing Speed	65 mph		58 mph
Rate of Climb	1200 ft./min	1050 ft./min.	1320 ft./min.
Service Ceiling	21,000 ft.	23,000 ft.	18,400 ft.
Range	1000 mi.	1000 mi.	485 mi.

of a record flight around the world. He soon lost interest in the DC-1 for that project and sold the plane to an Englishman in May 1938. After only three months on the British Register as G-AFIF, it was sold to the government of Loyalist (Republican) Spain and became EC-AGJ. After the fall of that government, it was used to evacuate officials from Spain to France. Taken over by the victorious Nationalists, it was put into scheduled airline service as EC-AAE. It belly-landed in December 1940, following engine failure on take-off, and was scrapped.

It is interesting to compare the 1934 "airline" specifications and performance of the DC-1 with the original 1932 TWA requirement and corresponding figures for the original 1933 version of the Boeing 247 (Table 2-1).

THE DC-2

The DC-2 (Fig. 2-13) was the production version of the DC-1 and incorporated enough minor refinements and significant structural changes to justify a new model number. Except for the two-foot length increase, it was outwardly identical to the finalized form of the DC-1, including the left side passenger door. Later DC-2s incorporated an enlarged vertical fin to improve directional stability (Fig. 2-14). Gross weight for the airliners varied from 18,200 pounds to 18,560 and some military cargo versions had a gross weight of 21,000 pounds.

From a revenue standpoint, the most significant change was the two-foot increase in fuselage length, which allowed seating of two more passengers. Powerplants were initially standardized with the Wright F-series Cyclones, but to satisfy customer demand, P & W Hornets were used in three DC-2As (Fig. 2-15) and British Bristol Pegasus VIs were used in two DC-2Bs (Fig. 2-16).

The DC-2 with 720-hp F-3 Cyclones received ATC A-540 on June 28, 1934. This was for the initial version designated DC-2-112. Different Cyclones varying from 710 to 875 takeoff hp plus minor variations made a customer request resulted in further designations under ATC-540:

DC-2 -115A, B, D, E, G, J/M
DC-2 -118A, B
DC-2 -120, -123, -124, -152, -171, -172, -185, -190, -192, -193, -199, -200, -210, -211, and -221.

Fig. 2-13. The first DC-2s, stretched versions of the DC-1, went to TWA, the airline that had ordered the development of the DC-1. This is a DC-2-112, NC13783. In 1942 it was drafted by the U.S. Army as a C-32A, 42-65578, and leased to Braniff Airways. (photo by Gordon S. Williams)

Foreign customers desired further changes, so the DC-2-115 with the 720-hp F-2 Cyclone was awarded ATC-555 on August 28, 1934. The DC-2-115H, or DC-2A, with 720-hp Pratt & Whitney R-1690-S8EG Hornets, received ATC-570 on May 20, 1935. Because of customer-requested differences, the other two DC-2As were identified by Douglas as DC-2-127 and DC-2-165H. Since the two DC-2Bs with Bristol Pegasus engines were not for U.S. operations, they did not receive ATCs but were identified as DC-2-115F.

Altogether, Douglas built 193 DC-2s as such between May 1934, and July 1936. The majority went to the world's airlines but a few served as executive transports. There were also significant military sales: five for the U.S. Navy as transports, three for the Army as transports, and 54 specialized freighters for the Army. The Army freighters, C-33s and C-39s, extended the production life of the basic DC-2 to September 1939.

Fig. 2-14. Following introduction of the DC-2, American-made airliners were exported in significant numbers for the first time. This DC-2-115K, sold to Czechoslovakia via Fokker in 1936, has the enlarged vertical fin used on some DC-2s. (Douglas photo)

23

Fig. 2-15. All but five DC-2s used Wright Cyclone engines. This is one of three DC-2As, the single DC-2A-127 for the Standard Oil Company, with Pratt & Whitney Hornet engines. (photo by A.U. Schmidt)

European manufacturing rights were acquired by the Dutch designer/builder A.H.G. "Tony" Fokker, but he didn't build any DC-2s. Instead, he imported and sold 39 to European customers. Five additional DC-2s were built in Japan by Nakajima from Douglas-supplied parts 1936 and 1937, to bring the DC-2 total to 198. Incidentally, these were used by the Japanese navy during World War II and received the Allied code name "Tess."

The Boeing 247 enjoyed its role as the first of the "new generation" airliners only briefly. On August 1, 1934, TWA put DC-2s on the transcontinental route—New York to Los Angeles via Chicago, Kansas City, and Albuquerque—in direct competition with United's 247s and clipped two hours off of United's time. Westbound, the elapsed time was 18 hours; eastbound it was 16 hours 20 minutes due to the prevailing winds. Boeing tried to counter the DC-2 with a cleaned-up 247D model (Fig. 2-17) featuring geared Wasp engines and controllable propellers that increased the cruising speed to 189 mph. United had all its existing 247s converted to 247Ds, but still couldn't compete. The 247 didn't have the growth capability already demonstrated by the DC-1/DC-2 stretch.

DC-4 AND DC-5

Although these two models followed the DC-3, detailed in the remainder of this book, they deserve brief mention here because of their interaction with the DC-3 and how they were treated differently by world events.

The DC-4 was unique in aircraft procurement history by being a joint development by the manufacturer and five major U.S. airlines. It was a big 42-passenger airliner with four 1450-hp P & W R-2180-S1A1-G engines. Negotiations began between Douglas and United Air Lines late in 1935. Douglas was not in a position to absorb development costs in anticipation of future sales as it had done with the DC-2, nor could UAL underwrite the cost by itself. Eventually, UAL persuaded four

Fig. 2-16. Two DC-2Bs with British Bristol Pegasus engines were delivered to Poland via Fokker. The B-designation was not official; factory identification was DC-2-115F. Note the left-hand propellers, the opposite of American engine practice. (Douglas photo)

24

Fig. 2-17. The Boeing 247, which had inspired the design of the DC-1, was soon outclassed by the DC-2. Boeing tried to catch up with the refined 247D model. In spite of its impressive performance gain, it was still no match for the DC-2. (photo by Peter M. Bowers)

other lines to put up $100,000 each toward development costs.

The DC-4 was a greatly advanced and complex aircraft, and as work progressed two airlines, TWA and Pan American, began to have doubts about its suitability. They withdrew from the DC-4 program and ordered smaller four-engine Boeing 307s instead.

The triple-tail DC-4 (Fig. 2-18) flew on June 7, 1938. After testing by Douglas, the remaining airlines tested it on their routes. At a gross weight of 65,000 pounds it was simply too much airplane for its revenue potential and maintenance effort. The single prototype was dropped and the lines got behind Douglas in the development of an entirely new and smaller design that was still designated DC-4 (Fig. 2-19).

When the new DC-4 program got underway the old one was redesignated DC-4E and was sold to

Japan early in 1940. Although the new 50,000-pound 40-passenger DC-4 flew in February 1942, the airlines did not get their DC-4s until early 1946; the U.S. Army requisitioned the 24 original airliners right on the production line before Pearl Harbor and they were completed as Army C-54 Skymasters. The C-54A and subsequent were revised for military cargo work with reinforced cabin floors and wide cargo doors. Some were diverted to the U.S. Navy as R5D-1 through R5D-6.

The postwar civil DC-4s pioneered transatlantic landplane passenger service, but that career, and transcontinental U.S. service, was brief; they were soon replaced by the new postwar generation of airliners, starting with the "stretched" DC-4 that was introduced in 1947 as the DC-6.

The DC-5 was intended to be a short-haul "feeder" airliner for routes then using the DC-3 that would use the upcoming DC-4 on their trunk routes.

Fig. 2-18. The single DC-4E was developed jointly by Douglas and five U.S. airlines, but proved to be too complex and uneconomical for service. Three of the airlines and Douglas then developed a smaller four-engine design still called DC-4. (photo by A.U. Schmidt)

Fig. 2-19. The new DC-4 appeared early in 1942 but the sponsoring airlines did not get their airplanes until after World War II; the U.S. Army requisitioned all production and assigned the designation C-54. This is the third article, 41-20139, built as an airliner. C-54As and on were built with military features. (photo by Gordon S. Williams)

Fig. 2-20. The little-known DC-5 was intended to be a short-range feeder airliner for airlines using larger Douglas equipment on their trunk routes. Production was curtailed by the U.S. Army's need for increased DC-3/C-47 production, and only four of 12 DC-5s built went to an airline customer. (Douglas photo)

Since the engineering and manufacturing facilities at the Santa Monica plant were overloaded in mid-1938, design and construction were assigned to the El Segundo (ex-Northrop) plant. Based on the high-wing tricycle configuration of the Model 7 attack bomber then in development at El Segundo, the DC-5 (Fig. 2-20) was a 16-passenger design with the fuselage rounded out for two double rows of passenger seats. The nose greatly resembled that of the DC-3, but there was no parts interchangeability.

Several airlines showed interest and placed orders. The U.S. Navy and Marines ordered seven as R3D-1 (3) and R3D-2 (4) with military features and cargo doors. However, the production life of the DC-5 was short. In 1941 U.S. Army Chief

General H. H. Arnold told Douglas that he was giving the firm so many military DC-3 orders that there wouldn't be room for a separate DC-5 production line.

Other than the prototype and the seven R3Ds, only four DC-5s were delivered to an airline customer. All four were in the Netherlands East Indies at the time of the Japanese attack. One was captured by the Japanese and the other three escaped to Australia, where they were drafted into the U.S. Army as C-110s. By this oddity, the same Army that had cancelled DC-5 production acquired 25 percent of the total built! The prototype, sold to William E. Boeing in 1940 as a replacement for his Douglas Dolphin, which he traded in, was taken over by the Navy as the sole R3D-3.

Chapter 3

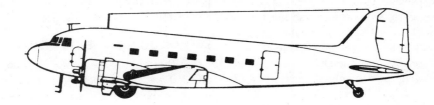

DST/DC-3, The Airplane

Although Douglas became well established as a major producer of transport planes with the DC-2, the following DC-3 was not simply an improved model developed by the builder for offer to the airlines. Like the DC-1, the DC-3 resulted from one airline's specific requirements, but this time the builder was initially reluctant to provide them.

THE REQUIREMENT

American Airlines operated primarily in the eastern part of the United States but had a transcontinental route that reached Los Angeles by the most southern route of the three (United, TWA, and American). The latter had a specialty not shared by the others—it was the only one providing sleeper service, using its slow but comfortable Curtiss Condor II biplanes for the purpose. However, due to the impact of the DC-2, the days of the Condor were numbered despite its slumber monopoly.

What American wanted as a replacement was a plane with the capacity and berth facilities of the Condor but the performance, maintenance, and economic advantages of the DC-2. American had already ordered DC-2s, but their fuselages were too narrow to permit the installation of double berths on each side and still leave an aisle between them. No American manufacturer had an airplane in production or on paper in mid-1934 that could meet American's requirements.

Obviously, it would take a lot of time and money to develop an entirely new model for such a relatively limited purpose; it would be easier to simply stretch an existing design by widening the fuselage. The DC-2 was the logical candidate and there was already a precedent—the 12-passenger DC-1 had been stretched into the 14-passenger DC-2. If the fuselage could be lengthened, why couldn't it also be widened?

Actually, the choice of a modified DC-2 as American's new sleeper is reported to be the result of a remark made by the line's president, Cyrus R. Smith, to his Chief Engineer William Littlewood. They were in Dallas, Texas, about to board a Condor for a continuing flight to Los Angeles in the summer of 1934.

"Bill," said Smith, "what we need is a DC-2 sleeper plane!"

Upon their return to company headquarters in Chicago, Littlewood and his assistant, Otto Kirchner, went to work on detailed suggestions to Douglas for what were intended to be relatively minor changes to the DC-2. Later and more powerful Cyclone engines were now available to handle the increased gross weight, so that presented no problem. The wider fuselage, to accommodate 14 berths or 21 day passengers, would of course not be interchangeable with other DC-2 components, but the stretched model was still expected to have 85 percent parts commonality with the DC-2. As it turned out, the DC-3 ended up with only 10 percent DC-2 commonality.

Douglas was not at all receptive to what was coming more and more to look like a new model, not a simple stretch. The plant couldn't even keep up with the flood of DC-2 orders, much less tool up for a new model—even if the Engineering Department, already busy with new military projects, could design it. Actually, much of the calculations and suggestions for needed structural change were worked out by the airline's engineers.

Douglas was still hesitant to commit its facilities to what promised to be only a relatively small order for a specialized model for one airline—no other line used sleeper planes or was planning to. Further, Douglas doubted American's ability to pay for the planes if they were built. In a prime example of the personal, man-at-the-top way of doing things in those days, C. R. Smith and Donald Douglas worked out a deal in a notable two-hour transcontinental phone call in late 1934. Smith assured Douglas that he could obtain a $4,500,000 loan from the government, which he did, and that the DC-3 need not be limited to the one-airline sleeper market only. The 2 foot 6 inch lengthening of the fuselage, in addition to the 26-inch widening, allowed the seating of 21 day passengers, thereby greatly expanding the market for the basic airplane.

The upshot of the conversation was that American agreed to purchase up to 20 of the new model, with the first 10 to be sleepers—all this over the telephone, with no lawyers, treasurers, or engineers kibitzing the proceedings, and Smith didn't even have his loan yet! Douglas then put his design team under Arthur Raymond (assisted by Ed Burton, Lee Atwood, and Dr. Baily Oswald) to work with no more than Smith's word that he would buy that many airplanes. A formal contract with American was not signed until July 8, 1935, only five months before the new model flew. The unit price for 10 sleepers was $79,500, less engines and other items supplied by the airline.

INTRODUCING THE DST/DC-3

Although the new model was logically the DC-3, it was not introduced as such upon its rollout in December 1935. It was the DST, for Douglas Sleeper Transport. The day-passenger models were identified as DC-3, but the DST designation soon phased out and all—even civil conversions of military versions built and initially operated under military designations—came to be called DC-3s in later years.

There was no prototype DST/DC-3 as such. The first one, with "Experimental" civil registration X14988, made its first flight on December 17, 1935, 32 years to the day after the Wright Brothers' first powered flight (Fig. 3-1). As the world's most advanced landplane transport at the time, it was a fitting milestone of aeronautical progress.

The test program progressed under Douglas and American Airlines pilots with relative few hitches until the airplane received Approved Type Certificate A-607 on May 21, 1936. In April, the airline had taken delivery of the first one—still with its X-license—for route-proving flights. As the first customer, American got delivery of the first 20 airplanes, eight DSTs and 12 DC-3s. Scheduled service with DSTs began between Chicago and Newark (then the terminal for New York) on June 25, 1936, another milestone date in DC-3 history. On September 18, American inaugurated one-plane through sleeper service from Newark to Los Angeles, which took 17 hours 30 minutes and only three stops compared to the Condor service that took 23 hours 23 minutes and nine stops.

Fig. 3-1. The first DST, developed from the DC-2 at the request of American Airlines. Note the absence of the dorsal fin, the use of eight cabin windows on each side of the fuselage, and that the prototype flew in airline markings. (photo by A.U. Schmidt)

NOT A STRETCHED DC-2

As mentioned, the DST/DC-3 turned out to be practically a whole new model, not simply a stretched DC-2. In addition to the dimensional changes and increased capacity, it had more powerful 850-hp engines, was some 7500 pounds heavier at first, cruised 6 mph slower, but had greater range. (Full specifications and performance figures will be found in Appendix A.)

The fuselage used the same structural details and materials as the DC-1 and DC-2. Outwardly, the notable difference was the nearly circular cross-section, more reminiscent of the Northrops than the flat-sided DC-1 and DC-2. The two landing lights were removed from the nose and placed one in each outer wing panel. The pilot's and copilot's windshields and side windows were similar to those of the DC-2 (Fig. 3-2).

In a switch from DC-2 practice, the 30 × 58-inch passenger door was moved to the right side of the fuselage at American's request, since its Fords and Condors had right-side doors and the line's ramp and loading procedures were set up for right-side loading. Later, most DC-3s had left-side doors, which led to interesting air terminal ramp complications (Fig. 3-3). The forward and aft bag-

Fig. 3-2. Standard DST/DC-3 windshield with two panels to a side. Some postwar-II modifications used one-piece windshields. Note the rectangular piece of aluminum skin aft of the TWA emblem. This is a removable "ice panel" that can be replaced easily after being dented by ice thrown off by the propeller. (Douglas photo)

Fig. 3-3. Aerial view of two DC-3s at Boeing Field, Seattle, Washington, in 1940, illustrating the different approaches to airline terminals dictated by right-side and left-side doors on the airplanes. United Air Lines DST-A-207A at the left and a Northwest Airlines DC-3A-269 at the right. (photo by Gordon S. Williams)

gage compartment doors remained on the left side for all DST/DC-3s.

The first DST had eight 14 × 27-inch rectangular windows on each side of the fuselage and the upper berths on each side were fitted with a single 5 × 27-inch window. These narrow upper windows were positive identification features that distinguished the DSTs and the few DC-3Bs from standard DC-3s. The production DSTs had only six lower-berth windows on the left side of the fuselage because of the location of the galley in the left forward portion of the cabin. Some DSTs retained four upper-berth windows on the left side but others had only three for the three berths on that side. It should be noted that most previously published drawings of DSTs show eight windows on the left side because they were based on photos of the widely publicized first article.

Standard 21-passenger DC-3s had seven passenger windows on each side of the fuselage, while 24-passenger DC-3s had eight. Postwar modifications increased some window counts to as many as nine to a side. Emergency escape hatches were built around the fifth window from the front on DC-3s, with those for DSTs in matching positions. Changing safety requirements soon made it necessary to fit an additional escape hatch to the next window aft on all versions.

The fuselage was 108 inches deep, 97 inches wide, and the height of the cabin was 79 inches. From the rear of the flight deck to the front of the aft cargo compartment, the cabin was 30 feet long.

The wing was similar in construction to that of the DC-1/DC-2 but with the span increased from 85 feet to 95 and the area increased from 939 square feet to 987. The wing attachment flanges were common to both models and the outer panels were therefore interchangeable in spite of their different lengths. Where the DC-2 had notably blunt wingtips, the DC-3 had double-elliptical tips in removable sections that came almost to a point. The tip chord of the DC-3 was slightly less than that of the DC-2 because the same taper was projected further outboard. As on the DC-2, the ailerons were

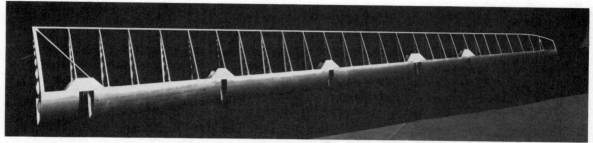

Fig. 3-4. The ailerons of the DST/DC-3, like those of the DC-2, were aluminum frame construction with fabric covering. The rudder and elevators were similar. (Douglas photo)

aluminum frame with fabric covering (Fig. 3-4). Only the right aileron was fitted with a controllable trim tab.

The airfoil was the relatively new NACA 2215 at the root and the related NACA 2206 at the tip. This meant that the DC-3 wing, like most tapered wings, had a depth at the root equal to 15 percent of the chord at that point while the depth at the tip joint was 6 percent of the tip chord. The wing used three full-depth aluminum-web spars. The ribs were also aluminum web, and those between the spars were shallower at the top to allow for installation of stiffening panels with spanwise corrugation.

The aspect ratio of the wing—the span divided by the average chord—was 9.15, higher than average for contemporary airliners and partly responsible for the high efficiency of the DC-3 wing. The long, narrow wing of the DC-3 had an ultimate load factor of 4.5, at 27,500 pounds, but was extremely flexible compared to earlier designs. (This was a somewhat unnerving sight to passengers who did not realize that the flexible wings were absorbing many of the rough-air "bumps" that would otherwise have been transmitted to the fuselage.) The taper ratio was also high for the day, 3.28:1. The hydraulically operated four-section split flaps (Fig. 3-5) covered 43.6 percent of the total wing span and from 18.4 to 19.3 percent of the chord. The flaps could be lowered 60 degrees for landing and were usually set at 10 degrees for takeoff.

Fig. 3-5. Closeup of a DC-3 showing the four-section split trailing edge flaps. Note the size of the wing root/fuselage fillet and the escape panel around the fifth window from the front. (Douglas photo)

Fig. 3-6. Aluminum rudder frame of the DST/DC-3, showing metal-covered trim tab. All of the area forward of the aluminum tube main spar is aerodynamic balance area. (Douglas photo)

For flight in icing conditions, the wings (and vertical fin) could be fitted with rubber de-icer boots. These contained flexible tubes that could be inflated by compressed air to crack accumulated ice from the leading edge by expansion.

The vertical tail surfaces differed notably from the DC-2 and took on the shape used on the contemporary Army cargo plane version of the DC-2 (the C-33) and the B-18 bomber variant. The shape and balance area distribution of the horizontal tail surfaces were also changed. The fabric-covered rudder (Fig. 3-6) and each elevator had an inset trim tab controlled from the cockpit.

The first DST first flew without the distinctive dorsal fin that was to become a trademark of the DC-3. It was added in March 1936 to improve directional stability at approach speeds (Fig. 3-7). This detail was added to the later Army C-39 variants of the DC-2.

The DC-3s landing gear was only slightly changed from the DC-2, and featured a greater shock absorber travel for softer landings and heavier structure to carry the higher gross weight (Fig. 3-8). Retraction and braking were hydraulic. As on the DC-2 and the Boeing 247, the retracted wheels did not go completely into their wells. This feature enabled emergency belly landings to be made with minimum damage to the airplane (Fig. 3-9).

Wheelbase was 37 feet 6 inches and wheel track was 18 feet 6 inches, allowing a slow-speed turn radius of 57 feet. The main wheels were 17.00 × 16 and carried 43 psi air pressure. The full-swivelling 9.00 × 6 tailwheel (Fig. 3-10) was non-retractable.

The DST/DC-3 certificated under ATCs A-607 and A-618 followed DC-2 preference in using the single-row Wright Cyclone engine, starting with the 850-hp SGR-1820-G2, which could deliver 1000 hp for takeoff. Other Cyclones in later production

Fig. 3-7. The first DST with a ''Standard,'' or ''NC,'' license after installation of the dorsal fin. The two tiny windows at the forward end of the fin are skylights for the right-side lavatory. Note that the escape hatch around the sixth window from the front is partially open. (Douglas photo)

Fig. 3-8. Two views of the DST/DC-3 main landing gear, which retracts forward and upward into the engine nacelle. (Douglas photo)

Fig. 3-9. When retracted, the main wheels of the DST/DC-3 projected partway out of the nacelles, enabling emergency wheels-up landings to be made with minimum damage as with this United Air Lines DC-3A-191 in March 1937. (Bowers collection)

DC-3s delivered as much as 1200 hp for takeoff. (These are presented in more detail in the individual DC-3 descriptions that appear later in this book, as do several engines of foreign design and manufacture.)

The alternate engine for the DST/DC-3 was the twin-row 14-cylinder Pratt & Whitney R-1830 Twin Wasp. This was similar to the nine-cylinder Cyclone in weight and power, starting at 1050 takeoff hp, worked up to 1200, and eventually became the most widely used powerplant. Its use was instigated by United Air Lines as discussed under the DC-3A writeup below.

In military use, powerplants are identified by type and displacement, as the Twin Wasp being identified as R-1830, a radial of 1830 cubic inch displacement. Minor differences are identified by

Fig. 3-10. The tailwheel of the DST/DC-3 did not retract, but was full-swivelling. (Douglas photo)

sequential dash numbers, as R-1830-92. Engines produced for the U.S. Army carry odd dash numbers; Navy engines have even dash numbers.

Cyclone and Twin Wasp DST/DC-3s could be distinguished easily by their engine cowlings. The Cyclones had straight-sided cowlings with a flat area across the top of the throat, and no cooling flaps (Fig. 3-11). The Twin Wasp cowling was more tapered, had a fully circular throat, and had circumferential cooling flaps (Fig. 3-12). No Cyclone-powered DC-3s were produced after early 1942.

The initial fuel load of 650 U.S. gallons was carried in four metal tanks in the center section; 25 gallons of oil were carried in each of the two nacelle tanks. Some later variants carried as many as 822 gallons of fuel in the center section.

The original DST was set up to accommodate 14 sleeper passengers in addition to the pilot, copilot, and cabin attendant. The berths (Fig. 3-13) followed the long-established Pullman details of railroad fame, converting to opposite-facing pairs of seats bridging two windows when taken down (Fig.3-14). Four double berths were on the right side of the cabin and three on the left. The DC-3 day planes were originally fitted with seven rows of seats for 21 passengers, two seats on the left side of the 18 inch aisle (Fig. 3-15). A few early DC-3s were fitted out as 14-passenger special fare transports similar to railroad parlor cars and had individual swivelling armchair-style seats (Fig. 3-16).

Later "high-density" versions had 28 to 32 seats paired on each side of a 10-inch aisle. Personal

Fig. 3-11. Closeup of the parallel-sided cowling of a DC-3 powered with Wright R-1820 Cyclone engines. An additional Cyclone identification feature was the small closed-off area at the top of the opening. Note the absence of cooling flaps. (Douglas photo)

Fig. 3-12. The cowlings of DSTs and DC-3s powered with Pratt & Whitney R-1830 Twin Wasp engines were slightly tapered, had fully circular throats, and were fitted with cooling flaps. Note position of oil cooler. (Douglas photo)

Fig. 3-13. Made-up upper and lower berths of a DST. Note the single small window for the upper berth while the lower berth has two full-size windows. (Douglas photo)

Fig. 3-14. For daytime use, the upper berth folded into the cabin ceiling and the lower berth made into the double pair of facing seats shown. (Douglas photo)

carry-on luggage was carried in overhead racks.

Standard DST comfort facilities were two washrooms with basin and chemical toilet—one for men and one for women—located at the rear of the cabin (Fig. 3-17). The buffet was at the front of the cabin. On DC-3s there was only one lavatory at the rear of the cabin; the galley was opposite it. Each seat was provided with an individual reading light, cabin attendant call switch, and adjustable cool-air ducts.

One original DST/DC-3 detail that was very unpopular with passengers, crew, and maintenance personnel alike was the cabin heating system. This operated on steam generated by the engine exhaust and was chronically too hot, too cold, leaking, or otherwise malfunctioning or inoperative. It was eventually replaced by a simple muff around each

engine exhaust that heated ram air and ducted it to the cabin.

Over the years, interior arrangements varied greatly at customer request (Fig. 3-18), but the cockpit, except for instrument variations, was similar for all (Fig. 3-19). Baggage and mail were carried in forward compartments between the cockpit and the cabin, loaded through the forward door on the left side. The rear baggage compartment, just aft of the lavatory, was loaded through an upward-hinging door on the left side.

DC MANUFACTURING

All of the DC-2s and the civil DSTs, DC-3s, and the following U.S. Army C-53s were built at the Santa Monica plant. When the Army placed large orders for the cargo plane variant designated C-47, a new plant was built for Douglas by the government on the airport at nearby Long Beach, California. When further military production of C-47s was needed, another new Douglas factory was built by the government at Oklahoma City, Oklahoma. The few C-117s (passenger versions of the C-47 with airliner features) were also built in Oklahoma, as were the DC-3Ds assembled from unfinished C-117s after the postwar cancellations of military contracts.

In 1942, with similar models being built in several factories, the Army added code letters to its airplane designations in order to identify the source, as follows:

Plant	Example
Santa Monica	C-53-DO
Long Beach	C-47-DL
Oklahoma City	C-47A-5-DK

COSTS

The prices for pre-Pearl Harbor DSTs and DC-3s ranged from $90,000 to $110,000 in 1936, increased to a top of $115,000 in 1939. Seldom was a plane sold "off-the-shelf" at a published price. There were significant reductions for quantity purchases. Prices were also affected by the amount of equipment (sometimes even engines) supplied by the customer and the amount of training given to customer flight and maintenance personnel by the factory and the amount of post-delivery fleet support provided by factory personnel.

DOUGLAS SERIAL NUMBERS

All Douglas airplanes starting with the Cloudster were assigned sequential serial numbers starting with No. 1. These are often referred to as

Fig. 3-15. Standard seating for a 21-passenger DC-3 was seven rows of paired seats on the left side of the cabin and single seats on the right. The 24-passenger versions had eight rows of seats and the 28-passenger versions had seven rows of paired seats on each side of a narrower aisle. (Douglas photo)

Fig. 3-16. As in railroad practice, some DC-3s were converted to aerial "parlor cars" with luxurious swivel chairs for only 14 passengers instead of 21. (Douglas photo)

C/Ns, for Constructor's Numbers, by aircraft data buffs who keep track of individual aircraft through changes of ownership, registration numbers, and even conversion from civil to military service and vice versa. The C/N remains constant throughout. (See Chapters 11 and 12 for exceptions.)

C/Ns are not necessarily consecutive over the production life of long-production series like the DC-2s and DC-3s; other models produced simultaneously get intervening C/Ns in sequence of their production orders. The Douglas C/N for the DC-1 was 1137; those for the 198 passenger DC-2s (including the five shipped to Japan as parts) ranged from 1237 for the first to 1600 for the last. The first of the 10,655 Douglas-built DST/DC-3s was 1494; the last DC-3D, completed after military production ended, was 42981.

A book of this limited size prohibits a listing of all Douglas C/Ns; only those significant to appropriate discussions are mentioned.

DC DASH NUMBERS

Starting with the civil Dolphins, Douglas adopted what has been called a "dash number" system that distinguishes between minor variations of the same basic model. Actually, these are Douglas specification numbers, with each specification tailored to the requirements of a specific customer. Very seldom were DC-3s with the same specification number sold to different customers, and then usually to airlines that were closely affiliated, as were United Air Lines and Western Air Lines in 1936. The same did not hold true for the

DC-2; several different airlines received DC-2-112s, for example.

A major customer would sometimes procure progressive variations of a basic model within a single specification identified by suffix letters, as DC-3-201, -201A, etc., on to -201G for Eastern Air Lines. Other lines would procure DC-3s under several different specifications over a period of time.

The dash numbers, to call them by their accepted term, were not exactly consecutive; there were large gaps at times for studies and proposals, unsold variants, cancelled orders, etc. Not all dash numbers were matched by consecutive C/Ns, ei-

ther. The first seven DST-144s had C/Ns 1494/1500 but the eighth had C/N 1549. The DST/DC-3 dash numbers started at -144 and ended at -1003, the U.S. Army C-117s. The postwar DC-3C and DC-3D were not assigned dash numbers, nor were the DC-3S "Super DC-3s."

DST/DC-3 DESIGNATIONS

The pre-Pearl Harbor DSTs and DC-3s carried a total of five designations between them and because of minor differences—mostly in powerplant details—were given seven separate Approved Type Certificates, or ATCs. Other designations were

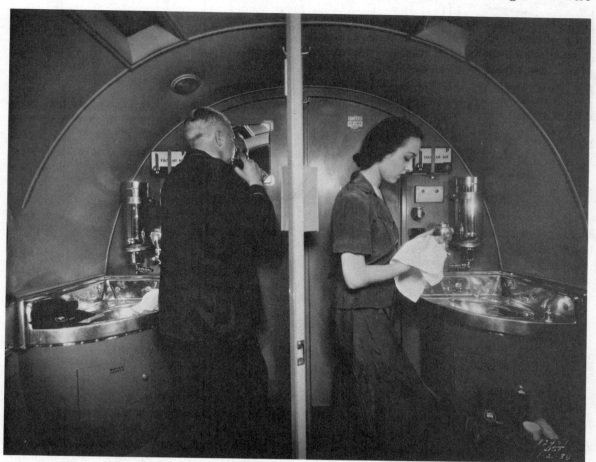

Fig. 3-17. The DST had separate lavatories for men and women, each with two skylights. The DC-3 had a single lavatory for all, with only one skylight. (Douglas photo)

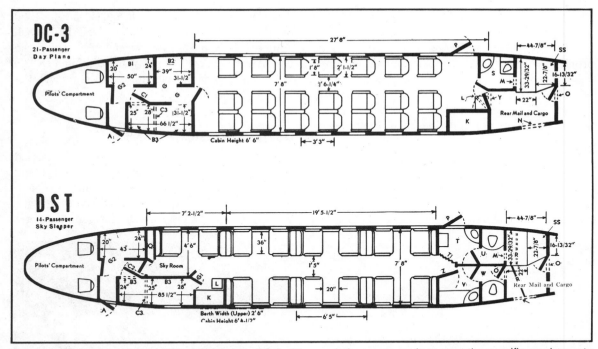

Fig. 3-18. Basic cabin layouts of the DST and the DC-3. Minor variations were made to meet the specific requirements of different customers. (courtesy Douglas)

assigned to modified versions after the war and still others were assigned by firms that undertook major modifications of the basic DC-3 airframe on their own. The government certified the DST/DC-3 under Douglas' basic designations, as DST, DST-A, etc., plus the engine installed.

DST—This was the initial sleeper version with 850-hp Wright Cyclone GR-1820-G2 engines developed for American Airlines. It received ATC A-607 as DST-G2 on May 21, 1936, but was identified by Douglas as the DST-144. Eight-144s were built including the prototype. The certificate was soon expanded to permit the use of G2E, G5, G102, G102A, G103, and G202A Cyclones, but not all were used.

Of 21 DSTs built under ATC A-607, only the first eight had the G2 engine. One had 900-hp G102 engines as DST-217, two with G102 were −217A, and 10 with 1000-hp G202A engines were −217B (2), −318 (3), −217A (2), −318A (2), and −406. All but −406, which went to Eastern Air Lines, were for American.

DC-3—The original 20-plane American Airlines order was completed with 12 21-passenger DC-3-178s with G2 engines that received ATC A-618 as DC-3-G2 on August 27, 1936. Engine options were the same as under ATC-A-607.

Outwardly, the DC-3 could be distinguished from the DST by the use of only seven passenger windows to a side and elimination of the upper bunk windows. American's monopoly of the DST/DC-3 soon ended, and other lines exercised equipment options that included galley and lavatory arrangements and left-side (rather than right-side) passenger doors. Both baggage doors remained on the left side of all DST/DC-3s, however. Seating was not standardized at 21; some deluxe versions marketed as the "DC-3 Skylounge" had 14 luxury chairs for premium-fare passengers. TWA led in this field with five DC-3-209s with left-side doors (Fig. 3-20).

DC-3A—The difference between the DC-3 and the DC-3A was the use of the 1050 to 1200-hp (take-

Fig. 3-19. Cockpit details of the first "production" DST-144, NC16001, for American Airlines. There was very little change in the cockpit details of subsequent DSTs and DC-3s. (Douglas photo)

Fig. 3-20. DC-3s could be distinguished from DSTs by the absence of the upper-berth windows, as on this TWA 14-passenger extra-fare Skylounge. Wright Cyclone engines were notorious for throwing oil—note the cowling. It was not common practice to embark or debark passengers with the door-side engine running. (courtesy Larry M. Peterson)

off) Pratt & Whitney R-1830 Twin Wasp, a 14-cylinder twin-row engine, in the DC-3A. The change from the Wright Cyclone was a relatively simple matter of modifying the nacelles and engine mounts to accommodate an equivalent engine by another manufacturer.

The Cyclone was a well-established design dating from 1928 but the Twin Wasp dated from 1933 and was used in only one civil airplane prior to the DC-3A, the famous Martin 130 China Clipper of 1935. Pratt & Whitney, seeking a wider market for the Twin Wasp, tried hard to sell it to Douglas for the DC-3, but Douglas was too busy to spare the necessary engineering time for a speculative project.

The picture changed when United Air Lines became interested in replacing its Boeing 247s with DC-3s. Since it had a long history of satisfactory service with P & W engines, it preferred to stay with them. Besides, its central transcontinental route was at higher elevation than either TWA's or American's, and the Twin Wasp delivered more power at altitude (900 hp at 6500 feet) than did the "Cyclone" (850 hp at 5,500 feet). When United negotiated for 10 DC-3s in January 1936, Douglas

agreed to develop a Twin Wasp installation with the engineering costs amortized over the cost of the airplanes. In other words, United had to pay for the engineering. In spite of Douglas' initial reluctance to use the Twin Wasp, it ended up as the most widely used engine for the DC-3.

To test the new installation, the second production DST on the American Airlines order was pulled off the production line with American's permission and used for the prototype Twin Wasp installation (Fig. 3-21). It was later refitted with Cyclones and delivered to American as a DST-144.

The initial Twin Wasp engines for United's 10 14-seat right-side door "Skylounge" DC-3A-191s and 12 21-passenger DC-3A-197s were R-1830-SB3G engines with 1100 takeoff hp and normal rating of 900 hp at 2500 rpm at 8000 feet. ATC A-619 was issued for the DC-3A-SB3G on November 28, 1936.

The 22 United planes (with two diverted to affiliated Western Air Express) were the only ones built under this ATC but did not have consecutive C/Ns in a single block. Subsequent DC-3As used later R-1830-S1CG engines with 1200 takeoff hp and 1050 hp at 2250 rpm at 7500 feet and were cer-

Fig. 3-21. The DC-3A differed from the DC-3 in being powered with Pratt & Whitney R-1830 Twin Wasp engines instead of Wright Cyclones. The change was instigated by United Air Lines, and the test installation was made on the second production DST, then registered NX 16002. (Douglas photo via United Technologies)

tified as DC-3A-S1CG under ATC A-669 on October 30, 1937 (Fig. 3-22). This became the major DC-3A model and included postwar conversions of the military C-47. DC-3As built under ATC A-619 came under this ATC when refitted with later series Twin Wasp engines.

DC-3B—This was a "half-and-half" airplane, with four DST-type double berths in the forward half of the cabin and deluxe reclining chairs for seven more passengers in the rear half. (Fig. 3-23). With GR-1820-G102 Cyclone engines rated at 900 hp (1100 hp takeoff) at 2200 rpm at 6000 feet, TWA's 10 DC-3B-G102s received ATC A-635 on May 3, 1937.

These 10 were the only DC-3Bs built. Even so, the C/Ns ranged from 1922 to 2028. All were later modified to DC-3B-G202A for operation under ATC A-618 by substitution of 1200 takeoff hp GR-1820-G202A engines delivering 1000 hp at 2300

rpm at 5000 feet in March 1941.

DST-A—With Twin Wasp engines approved for the DC-3A, it was logical to provide a DSTA for customers who desired the twin-row engine. Again, United Air Lines became the initial customer with an order for 10. The right-side-door DST-A-207s were first delivered in December 1937 under ATC A-647, issued June 30, 1937. Only the United planes, with consecutive C/Ns 1952/1960, were built under this ATC; nine others, using improved S1CG engines, were delivered to United as DSTA-207A under ATC A-671 for DST-A-S1CG issued October 30, 1937 (Fig. 3-24). Again, United was the only customer under that ATC and did the engineering work for the change at its facility in Cheyenne, Wyoming. Douglas approved the drawings and United made the engine changes in its own shops.

Later, when the DST-As were withdrawn from

Fig. 3-22. A United Air Lines DC-3A-197B, certified under ATC A-669. Earlier United DC-3As were certificated under ATC A-619. Note the taller but narrower ice panel on the fuselage in line with the propellers. (photo by Gordon S. Williams)

Fig. 3-23. The eight DC-3B-202s and two DC-3B-202As were mixed day-passenger and sleeper planes with four double berths forward and standard seats aft. The external recognition feature was the unique window spacing. This DC-3B-202 was later drafted by the Army as C-84, 42-57157, and returned to TWA in 1944. (photo by Jack Binder)

sleeper service, the airplanes were modified for conventional seating and relicensed under ATC A-669.

The left-side upper berth window arrangement differed on some sleepers. Although there was no left-forward berth opposite the one on the right side, some retained the upper berth window as a skylight for the galley (Fig. 3-25).

DC-3C—This was a postwar designation given to war-surplus military C-47s converted for civil use in 1946 and on under ATC A-669 (see Chapter 11). Outward recognition as such is difficult, since many had the double cargo doors replaced by standard DC-3 doors, deleted the navigator's astrodome, and installed a DC-3 tail cone over the glider tow hook mount at the rear of the fuselage. There was also considerable variation in the cabin window count.

Douglas converted 21 C-47s and assigned new serial numbers to them, but did not add them to the DC-3 airframe total; nor did the company assign dash numbers as had been done with the prewar DC-3s. (See Chapter 11 for further details.)

DC-3D—Another postwar designation assigned by Douglas to 28 civil DC-3s completed in the Oklahoma City plant from parts for Army C-117 personnel transports cancelled after V-J Day. These were the last DC-3s built as new aircraft and are included in the DC-3 airframe total. They were licensed under ATC A-669 without dash numbers (see Chapter 11).

DC-3S—This designation was applied to former

Fig. 3-24. United Air Lines DST-As with Twin Wasp engines were the first airliners to be fitted with full-feathering propellers, as shown on this DST-A-207A in one-engine flight over New York City in April, 1938. This airplane was later taken by the U.S. Army as C-48B, 42-56101. (courtesy United Technologies)

Fig. 3-25. These matched photos of United Air Lines DST-A-207, NC18109, taken from opposite sides show the different window spacing on opposite sides of the sleeper planes. Note that there is a forward upper berth window on the left side but no corresponding lower berth windows. Compare with Fig. 3-3, which shows different arrangements. (photos by Jack Binder)

DC-3s and surplus military C-47s converted to "Super DC-3" in 1950 and on. Only four were sold to civil customers but the Navy had 100 of its R4Ds (C-47s) converted (see Chapters 12 and 14).

Turbo-Three—A designation applied by a modification firm to its DC-3 conversion that featured two turbine-propeller engines. (See Chapter 15.)

Tri-Turbo-Three—Another turboprop conversion, this time with three engines. (See Chapter 15.)

Super Turbo-Three—Turboprop conversion of a DC-3S. (See Chapter 15.)

DC-3 Turbo Express, or **DC-3-TP**—The only DC-3 turboprop conversion to enter revenue passenger service. (See Chapter 15.)

Chapter 4

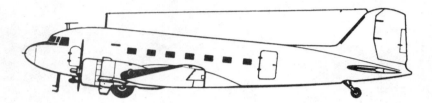

The DC-3 Covers the World

After two of the four U.S. Army DWCs that started the first flight around the world in 1924 completed it, the Douglas Aircraft Company adopted a picture of the globe as its trademark and included the slogan "First Around the World" (Fig. 4-1). By the end of 1938, when the DC-3 had been in production for three years, it could easily have adopted another: "The DC-3 Covers the World."

The excellent performance of the plane, plus its relatively easy maintenance, increased revenue potential over the DC-2 at a relatively small increase in initial and operating costs, and a large modern manufacturing facility that could ensure prompt delivery to any customer made the DC-3 the world's best-selling airliner. It is reputed to be the first airliner that could make a profit for its operators without the need for a government subsidy. The orders received from airlines all over the world bore out that statement.

PIONEERING EXPORTS

Prior to the DC-2, the sale of American airliners

to Europe was practically zero. The DC-2 soon changed that and became the first American airliner sold outside the western hemisphere in significant numbers (Fig. 4-2).

In Europe, the DC-3 finished the job that the DC-2 had started, replacing pre-1935 Fokker trimotors, plus assorted obsolescent biplanes, that made up most of the European airline fleet. Improved designs were on paper or flying as prototypes, but there were no production models available to stem the Douglas invasion. The DC-2/DC-3 influence was very evident in European airliners developed from 1935 to World War II. While European designers copied the DC-2/DC-3 and later American airliners, they never fully caught up. Since export sales of the DC-2 began in 1935, the United States has been the principal supplier of airliners to what is presently called the Western World.

By the time civil aircraft production ended in the U.S. after Pearl Harbor, Douglas had delivered a total of 430 civil DC-3s, mostly as airliners. Again,

Fig. 4-1. The Douglas trademark, proclaiming the fact that Douglas was "First Around The World." (courtesy Douglas)

manufacturer in history. Comparative production figures for the DC-3 and the principal two and three-engine trunk airliners of other firms in the U.S. and Europe that were in service in the early 1930s are presented in Table 4-1.

NO COMPETITION

Throughout its 50-year service the DC-3 has had no directly comparable competing design. There have been somewhat similar transports larger and smaller, but none of the *same* size, power, and capacity doing the *same* job at the *same* time, as was the case with the World War II rivalry between the Boeing B-17 and the Consolidated B-24 Army bombers.

The only American firm to come close to matching the DC-3 in its early years was the Lockheed Aircraft Company of nearby Burbank, California. In 1934, the reorganized Lockheed firm (the original had succumbed during the Depression) introduced a 10-seat twin-engine transport called the Model 10 Electra. This, like the DC-1 and -2, was inspired by the Boeing 247, but secured only a small role with the trunk airlines because of the DC-2.

After the DC-3 entered the scene, Lockheed responded with the Model 14 Super Electra, a 14-seater (Fig. 4-3). The Model 14 was awarded four ATCs late in 1937 and used both P & W Hornet and Wright Cyclone engines. However, the Super Electra beat the DC-3 in only one area—

Fokker was the European distributor, having sold 63 up to the outbreak of World War II in Europe in September 1939. This DST/DC-3 total should be expanded to 579 because 149 ordered by civil customers were requisitioned by the U.S. Army while still in the factory and were delivered under military designations (See Chapter 8).

From the end of 1935, when the first DST flew, to early 1942, Douglas had built more examples of a single airliner model than any other aircraft

Fig. 4-2. This much-travelled DC-2-115E was sold by Fokker to KLM; it then went to Sweden and was later donated to the Finnish Red Cross. It was acquired by the Finnish Air Force during the war with Russia and is shown here in postwar-II markings. It last flew in May 1955, and is presently preserved in Finland. (photo by Charles W. Cain)

47

Table 4-1. Principal Trunk Airliners in Use—Early 1930s.

Make/Model	Country	Production Years	No. Built	
Boeing 80/80A	USA	1928 - 1930	16	
Boeing 247/247D	USA	1933 - 1935	75	
Caproni CA97/CA-101	Italy	1927 - 1933	100	+ (1)
Curtiss Condor II	USA	1933 - 1935	45	
Douglas DC-2	USA	1934 - 1937	198	(2)
Douglas DC-3	USA	1935 - 1946	10,655	(3)
Fokker Trimotor F-VII	Holland	1926 - 1932	197	(4)
Fokker Trimotor F-X	USA	1927 - 1931	63	
Ford 4AT/5AT	USA	1926 - 1932	94	
Junkers JU23/24/31	Germany	1924 - 1929	73	
Junkers Ju52-3M	Germany	1932 - 1947	4835	(5)
Stinson 6000/U	USA	1930 - 1932	80	
Stinson A	USA	1934 - 1936	35	

(1) Civil and military production cannot be separated
(2) Includes five delivered unassembled
(3) 579 ordered as DST/DC-3, 1935-1941. 28 cancelled Army C-117's completed as DC-3C to end production in 1946.
(4) Includes F-VIIB, F-IX, F-XII, F-XVIII, F-XX, and production by six licensees.
(5) German production through 1944. Major military production after 1939. Also built under license in France and Spain into postwar years.

speed. Its cruising speed was 235 mph, but it carried only two-thirds the passengers and half the fuel, and was 10,000 pounds lighter. Only 110 Model 14s were built as civil aircraft; Lockheed sold more of them abroad than it did on the American market.

Civil Model 14 production was dropped in favor of a stretched Model 18 Lodestar in 1939, but the basic design was quickly adapted to a patrol bomber, the famous RAF Hudson of World War II. Over 2900 were built into 1943.

By 1940, the Lockheed Model 14 had been stretched to become the Model 18 Lodestar using the same wing and tail and the engine options stretched to include the P & W Twin Wasp (Fig. 14-4). The five-foot-six-inch fuselage stretch was not made to increase passenger capacity as with the DC-1 and -2, but to improve longitudinal stability. The 18 was nearly 20 mph faster than the 14 and 3500 pounds heavier, but had the major handicap of short range; a slower DC-3 could beat it over distances like 1000 miles by being able to fly

Fig. 4-3. A Lockheed Model 14G3B Super Electra in Japan. The Model 14 appeared after the DC-3 but was smaller and not directly competitive. (courtesy Hideya Ando)

Fig. 4-4. The Lockheed Model 18 Lodestar was a stretched version of the Model 14 but did not use the added fuselage length to increase passenger capacity. (Lockheed photo)

nonstop while the Lodestar had to make several fuel stops.

Relatively few Lodestars served U.S. airlines; most production was taken over by the military. Army models were C-56, C-57, C-69, and C-60; the Navy had over 100 R5Os and the RAF also got some. There was also a bomber derivative, the Model 37, called Ventura by the RAF, B-34 and B-37 by the U.S. Army, and PV-1 by the Navy.

The final prewar-II challenge to the DC-3 was the 36-passenger twin-engine Curtiss-Wright C-W 20 that flew in 1940. This was larger than the DC-3, with a wingspan of 108 feet 1 inch and a gross weight of 40,000 pounds. Powerplants were the new 1700-hp twin-row Wright R-2600 Twin Cyclones. Cruising speed of the twin-tail prototype was 222 mph at 10,000 feet.

The prewar C-W 20 was never certificated. After ordering higher-powered cargo versions with 2000-hp P & W R-2800 Double Wasp engines as the C-46, the U.S. Army bought the existing prototype as the C-55 for testing before the C-46s were built. Surplus C-46s received six different ATCs after the war, but did not serve the trunk airlines. Most were used as freighters and could carry heavier loads than the DC-3 but could not match its versatility.

Oddly, the one European airliner that the DC-3 did not replace was a true aeronautical anachronism, the 16-passenger German Junkers Ju52/3M (Fig. 4-5). This all-metal trimotor, nicknamed "Tante Ju" (Auntie Ju) by its airline and Luftwaffe crews, was a straight-line development of the similar Ju23 trimotor of 1923. The unique Junkers metal-frame construction with corrugated sheet aluminum covering was developed in 1917 and was used on the American Stout designs of the early 1920s that evolved into the Ford trimotor, the famous Tin Goose.

The first six Ju52s, which had a wingspan of 95 feet—the same as the DC-3—were single-engine cargo planes with 690 to 800-hp engines. For passenger work, the reliability was greatly increased by the use of three engines, soon standardized as 525 to 750-hp American Pratt & Whitney Hornets built under license by BMW.

The Ju52/3M had a career remarkably parallel to that of the DC-3. Both were refinements of previous designs, and both started their careers as civil airliners but were to see there major produc-

49

Fig. 4-5. The German Junkers Ju52/3M was a much older design than the DC-3, with structural features dating back to 1917. However, the Ju52/3M stubbornly resisted replacement by the DC-3 and actually remained in production later than the DC-3. (courtesy LuftHansa)

tion as military cargo planes (Fig. 4-6). The Ju52/3M had an early diversion as a bomber, quickly adapted in 1934 to form the bomber nucleus of Hitler's still unrevealed new Luftwaffe.

Prior to the DC-3, the Ju52/3M was the world's most widely used airliner, with sales all over the world except to North America. Luft Hansa, the German national airline, had 51 on hand in December 1935, and 78 in December 1940. Of the 4835-plane total, 2804 examples of this obsolete but highly reliable and unreplaceable slowpoke were built from 1939 on—not only in Germany, but by the captive French aviation industry on Luftwaffe orders and under license in Spain.

Again as an oddity, the production life of the Ju52/3M passed that of the DC-3; of 400 or more built by the French firm Ateliers Aeronautiques de Colombes (AAC) after V-J Day, and into 1937, some 113 were completed as airliners. In still another oddity, Air France, not Luft Hansa,* had the largest fleet of Ju52/3Ms at one time, with 85 on hand in 1946-47. In England, 20 captured Ju52/3Ms were

refurbished and used by British European Airways and others in 1946-48.

The Ju52/3Ms faded from the airline scene quickly in the 1960s and were replaced—principally by DC-3s. At this writing (July 1985), three are still in service with the Swiss Air Force, giving that model to date a longer military life than the DC-3, which did not join the U.S. Army until 1938.

EARLY DELIVERIES

For U.S. airlines, delivery of new DST/DC-3s was easy—just send a company crew to Santa Monica and have it fly the new bird to the home base. Overseas deliveries at the time were a different matter. The airplane did not have transoceanic range, so had to be shipped by sea as deck cargo. For protection against salt water, the fuselages were extensively sealed and sometimes given overall protective coatings of grease or cosmoline (Fig. 4-7).

This was costly and time-consuming, and of course delivery by air was preferable. However, special measures had to be taken to give the airplanes the necessary range. Temporary fuel tanks were installed in the cabin (Fig. 4-8). Removal

---

* Actually, "Deutsche Luft Hansa" until May 1945. Dormant until reorganized in August 1954 as "Lufthansa."

of the normal cabin furnishings and revision of the fuel system to accommodate the cabin tanks made it necessary to ferry the airplanes on restrictive "Experimental" rather than "Standard" licenses. The first overseas delivery of DC-3s by air was a trio for Hawaiian Airlines in August 1941 (Fig. 4-9).

After establishment of the North Atlantic Ferry Route for the delivery of U.S. warplanes to Europe in 1941, delivery of military DC-3s to Europe by air became commonplace. Since transpacific distances were too great, initial deliveries to Asia went the long way—across the South Atlantic and Africa and on through India to China and Australia. Late in the war, however, military DC-3s were island-hopping their way across the Pacific.

CHANGE OF OWNERSHIP

Not all of the early DC-3s delivered to Europe remained long in the hands of their original purchasers. When Germany annexed Czechoslovakia in March 1939, it took over a number of Czech airliners, including DC-2s and DC-3s. These were turned over to Luft Hansa and received new German civil registrations. Three DC-2s and four DC-3s were confiscated in Czechoslovakia, with one DC-2 being assigned to the Luftwaffe.

After Germany's invasion of the low countries in May 1940, seven more DC-2s were taken from Holland, along with five DC-3s plus another DC-3 captured in Belgium. The five Dutch DC-3s served temporarily in the Luftwaffe before being released to Luft Hansa (Fig. 4-10). Since the U.S. Army had only two DC-3s in service at that time, Germany had more DC-3s in military service than did the U.S.

Some prewar DC-3s operating outside the U.S.

Fig. 4-6. The military cargo versions of the Ju52/3M underwent essentially the same changes as the DC-3/C-47 conversion—the addition of large cargo doors and reinforced flooring. This variant has the designation Ju52/3Mg10e. (H.J. Nowarra collection)

Fig. 4-7. Early overseas delivery of DC-3s was by ship. Here a KLM DC-3 is being hoisted aboard. Note that all openings have been sealed and the skin protected with a heavy coat of grease. (courtesy Robert Esposito)

were not owned by the countries in which they were based in spite of their markings. In some cases an airline, as CNAC (China National Aviation Corporation), was partly American-owned and the airplanes carried American registration numbers, which may or may not have been painted on the airplane (Fig. 4-11).

UNIVERSAL TRANSPORT

The DC-3 became historic before World War II when it was produced in greater numbers than any other civil transport plane. The Ju52/3M might have been sold to more individual countries of that time, and built in greater numbers, but the majority after 1935 were produced for military, not civil, use.

When World War II ended the DC-3 came into its own as the world's most widely used single airplane model. Other wartime models had been built in greater numbers—for example, 19,256 Consolidated B-24 Liberators and over 30,000

Messerschmitt Bf 109s—but these were specialized military types that were of no use in civil work. The majority of DC-3s built from 1942 on were U.S. Army C-47s, relatively minor adaptations of the civil airliner for military cargo and transport work, but there were also the Army C-53s which were more like true DC-3s. Thousands of C-47s and some C-53s became available on the surplus market at very attractive prices, and very little work was required to readapt them to purely civil missions.

The combination of low price, easy adaptability, reliability, and performance that fulfilled most short-to-medium-haul needs made the surplus C-47 and the surviving prewar DC-3s the world's most widely used civil transport plane, both in actual airframe numbers and the number of using nations. Altogether, civil DC-3s have been registered in 159 separate countries, both as conventional passenger planes stripped of military features (Fig. 4-12) and as cargo planes with their original C-47 doors (Fig. 4-13). Considering that there are cur-

Fig. 4-8. To enable DC-3s to be delivered overseas by air, the relatively short airliner range was increased by the temporary installation of additional fuel tanks in the cabin. (Douglas photo)

Fig. 4-9. First aerial delivery of DC-3s overseas was a trio of DC-3A-375s on a 2400-mile flight from Oakland, California, to Hawaii in August 1941. Because of the auxiliary fuel tanks, the planes flew on temporary Experimental licenses. Note eight cabin windows to a side on this short-range 24-passenger version. (photo by Peter M. Bowers)

Fig. 4-10. This DC-3-194B was sold by Fokker to KLM. It was impressed into the Luftwaffe in 1940, then transferred to Luft Hansa as shown. In 1945 it was returned to KLM and was sold to England in August 1946. It was scrapped in May 1950. (courtesy John Stroud)

rently (1985) only 163 recognized independent nations in the world, the global coverage of the DC-3 can truly be appreciated.

However, the figures are somewhat misleading. In some cases, individual countries have undergone changes of name, as Ceylon to Sri Lanka, so appear twice. In others, countries have broken up, as part of India breaking away to become Pakistan, part of which later broke away to become Bangladesh. Further, separate countries have

joined to become one and then have broken apart again.

Some colonial powers are recognized as a single nation, but have colonies with separate aircraft registries from the mother country. Hong Kong, for instance, is treated as a country of its own in tallying aircraft registrations but as a British Crown Colony does not appear on any listing of independent nations. If British possessions other than Commonwealth Nations such as Australia, Canada, and

Fig. 4-11. China did not use a conventional aircraft registration system in the immediate prewar-II years, so identification from photos is difficult. This is either a DC-3-227 or -228B with CNAC in large letters on top of the fuselage and wings. (courtesy Arthur Pearcy)

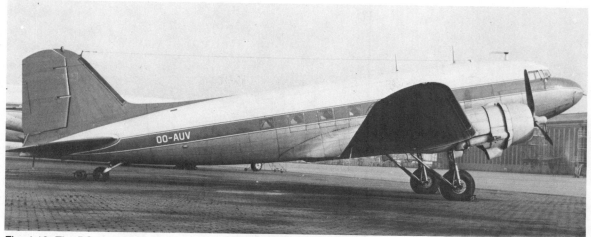

Fig. 4-12. The DC-3's prewar status as the world's leading airliner was increased in postwar years as surplus military variants became available. This former C-47A-45-DL, 42-24097, is shown in the markings of the Belgian Delta Air Transport, which it served from 1968 through 1972. (courtesy Alain Pelletier)

New Zealand, which have their own registrations, plus surviving French and Portuguese colonies are included, the listing of "nations" would be somewhat higher.

Many colonies that became independent nations in the decades following World War II quickly formed new airlines, either as private enterprises or government-owned endeavors. Not surprisingly, a DC-3 or former C-47 was often the first airplane to appear on the civil register of a new nation (Fig. 4-14).

Because of the constant increase in new nations and the disappearance of some others, it is impossi-

ble to make a completely accurate count of every different nation or colony that has used civil DC-3s. Despite such inaccuracy, no one can dispute the universal use of the DC-3. No single transport airplane has been used in so many places or in such numbers. Because of changing world politics and economics, no other airplane in existence or projected can expect to match the record of the ubiquitous DC-3.

The same circumstances of availability, suitability, and the right price also made the surplus C-47 popular with postwar-II military services. Counting these countries receiving C-47s under

Fig. 4-13. Some surplus C-47s used by European airlines retained many of their military features. This former C-47A-65-DL, 42-100612, for Air France not only has its military cargo doors but the military navigator's astrodome. (courtesy Alain Pelletier)

Fig. 4-14. Most nations of the world use letters rather than numbers for aircraft registration. Several of the new nations formed in the decades after World War II had a DC-3 as the first airplane on their new registers. This former C-47A-45-DL, 42-24116, was registered 8P-AAA in Barbados, a former British colony that became independent in 1966. (photo by Harold G. Martin)

Lend-Lease in World War II, the armed forces of 105 nations besides the U.S. have used it. This total does not include such organized guerrilla forces as the current "Contras" of Nicaragua.

Chapter 5

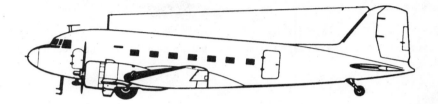

Foreign Manufacture

The DC-3 became such a popular airliner before World War II that Douglas could not keep up with the demand. Consequently, licenses to manufacture it were issued to three countries: Holland, Japan, and Russia. The Dutch licensee was Fokker, which had been the European distributor for the DC-2 and early DC-3s. Although Fokker did not actually build any DC-3s, it continued to distribute them to a total of 63 until war ended the operation. Japan and Russia, however, became major producers of civil models under the prewar licenses and then went on to develop their own "C-47" military equivalents with no help from Douglas.

JAPAN

In 1934, Japan secured manufacturing and certain geographic distribution rights for the DC-2, and five Japanese models assembled from Douglas-supplied parts (Fig. 5-1) took to the air early in 1936. When the DC-3 came along (Fig. 5-2), similar rights were obtained for it, in February 1938, at a

cost of $90,000, but the situation then was quite different.

Where the DC-2s had been built by the long-established Nakajima Aircraft Company, the DC-3s were built by a new firm, Showa Hikoki Kogyo KK, a subsidiary of Mitsui Bussan Kaisha KK, or Mitsui Trading Company, Ltd. Although outwardly for civil airlines, Japanese production of the DC-3 was sponsored by the Navy, which carried it as the "Type 0" transport for the same reason the famous "Zero" fighter carried the same number—it was ordered in the Year 2600 of the Japanese calendar (actually, it would seem that the number should be 00, since earlier "calendar" types like the "Type 97" used two digits). The assigned airplane designation was L2D2 for transport (L), second Navy type (2), and the second Douglas design (D2). This did not mean that the DC-3 followed the DC-2; the designation L2D1 was assigned to the imported DC-3s, which the Navy also controlled. Detail distinctions within the model were indicated by suffix letters and dash numbers.

Fig. 5-1. One of the five DC-2s shipped to Japan in parts for final assembly by Nakajima. (courtesy Hideya Ando)

Fig. 5-2. A DC-3A built under license in Japan by Showa. Note added small window aft of cockpit, unidentified structure above it, antenna mast, and fuel dump chutes at trailing edge of wing.

Fig. 5-3. A Douglas-built DC-3 (note trademark on fin) sold to Japan before World War II. Prewar Japanese registration records are incomplete, so this cannot be verified as either a DC-3-237C or a -260, four and six each, respectively, having been exported to Japan. (courtesy Shiro Ogiwara)

Since the Allies later had a tough time determining, much less understanding, Japanese aircraft designations, they gave one-word code names to all Japanese military aircraft during the war. Thus, the DC-2 became "Tess" and the DC-3 became "Tabby."

Starting in 1937 and continuing after the first L2D2 rolled out in September 1939, Japan imported

19 Santa Monica-built models, 12 DC-3s (Fig. 5-3) and seven DC-3As, plus two unassembled airframes for patterns. Thirteen of these went to Japan's Great Northwest Airways and six, all Cyclone-powered DC-3s, went to the Far East Fur Trading Company.

To help get production rolling, Douglas sent technicians and planners to Japan. Since completion of the Showa factory was way behind schedule, the Navy got Nakajima to follow its DC-2 production with some DC-3s, which despite the change of manufacturer were still called L2D2s. Nakajima built 71 in 1940-41, while Showa produced 416 from 1939 through 1945, including finishing the two that

came from Douglas as parts.

The L2D2 model (Fig. 5-4) broke down to eight separate subtypes with two basic configurations: straight airline-type transports and a cargo plane with reinforced floor and double cargo door on the left side as on the American C-47 but preceding it in service. However, the Japanese model did not have the C-47's canted floor at the rear of the cabin.

Where the airline DC-3s were almost exactly like the American originals externally, the military models were quite distinctive. Most noticeable were the extra windows behind the cockpit, differently contoured engine cowlings, and large spinners on the propellers. The subtypes are:

Model	Type	Powerplant	Remarks
L2D2	Passenger	Mitsubishi 43, 1000 hp	
L2D3	Passenger	Mitsubishi 51, 1300 hp	
L2D3a	Passenger	Mitsubishi 53, 1300 hp	
L2D3-1	Cargo	Mitsubishi 51, 1300 hp	
L2D3-1a	Cargo	Mitsubishi 53, 1300 hp	
L2D4	Passenger	Mitsubishi 51, 1300 hp	Dorsal gun
L2D4-1	Cargo	Mitsubishi 51, 1300 hp	Dorsal gun
L2D5		Mitsubishi 62, 1560 hp	Unfinished wooden version, 1945

Fig. 5-4. The Japanese made their own conversion of the DC-3 to a military cargo plane. This is the Showa L2D-3 Tabby. Note the different shape of the double cargo doors, the additional cockpit windows, observation blister, and propeller spinners on the 1300-hp Mitsubishi 53 engines. (photo by Peter M. Bowers)

Fig. 5-5. Tabbys flown by the Japanese during the surrender negotiations were painted overall white. This one was later taken over by the Chinese Air Force. Note the additional cabin window in the forward portion of the cargo door. (photo by Peter M. Bowers)

Wartime materials shortages in Japan soon brought other undesignated changes to the L2Ds. Some components such as the fabric-covered movable control surfaces were made of wood, and some fairings and the tail cone were plywood. The unfinished wooden L2D5 inspected after the war revealed some steel parts in critical areas.

The prewar DC-3s continued to serve the Japanese airlines during the war and the military models paralleled Allied C-47/R4D operations. After its defeat, Japan had hopes of being allowed to continue airline operations and had some American-made DC-3s ready, but this was not to be. Unlike the situation in Germany, where useful airliners were saved from the scrapping edict and put to work on the victors' airlines, all DC-3s and L2Ds in Japan were soon scrapped. The only survivors were flyable or repairable examples that the Chinese rounded up in their country (Fig. 5-5). The U.S. tested some examples captured in the Philippines (Fig. 5-6) but did not preserve any. Surprisingly, the late-model "Japanese copies" outperformed the U.S. originals in some areas.

RUSSIA

Russia got on the DC-3 bandwagon in a very systematic way. It imported 22 DC-3s, plus two

Fig. 5-6. A Tabby tested by the U.S. Army in the Philippines after the war. Note the fuel dump valves present on prewar Showa-built DC-3A but not on the two previous Tabby photos. (USAF photo)

Fig. 5-7. A Russian-built DC-3 powered with Russian Shevstov M-62 engines, which were license-built versions of the American Wright Cyclone. Originally designated PS-84, the Russian DC-3s were redesignated Li-2. (courtesy H.J. Nowarra)

unassembled airframes to serve as patterns after manufacturing rights were obtained. To prepare for production in State Aircraft Plant No. 84, near Moscow, the government sent Boris P. Lisunov to Douglas in 1938 to study Douglas' methods. He remained in Santa Monica for two years and upon his return was able to adapt the DC-3 to Russian procedures.

Production of the Russian DC-3 began near Moscow under the designation of PS-84 (for the factory) but it was changed to Li-2 (Lisunov) on September 17, 1942. Because of the German invasion, production was transferred to a new factory in Tashkent in South Central Russia, not far from the border with Afghanistan.

The Russians also took liberties with the design. Their initial powerplant was the 900-hp Shevstov M-62, which was the Wright Cyclone built under license (Fig. 5-7). It was also used on the well-known Polikarpov I-16 fighter. Other than larger cargo doors on some, the major alteration was to fit a power turret for a 7.2mm machine gun to the

Fig. 5-8. The Russians also made their own military adaptations of the DC-3. This Li-2 has a powered machine gun turret in the center of the cabin but standard right-side airliner door. (courtesy Arthur Pearcy)

Fig. 5-9. In the postwar-II years, the Russian Li-2s played the same role in Iron Curtain countries that the DC-3/C-47 played in the west—serving both the civil airlines and the military. This Li-2 has a DC-3 type aft baggage compartment, a left-side cargo door, and a right-side passenger door. Note the attached steps. (courtesy Arthur Pearcy)

top of the fuselage, somewhat farther aft than the Japanese L2D4 installation (Fig. 5-8). Gun turrets and bomb racks seem to have been extras that did not affect the airplane designation. Beside the basic Li-2 designation, there were seven subtype designations for the approximately 2,930 built:

Li-2   Basic DC-3 airframe; some fitted with turrets and bomb racks.
Li-2R   Photoreconnaissance; some with extra windows and PBY-style side blisters.
Li2P   Civil passenger version.
Li-2G   Cargo version for Aeroflot.
Li-2PG   Civil mixed cargo/passenger.
Li-2T   As Li-2G with upward-opening cargo door on left side.
Li-2F   Czech military designation for Li-2R.
Li-2V   As Li-2P with supercharged engines.

There was also an Li-3, apparently Russian-built Li-2 airframes fitted with American-made Wright Cyclone engines.

The Li-2s were used for long-haul transportation within Russia and for support of the troops on the German front. After the war the Li-2 played the same role in Iron Curtain countries that the DC-3/C-47 played in the rest of the world; it remained in military service and also became the mainstay of Aeroflot, the Russian national airline, into the 1970s. Some still serve satellite countries today (Fig. 5-9).

Chapter 6

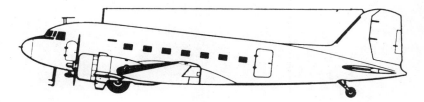

U.S. Army Production DCs—XC-32 to C-117

It did not take long for the U.S. Army and Navy to follow the airlines in their desire to update their transport plane fleets. Both got early starts by ordering virtually off-the-shelf DC-2s for evaluation.

Although the Navy obtained DC-2s prior to the Army, the Army models are described first in this separate chapter because all of the later Navy DC-3 procurements followed Army procurement and in most cases were existing Army models given Navy designations.

U.S. ARMY DESIGNATION SYSTEM

A better understanding of U.S. Army DC procurement will be had through an understanding of the Army Aircraft Designating system. Essentially the U.S. Army (U.S. Air Force after September 18, 1947) uses what is known as the Type-Model-Series System (TMS). The full TMS designation, along with the airplane's Army serial number and other data, is painted in one-inch stencil figures on the left side of the fuselage near the cockpit. For most Army DCs, this was directly below the pilot's side window (Fig. 6-1).

Type—Aircraft are designated by a *type* letter that identifies the primary mission, as A-for-Attack, B-for-Bomber, C-for-Cargo/Transport, etc.

Model—The type letter is followed by a *model* number that shows the sequence of model procurement. The Douglas C-33 was the 33rd model of a C-type procured since the system began in 1924. It should be pointed out that not all models contracted for were actually built.

Series—Successive variations of each type/model are identified by *series* letters, as C-47A, C-47B, etc.

Block Numbers—In 1942, with almost day-to-day changes being made to production aircraft, a *block number* system was set up to keep track of minor changes that did not justify a change of series letter.

The block number started with -1 for a block of identically-equipped planes, then jumped to -5 for a block with notable differences, then -10, -15, etc., in multiples of five. The intermediate numbers were used for field modifications and post-production changes.

Fig. 6-1. Data block on a U.S. Air Force JC-47A, giving Type, Model, and serial number as well as the crew weight (200 pounds per man) and the grade of fuel to be used. (photo by William T. Larkins)

Factory Identification—By early 1942 the rapidly expanding Army Air Forces not only had similar models being built in separate plants of the same manufacturer, but had different manufacturers building the same airplane model. The Army C-53s were built at the same Douglas Santa Monica plant as the DC-3s, which received the identification -DO. This was added to the airplane designation as C-53-DO (the C-53s were not assigned dash numbers). Similarly, the C-47s built at the new Douglas Long Beach plant, built especially for them, were C-47A-1-DL, etc., while C-47Bs built in Oklahoma City, Oklahoma, were C-47B-1-DK, etc.

The six wartime Douglas plants are identified below as to principal U.S. Army models produced:

Status Prefixes—The Army prefixes the standard TMS series with three prefix letters to identify the status of the airplane.

X—The letter X has been used since 1924 to identify true experimental models, as the prototype of a new model, or for existing "standard" models diverted to an experimental test program. In this case, the experimental status protects the program from delays caused by airplane compliance with routine maintenance and upgrade directives.

Very few Xs appear among the Army's DCs—the XC-32 as a "new" model, the XC-47C and XC-53A, standard C-47s and 53s modified for experimental programs. On prototypes, the X-designation is usually retained for the life of the

Abbreviation	Plant	Army Models
DO	Santa Monica, Calif.	A-20, C-53, C-54
DE	El Segundo, Calif.	A-24, but mostly Navy models
DL	Long Beach, Calif.	A-20, A-26, B-17 (licensed), C-47
DK	Oklahoma City, Okla.	C-47, C-117
DT	Tulsa, Okla.	A-24, A-26, B-24 (licensed)
DC	Chicago, Ill.	C-54

airplane; on modifications it can be dropped if the airplane reverts to standard configuration.

Y—The letter Y has been used since 1929 to identify the Service Test status of a new model, such examples usually following the order for an X-model. Examples are rare among the Army DCs—the two YC-34s of 1935 and the YC-129 (redesignated as YC-47F) of 1949.

Z—This is a paperwork designation used to indicate that an airplane has become obsolete but is still a useful machine to keep in service. The designation was seldom painted on the airplane—and certainly not on the many C-47s that remained in service nearly 30 years after they were built.

Special-Purpose Prefixes—Starting during World War II, the Army began to add various special-purpose prefixes in addition to the status prefixes to airplanes that were used for other than their designated missions. For Army C-47s the practice applied mostly in postwar years and past the change to U.S. Air Force. During the war, many C-47s were given unidentified modifications or were used for purposes that in later years would have rated a prefix.

Single letters were used, but these are sometimes misleading today because the same letter has meant different things at different times. The special-purpose prefixes known to have been used by U.S. Army/Air Force C47s, C-53s, and C-117s are presented below:

A (1)—Airway verification. The first use of A on a C-47 was for AC-47As and Ds fitted with electronic equipment in 1953 for checking the accuracy of airway beams. Such C-47s were usually distinguished by an elongated nose cone containing electronic equipment.

A (2)—Tactical Support. This can be translated as A-for-Attack. After 1962, the prefix A identified an airplane adapted to tactical support missions and the electronic function was taken over by the letter E.

E (1)—Exempt. From 1946 to 1954, the E-prefix indicated an exempt status for Army airplanes leased to civil firms under a Bailment Con-

tract. While many C-47s were leased out this way, it is not known that any carried an EC-47 designation at the time. The E was also applied to many airplanes of the Air Research and Development Command (ARDC) to exempt them from compliance with routine technical orders.

E (2)—There was an overlap here, with the second E-prefix, adopted in 1948, identifying special electronic equipment, which could vary from the airways checking equipment originally covered by A to exotic and still hush-hush electronic countermeasures (ECM) and detecting equipment widely used in Vietnam. After 1962, when the Navy changed to Air Force-type designations, Navy R4Ds with Q suffixes got E-prefixes, as the R4D-6Qs that were redesignated as EC-47J.

F (1)—Photographic. Airplanes modified for photographic purposes, 1945-47. C-47s were used for photo work in this period but are not known to have been given F-prefixes.

F (2)—Fireship. A very briefly-used prefix for the C-47 gunships that were later designated AC-47 in 1966-67.

H—Search and Rescue. A new prefix adopted in 1962 to replace the old S-for-Search used on planes equipped for search and rescue. Many C-47s carried the S-prefix but the type had been largely replaced in the role when the H came along.

J—Temporary Special Test. In the past, it was common practice to add an X-for-Experimental to airplanes diverted and modified for special test programs. Since August 1955, the letter J has been used to identify such airplanes that can be reconverted to their original configurations relatively easily. Quite a few guinea pig C-47s were in the J category.

L (1)—Liaison. From 1948 to 1962, the prefix L-for-Liaison was assigned to airplanes not built as L-types but assigned to liaison roles, particularly during the Korean War. C-47s were used in many roles there, but it is not known that any officially became LC-47s.

L (2)—Winterized. After 1962, the L prefix was used on Navy R4Ds that had been winterized for Arctic/Antarctic missions and identified as such by the addition of an L-suffix, as R4D-5L. In the redesignation of 1962, these became LC-47H.

M—Medical Evacuation. The widest use of the C-47 for MedEvac came long before the prefix was adopted in 1951, but some are known to have carried it in Korea. After 1962, M identified a missile carrier but it is not known that any C-47s were so designated.

N—Permanent Special Test. Since 1955, the N-prefix has identified planes that have undergone such extensive structural or equipment changes for special test purposes that they cannot be conveniently restored to their original configurations. Numbers of C-47s were in this category.

R (1)—Restricted. The letter R was one of the first prefixes adopted late in 1942 and was intended to restrict obsolete airplanes from being used for their designated mission, as fighting or bombing. This, of course, never applied to the C-47.

R (2)—From 1948, the letter meant Reconnaissance, and was mostly applied to photographic conversions that later reverted to original type. The B-17s that became F-9s (F-for-Foto) in WW II became RB-17s in 1948. Some C-47s had been fitted with search or pathfinder radar during WW II but did not get special prefixes or redesignations because of it. Some so equipped after 1948 became RC-47s. Some with this same equipment were later used as electronic and navigation trainers as TC-47s. RC-47s were used extensively in Korea, sometimes in such dangerous tasks as dropping flares over enemy territory in support of tactical operations.

S—Search and Rescue. In 1948, the S prefix was added to various airplanes, mostly bomber and transport types with good range and load capacity, that were assigned to Air-Sea search and rescue missions (ASR). Some of these carried lifeboats to drop at sea, but although the C-47 was widely used for ASR, none are known to have carried boats. They did, however, carry the special ASR markings. After 1962, the S was replaced by H for USAF airplanes but was inconsistent overall because Navy R4Ds used in search missions, as R4D-6S, used the S prefix when redesignated SC-47J.

T (1)—Trainer. This was the only special-purpose prefix assigned to Army C-47s during WW II. A particular rarity is the fact that 133 airplanes were built as TC-47Bs and did not pick up the T later as did others. They were built specifically as instrument and navigation trainers, not transports. Other C-47s were pressed into many different training roles in later years.

T (2)—Transport. Navy R4Ds that were specifically Staff transports, such as R4D-5R, became TC-47H after 1962 but were still transports, not trainers.

V—Staff Transports. Since the end of WW II, standard transports and some obsolescent bombers fitted with deluxe cabin furnishings for the use of high ranking officers have been given the V prefix that is generally considered to mean VIP. No standardization was involved for the many VC-47s. Some retained their two-section cargo doors and needed a ladder for access. Others had one part of the door sealed and the other modified to drop-down "airstair" type, and some even had adjacent center cabin windows merged into large single view windows. Some C-53s became VC-53 after the war, and Navy R4D-8s that carried the Z suffix denoting staff transport became VC-117Ds in the 1962 redesignation.

W—Weather. Starting in 1948, the prefix W was applied to airplanes used for weather reconnaissance and reporting, and in the famous "Hurricane Hunting" missions. These missions generally went to longer-range airplanes like bombers, but a few C-47s were equipped specifically for the role.

ARMY SERIAL NUMBER SYSTEM

The serial numbering system for U.S. Army airplanes, under which they are procured and thus identified in service, is very simple. Since 1922, the system has operated on a Fiscal Year basis. The Douglas XC-32 had Army serial 36-1, meaning that it was the first Army airplane contracted for in the government's Fiscal Year 1936, which ran from July 1, 1935 to June 30, 1936.

Note the words "contracted for." These explain the apparent puzzle of airplanes with fiscal serials a year or more later than that of a particular plane of similar type flying long before that

Fig. 6-2. Two C-47A-90s from the same production block photographed 17 years apart, 1945-1962. 43-15988, left, has the original eight-inch Army serial number on the fin in yellow on camouflage. 43-15957, right, has only the last five digits of the serial in 12-inch figures, prefixed by the zero-dash that identifies USAF airplanes that are over 10 years old. (photos by Peter M. Bowers, Victor D. Seely)

airplane's first flight. For example, the first C-47, 41-7722, was ordered as the first of a batch of 145 that were to be built in a factory that did not yet exist. On the other hand, various DC-3s drafted from the airlines and out of the factory were given Fiscal 1942 serials upon their acquisition, so were flying with late serials before the first C-47 flew in December 1941, halfway through the Fiscal Year 1942.

For presentation in this book, a range of Army serial numbers, such as 36-70 through 36-87, inclusive for the 18 C-33s, is written as 36-70/87.

In January 1942, the Army performed a great service for subsequent historians by applying the airplane serial numbers in large block figures to each side of the vertical fin. Since 1932 it had been in one-inch figures on the left side of the fuselage near the cockpit. However, the tail presentation was slightly different—the first digit of the Fiscal Year was deleted. Serial 43-15788 for a C-47A-90-DL appeared as 315788 (Fig. 6-2). If the number was short, as 36-1, zeroes were used to bring it up to four digits, as 6001. Later, some long numbers were reduced to use only the last five digits. Tail numbers were usually yellow, but sometimes black, on camouflaged planes, and black on natural metal finish.

Since military airplanes of the time were not

expected to last more than 10 years, no conflict between a serial like 41-7722 (for the first C-47) and 51-7722 was anticipated. When Army/Air Force planes survived past 10 years in postwar years, the prefix 0- was added to the tail number to indicate that the plane was more than 10 years old (Fig. 6-2). This has often been misrepresented as O-for-Obsolete, but is not so. No different prefix was used for a third or even fourth decade of service that some C-47s reached.

All of the Douglas DC variants built for the U.S. Army from 1935 to the end of World War II, less the C-47 which is treated separately, are detailed in this chapter. Those DCs drafted by the Army from the airlines or the factory are detailed in Chapter 8.

U.S. ARMY DC-2s

XC-32—The single XC-32, Army serial 36-1 (Fig. 6-3), was an "off-the-shelf" DC-2 with only minor changes to accommodate Army-type radio. Douglas identified it as DC-2-153, and the civil SGR-1820-F2 Cyclone engines were redesignated R-1820-25 to fit them into the Army's engine identification system. Delivery was on September 30, 1935.

Since the DC-2 was a type-certified civil transport, in wide airline use and already operating

Fig. 6-3. The U.S. Army's first DC was a DC-2-153 with only minor changes to accommodate military equipment. Note the Airplane Commander's astrodome above the cockpit and the added antenna mast. The marking on the fuselage is the insignia of the GHQ Air Force, used from 1935 through 1937. (photo by Gordon S. Williams)

with the U.S. Navy, it is hard to understand the assignment of an experimental (X) classification, but tradition dies hard. A Service Test Classification (Y) would have been more logical, especially since it had been applied to several previous off-the-shelf transport procurements.

The experimental classification was soon dropped. As plain C-32, 36-1 was damaged extensively in a landing accident at Spokane, Washington, on September 4, 1942, and was turned over to a mechanics' school as "Class 26 materiel," a non-flying instructional airframe. Total flight time was 2321 hours.

C-33—The 18 C-33s, 36-70/87, started the development of the C-47. They were essentially DC-2s adapted to bulk cargo work by reinforcement of the floor and installation of a two-section 63 by 69-inch cargo door at the rear of the cabin, where the floor was angled to be level when the airplane was in normal ground attitude. In the absence of available forklifts or other ground-based loading facilities, bulk cargo could be hoisted aboard by a chain-hoist suspended from a portable tripod assembly (Fig. 6-4). The larger vertical tail took on the contours of the new DC-3 (less the dorsal fin) to start the unofficial "DC-2 1/2" identity (Fig. 6-5). Douglas identified the C-33s as DC-2-145. The engines were the same military R-1820-25 Cyclones used in the XC-32.

Deliveries started in September 1936, with one held back for modifications that made it the C-38.

Only one, 36-80, survived the war. The high-time airplane was 36-82 with 3602 flight hours.

Note: Since the C-33s and subsequent Army

Fig. 6-4. External cargo hoist as used on U.S. Army C-33s and C-39s. Note the double-section cargo door common to both models and the upward-sloped rear cabin floor that is parallel to the ground when the airplane is at rest. (Douglas photo)

Fig. 6-5. Aside from its cargo doors, the C-33 could be distinguished from the civil DC-2 by the DC-3 style vertical tail that was not fitted with a dorsal fin. The rudder striping is erroneous, with the blue extended to the leading edge. (photo by Peter M. Bowers)

cargo plane DCs were built on regular Army contracts, the Army provided much of the equipment such as engines, propellers, instruments, and radio as Government Furnished Equipment (GFE). Published statistics for military aircraft neglect to mention this, so the unit costs appear to be notably lower than they would for "off-the-shelf" sales of an equivalent model to a civil customer.

C-33A—This designation does not appear in the official document "Model Designation Army Air-craft," although other unused designations do. However, it does appear in several unofficial postwar DC-3 references. It is alleged to be the first C-33, 36-70, after modification before it officially became the C-38. Apparently the modifications were considered enough to justify a new model number instead of merely a new series letter.

YC-34—The two YC-34s (Fig. 6-6) were service test versions of the XC-32, still with R-1820-25 engines. Although built on a later contract and with

Fig. 6-6. One of the two YC-34s, essentially off-the-shelf civil DC-2s with enlarged vertical fins used for high-ranking officials. This one carries the flag of the then-Secretary of War Harry Woodring. (photo by Howard Levy)

Fig. 6-7. The single C-38 was the first C-33 with modifications that made it the prototype of the C-39 series. Note the addition of a DC-3 dorsal fin. When photographed, the C-38 was being used at Wright Field as a flying electronics laboratory. (photo by William T. Larkins)

later Army serials, they had the next Douglas C/Ns after the XC-32. Douglas designation was DC-2-173 for 36-345 (delivered April 25, 1936) and DC-2-346 for 36-346 (delivered April 1).

C-38—The single C-38 was the first C-33, 36-70, kept at the factory for modifications that justified a change of designation. Control surfaces were changed even more to take on DC-3 features, including the dorsal fin (Fig. 6-7). Engines were changed to the more powerful Wright R-1820-45 that produced 930 hp at 2200 rpm and were fitted with constant-speed propellers.

In spite of all the changes, Douglas did not change the DC-2 dash numbers; it was still a DC-2-145. Since there was still room for improvement, further changes were made in the production version, which was designated C-39. The C-38 lasted until March 1945, surviving all but one of the C-33s.

C-39—Thirty-seven airplanes were ordered on the C-39 contract, but only 35 were delivered as such (Figs. 6-8 through 6-10). Army serials were

Fig. 6-8. With its DC-3 tail, the C-39 earned the nickname "DC-2 1/2." Here the rear portion of the cargo door has been removed to permit the exit of trainee paratroopers. (USAF photo)

Fig. 6-9. Starting in February 1941, U.S. Army transport planes began to use camouflage. This C-39 is a rare exception to the standard: The fuselage star that should go with the camouflage has not been added and the rudder stripes, used only on non-camouflaged airplanes after February 1941, have not been deleted. (photo by Logan Coombs)

Fig. 6-10. The spartan interior of a C-39 with 14 passenger seats. Note the radio operator's station at the extreme rear of the cabin. (Douglas photo)

38-499/537 and the Douglas designation was DC-2-243.

The C-39s were even more true "DC-2 1/2s," since a DC-3 center section had now been added to the narrow DC-2 fuselage and short outer wing panels. Engines were still more powerful R-1820-55s delivering 975 hp at 2200 rpm; deliveries began in January 1939.

The fourth airplane on the contract was not a DC-2 variant; it was a DC-3 and not even in the same C/N range. It was delivered as the C-41 (see following heading). The fifth airplane was delivered in March 1939, as the first C-42. Two other C-39s became C-42s later.

C-39s were the first U.S. Army DCs to be involved in World War II. At least five based in the Philippines managed to escape and continue service in Australia and India. In 1944 the Army released 17 or more to Mexican and other Central and South American airlines.

C-42—This is the model that was actually a converted C-39 (Fig. 6-11). The conversion of 38-503, the fifth airplane of the C-38 contract, was done in the factory by modifying the cargo door and installing an executive interior (Fig. 6-12) before delivery as a C-42 (DC-2-267). Engines were R-1820-53s, delivering 1000 hp at 2200 rpm. Later, C-39s 38-513 and 528 were similarly converted and redesignated C-42s. 38-503 and 528 were both retired in April 1945; 38-315 was transferred to TACA Airways of El Salvador, Central America, in December 1944.

Several stateside C-39s survived the war and were added to the DC-2 ATC-540 for civil operation. At least one was being used as a sprayer in Oregon in the 1960s and is now in the Air Force museum.

THE B-18

Although not a true DC-2 or DC-3, another Douglas model that influenced the DC-3 should be mentioned at this point in the military DC development. This is the B-18, developed for a U.S. Army fly-off multi-engine bomber competition in 1935. Essentially, the B-18 was a DC-2 fitted with a new bomber fuselage. Airliner characteristics were retained in that the bomb bay was entirely under the cabin floor. This feature made surplus B-18s popular as cargo planes after World War II.

The prototype of the B-18, Douglas Model DB-1, won the competition and received orders totalling 134 B-18s (Fig. 6-13) and 217 B-18As (Fig. 6-14). Some B-18 details—notably the enlarged vertical tail, reshaped wingtips, and revised center section structure—were incorporated in the DC-3.

A few B-18As, some fitted with search radar and redesignated B-18B, were used for antisubmarine patrols during the war but most served as trainers and squadron hacks. Two B-18As were redesignated as C-58 transports during the war. Others were used for the purpose without redesignation.

Fig. 6-11. The fifth airplane on the C-39 contract was completed at the factory as the C-42 executive transport. The marking HQ1 on the fin and under the left wing indicates that it is the No. 1 airplane assigned to U.S. Army Air Corps headquarters. (USAF photo)

Fig. 6-12. Deluxe executive interior of the C42; compare with standard C-39 from which it was converted. Two other C-39s were converted to C-42 later. (Douglas photo)

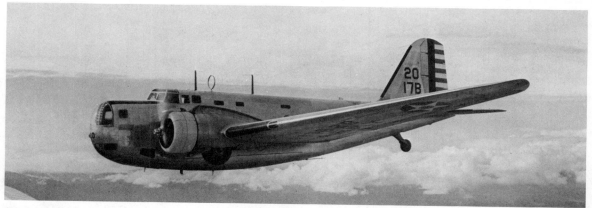

Fig. 6-13. The B-18, ordered in quantity, was basically a DC-2 with a new bomber fuselage, C-33 tail, and a longer wing. The 20 17B on the fin identifies Airplane No. 20 of the 17th Bomb Group in the 1940-41 unit designator system. (photo by Boardman C. Reed)

Fig. 6-14. The B-18A was distinguished by a revised "shark" nose with the bombardier's window above the machine gun turret. This one was used as a transport by the First Staff Squadron in March 1941. (photo by Peter M. Bowers)

At least 38 B-18s through B-18B were on the U.S. civil register after the war, licensed as freighters under Category 2 type certificate A2-577, issued March 31, 1947.

U.S. ARMY DC-3s

The first U.S. Army DC-3, the C-41, was given a lower model designation than the C-42, which was a converted C-39 (DC-2-243) because it was contracted for and given a new model number before the decision was made to convert a C-39 to the C-42. **C-41**—The single C-41, the first U.S. military DC-3 (Fig. 6-15) has been incorrectly identified as a modified C-39 ever since it was built and it still appears as such in some current publications. Because

of this error, photos of it have consistently been identified as the C-41A, an acknowledged DC-3, and its absence from some official DC-3 lists (even at Douglas) has resulted in an error in the total DC-3 count.

The confusion with the C-39 results from the fact that the C-41 was ordered as one article on the 37-airplane C-39 contract. The description in the Army's Model Designation Book did not say that the C-41 *was* a C-39 converted from cargo to passenger work; it said that it was *similar to* such a C-39. One of the C-39s on the same contract was converted to passenger interior and actually delivered as the first C-42. It was fairly common practice for one or more planes on a contract to be held back for conversion to a different configuration to

Fig. 6-15. The C-41 is a "lost" DC-3, having been misreported for many years as a modified C-39. It was a DC-3A-253 delivered as a staff transport in October 1938. Note the curtained windows, directional loop antenna, and the fuel dump chutes at the rear of the center section. (USAF photo)

be delivered under a different designation. Even a separate model could be slipped in, as was done with the C-41/DC-3.

While the Army serial, 38-502, gives the impression that it was the fourth C-39, the C-41 was actually an off-the-shelf DC-3A with a C/N four units ahead of the first C-39. In keeping with the Douglas practice of using a different dash number for each DC-2/DC-3 variant, it was identified in the factory as a DC-3A-253. It was delivered for General "Hap" Arnold on October 11, 1938, three months ahead of the first C-39, and differed from straight commercial configuration only in interior appointments for 14 luxury passenger military executive use, plus installation of military radio. The civil Pratt & Whitney R-1830 Twin Wasp engines, which generated 1200 hp at 2700 rpm, were given the Army designation of R-1830-21.

The C-41 accumulated 2739 flying hours to April 1945, and then was leased to Alaska Airlines by the government. It operated as NC15473 until transferred to the Civil Aeronautics Authority (CAA, later FAA) in 1948 and became N12 and then N43. In 1974 it was scheduled for donation to the Air Force Museum, but never got there.

C-41A—The single C-41A, 40-70 (Fig. 6-16), was another stock DC-3, specifically the DC-3A-253A, delivered on a one-airplane contract on September 11, 1939. It and the C-41 were the only Army planes to use the R-1830-S1C1G (Army -21) engine. The C-41A also carried General Arnold's flag and, until serial numbers were put on the tail early in 1942,
could be distinguished from the similar C-41 only by the fact that it was a partial sleeper like the DC-3B, with two small upper-berth windows above the first and third regular windows on each side of the forward cabin.

The C-41A survived the war and carried several registration numbers for different owners—N4720V, N65R, and N598AR.

C-47—The C-47, the most numerous example of the DC-3 series, is covered in detail by itself in Chapter 7.

THE MIXED C-53 SKYTROOPER SERIES

The second major production DC-3 variant ordered by the Army was the C-53. Douglas identified it as DC-3A-405 and the government named it Skytrooper shortly after it appeared in October 1941. Altogether, 379 C-53s were built on military contracts at Santa Monica, together with 19 drafted from the airlines and at least one special acquisition that made up a total of 399. The drafted C-53s are listed in this chapter because of their C-53 series designations.

The C-53s were essentially civil DC-3s built at Santa Monica and adapted to military use without structural change. The engines were the same R-1830-92 as on the C-47. The major alteration was the use of troop benches in most, and later the addition of astrodomes and rifle grommets to the windows. C-53s retained the civil baggage door on the left side, but the standard airline door was a signifi-

Fig. 6-16. The Army's second DC-3 was the C-41A, a unique one-only DC-3A-253A for General Arnold with four berths in the forward part of the cabin like the DC-3B but with Twin Wasp engines. (USAF photo)

Fig. 6-17. Although built on military contracts, the C-53s were essentially civil DC-3s. The standard airliner doors were a handicap to the loading of bulk cargo. (USAF photo)

cant handicap in hauling bulk cargo (Fig. 6-17). Cabin capacity, whether troops or litters, was the same as for the C-47, and the gross weight was the same. Many early C-53s were turned over to the airlines for contract operations in support of the Army. Later versions got over enemy territory as paratroopers.

Dash numbers were not used in C-53 designations.

C-53—There were 218 C-53s built on four contracts (Fig. 6-18). To those were added three draftees, two DC-3A-447s from Pan American and the Douglas-owned DC-3A-408. It was unusual to give drafted airplanes identical designations to models being built on military contracts. Of these,

nine went to the RAF as Dakota IIs, plus others to the Royal Australian Air Force. The U.S. Army got some back from the British for use in North Africa. A further 18 went to the U.S. Navy as R4D-3.

Army serial numbers: 41-20045, 41-20046, 41-20051, 41-20053/20056 (4), 41-20060/20136 (77), 42-6455/6469 (25), 42-6481/6504 (24), 42-15530/-15569 (40), 42-15870/15894 (25), 42-47371/47382 (12), 43-14404, 43-14495. Prices ranged from $147,265 to a low of $136,399.

XC-53A—One C-53, 42-6480, was modified to test full-span wing flaps and heated leading edge de-icing and was given an experimental designation (Fig. 6-19). Neither feature was adopted for war

Fig. 6-18. What appears to be streets, trees, and houses behind C-53D, 42-68818, is really camouflage covering erected over the Douglas Santa Monica plant after Pearl Harbor. (Douglas photo)

Fig. 6-19. The single XC-53A was a stock C-53 modified to test full-span wing flaps and hot-air deicers for the wing leading edge. It was reconverted to standard and had several different owners in postwar-II years. (photo by Harold G. Martin)

production, but the heated leading edge de-icing replaced the old rubber boot for new designs right after the war.

C-53B—Eight C-53s were modified for Arctic operations with extra fuselage fuel tanks, improved cabin heating, and a C-47 type navigator's station complete with astrodome. Army serial numbers were 41-20047/20050 (4), 20052, 20057/20059 (3). In spite of the modification, the C-53Bs were on the books at the lowest C-53 price of $136,399.

C-53C—Seventeen DC-3A-453s, 43-2018/2034, acquired from three airlines at a price of $150,470. Two more went to the Navy as additional R4D-3s.

C-53D—The 159 C-53Ds (DC-3A-457, 42-68693/-68851), differed from the earlier C-53s mainly in having a 24-volt electrical system and price tags of $140,944 (Figs. 6-20, 6-21). The last C-53D, 42-68851, C/N 11778, was also the last of the 961 DC-3s built at Santa Monica. Postwar survivors were redesignated ZC-53D-DO in 1948.

THE C-117 SERIES

By late 1944, the military situation was well enough in hand to allow some Army transport planes to be built strictly as plush airliner types for high-ranking staff officers, etc. Consequently, a new contract was written to allow 131 of the C-47Bs on order at Oklahoma City to be completed as C-117-1-DK. These had the Douglas designation of DC-3A-1003 and were structurally similar to prewar DC-3s and early C-53s in having 21-passenger airline-style interiors plus the rear baggage compartment. As converted C-47Bs, however, they used R-1830-90C engines and 24-volt electrical system, so had no direct civil DC-3 counterpart.

Fig. 6-20. C-53D 42-68770 was a wartime rarity, an Army transport operating in natural metal finish several months before the Army authorized the deletion of camouflage from most aircraft expected to fly in combat zones. (photo by Ken Sumney, Myitkyna, Burma, September 1944)

Fig. 6-21. The C-53D was similar to the C-53 except for a change to a 24-volt electrical system. Three stars on the fin identify the personal transport of a Lieutenant (three-star) General. Seen in India in 1945. (photo by Peter M. Bowers)

Because of some seemingly illogical redesignations, the post-production C-117 picture became very confusing.

C-117—There were no plain C-117s as there had been C-47s and C-53s. By the end of WW II the Army decided that the first production version of a new model would carry the series letter A, hence C-117A.

C-117A—The end of the war brought on large-scale cancellation of airplane contracts, and only 17 of the 131 C-117A-1s ordered by the Army were delivered (Fig. 6-22). Douglas completed 28 of the military cancellations as civil DC-3Cs, which were

licensed under the prewar ATC-669. Since there was no need for high-altitude performance, most C-117As were eventually converted to C-117B by deletion of the second-stage blower, as on the C-47B-to-D change.

Although the C-117As were built specifically as VIP airplanes, several were given the V-prefix in postwar years and, for some strange reason—possibly an engine change to -90C—some C-117C-DLs were redesignated as VC-117A-DL. No C-117s as such were built at Long Beach.

The Army serial number range for the 131 C-117As ordered was 45-2545/2675, but the

Fig. 6-22. The C-117As were C-47Bs completed as executive transports with civil DC-3 passenger and baggage facilities and were delivered without camouflage. The white rectangles were added to the U.S. star insignia at the end of June 1943. (photo by Peter M. Bowers)

Fig. 6-23. The C-117Bs were C-117As with engine modifications. The red bars were added to the U.S. insignia in January 1947, and white fuselage tops were added to personnel transports in 1953. (photo by Gordon S. Williams)

postwar cancellations ended this block at 45-2561.

C-117B—No C-117Bs were built as such; all were C-117As redesignated after their R-1830-90C engines were modified to R-1830-90D by deletion of the high blower. By the end of 1946, only two C-117s were on record as having become C-117Bs: 45-2546 was a C-117B-1-DK and 45-2549 was a -5. Most of the other As eventually became Bs (Fig. 6-23), but there is no record of DC-3 dash numbers.

C-117C—The C-117C designation was assigned twice—in 1946 to a C-117A modification that was not produced and in 1953 to 11 former C-47s in a rare case of reassigning a previous series designation (Fig. 6-24).

The eleven C-117Cs are also an odd example of redesignation within type. At the end of World War II, the government leased quite a few older C-47s and C-47As to airlines and other organizations and allowed some to be converted from freighters to regular passenger airliners. The changes were quite extensive, and included leveling the rear cabin floor, eliminating the cargo doors and replacing them with a DC-3 type, increasing the cabin windows to as many as eight on each side, and adding DC-3/C-53 aft baggage compartments and tail cones.

When some of the airliner conversions were returned to the Air Force, they were put into service as VIP transports with the appropriate VC-47 designations. However, because of their many airliner features, they now had much more in common with the C-117s than they did with freighter C-47s. In 1953 the logical move was made and eleven "airline" VC-47s were redesignated C-117C. Other

Fig. 6-24. The C-117Cs were not delivered as such; they were C-47s that had been leased to airlines in early postwar years and modified to airline standards. Note eight left-side windows instead of C-47's six, DC-3 size hinge-down door, and DC-3 baggage compartment and tail cone on former C-47-DL, 41-18384. (photo by Gordon S. Williams)

VC-47s with fewer modifications remained C-47s. Some of the C-117Cs are reported to have been redesignated again, as C-117As, plus one to SC-117A.

Army serial numbers: 41-18348, 41-18384, 41-18392, 42-32921, 42-92753, 42-15265, 42-92967, 42-93152, 42-93558, 42-93601, 42-100769.

C-117D—Another series designation that was assigned twice. In 1946 C-117A 45-2553 was redesignated C-117D with unspecified modifications but was apparently redesignated soon afterward as C-117B and remained in service through 1969, thereby overlapping the next C-117Ds.

In 1962, all U.S. Navy R4D-8 "Super DC-3s" were redesignated as C-117D in the new tri-service designating system. See Chapter 12 for details and Navy serial numbers.

Chapter 7

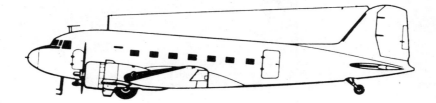

The C-47 Skytrain Series

The C-47 was the major production version of the DC-3, with 9283 examples built from 1941 through 1945. It had the same relationship to the DC-3 that the C-33 and C-39 had to the DC-2, principally, reinforced flooring, a large two-section cargo door on the left side (Figs. 7-1 through 7-3), and the rear portion of the main cabin floor tilted up to be parallel to the ground when the plane was at rest. The auxiliary door behind the cockpit was carried over from the DC-3, as were the forward cargo compartments, which easily converted to navigators' or radio operators' stations with suitable seats and tables. The instrument panel and controls were essentially the same as for the DC-3 (Fig. 7-4).

THE C-47 DESCRIBED

Like the Army DC-2 variants, the production C-47s had corresponding DC-3 designations in Douglas records. The minor differences were no problem in qualifying surplus C-47s for postwar civil license under existing prewar ATCs for DC-3As. Only C-47s through XC-47B were delivered from the factory; all higher designations through C-47R were conversions, modifications, or 1962 redesignations of Navy R4Ds. All qualified for civil licenses under ATC-669 regardless of cargo doors, window count, or dash number changes in the engines. C-47s modified for postwar civil use by Douglas or other shops became DC-3Cs (see Chapter 11).

Since the C-47 was essentially a cargo plane and trooper, the standard seating was fold-down benches on each side of the cabin (Figs. 7-5, 7-6), but some were delivered with airline seats and VIP accommodations. A new feature was a navigator's astrodome on top of the fuselage behind the pilots. With troop seats folded down, 24 litters could be installed at these levels (Fig. 7-7). Rifle grommets in the center of each cabin window were introduced on this model (Fig. 7-8). Normal window count on the C-47 series was seven on the right side and six on the left (civil DC-3s usually had seven on each side of the fuselage while DSTs had six left and eight right). Some postwar VIP conversions that reduced the door size got seven and sometimes

Fig. 7-1. Principal differences between the Army C-47 and the civil DC-3 were the reinforced cabin floor with tilted rear portion, and the double cargo doors. This is an early-series C-47 with the rear door section hinges right at the opening. Note that the wartime censor has blocked out the Army serial number. (Douglas photo)

Fig. 7-2. A later series C-47 with the rear-section door hinges mounted farther aft and on the outside of the fuselage. The hinges are streamlined by fairings on the door and on the fuselage. (USAF photo via Douglas)

Fig. 7-3. Inside view of the C-47 cargo door. The two large sections open outward; the small insert in the forward section opens inward. (Douglas photo)

eight on the left side. Radio and other "black boxes" were military.

Initial powerplant was the Pratt & Whitney R-1830-92 Twin Wasp engine built on Navy contracts. This was equivalent to the civil R-1830-S1C3G. Published takeoff power was 1200 hp at 2700 rpm, but some military manuals say 1300 hp at 2800 rpm. Normal output was 1050 hp at 2250 rpm at 7500 feet. The majority of the R-1830s used in the C-47s were built by Chevrolet. There were various dash number changes in the C-47 series and some changes to larger engines.

Structurally, the C-47 was identical to the DC-3 except for a minor difference in the center section that added six inches to the wingspan. Built-in fuel

capacity was reduced from the DC-3's 882 U.S. gallons to 804, but up to eight 100-gallon ferry tanks could be installed in the cabin (nine in later models). The length was shorter than the DC-3 by nine inches, and even more when the tail cone was removed for access to the glider tow hitch that was built into the rear fuselage structure. This detail was added after the first 200 C-47s and on all subsequent As and Bs (Fig. 7-9). The presence of the glider hitch resulted in installation of a notably shorter tail cone (Fig. 7-10).

The C-47 did not have a built-in cargo loading/handling system, not even the bolt-on external hoist of the C-33 and C-39. Loading was manual from truck beds (Fig. 7-11), assisted from ground level by forklifts—and in some places even elephants, which did an excellent job of loading 55-gallon fuel drums. Wheeled vehicles were pushed, pulled, or driven up on a pair of sloping ramps under their own power (Fig. 7-12). Once inside, the cargo was tied down to rings in the floor and to rails in the walls (Fig. 7-13). Sometimes the cabin of a C-47 was so jammed full of cargo (Fig. 7-14) that the crew had to reach the cockpit by means of an external ladder to the forward baggage door.

The C-47 was also the first Army DC-3 to be given a "popular" name—Skytrain. In October 1941, the U.S. government adopted the British practice of identifying military airplanes by a name in addition to the established alpha-numeric designation. This was allegedly a security measure intended to hide the development stage of a particular model from the public and, consequently, spies. It might have made sense with bombers— all Boeing B-17s, for instance, simply being referred to in press releases as "Flying Fortress" rather than a specific designation such as B-17G. There was no such sensitivity with transports, but the C-47s were all Skytrains in the press releases of the time. Of course, the names were ignored by the users of the airplanes and all to whom the actual designations were significant.

However, the C-47 and other military DC-3s acquired a nickname on their own—"Gooney Bird." This was also the nickname for the albatross, an awkward bird on the ground but a magnificent flier.

Fig. 7-4. The cockpit arrangement of the C-47 was not significantly different from that of the civil DC-3 (USAF photo)

Fig. 7-5. The 28 troop seats of a C-47 in extended position. There are three separate segments on each side of the cabin, with five seats in the two forward segments and four seats in the single rear segments. (Douglas photo)

After the war all C-47s through C-47B qualified for standard civil licenses as DC-3C under prewar ATC 669 issued to the DC-3A.

C-47 VARIANTS

C-47—This was DC-3A-360 in Douglas records, and 965 were built as the first product of the new Long Beach plant (Fig. 7-15). First flight was made in November 1941, and the first delivery to the Army was on December 23. Thirty-three C-47s on Army contracts were transferred to the Navy as R4D-1; 51 others were delivered to the RAF as Dakota I. All plain C-47s (C-47-DL, since this version was built only at Long Beach) were

completed before the block number system came into use.

The early C-47s had the small carburetor air scoop on top of the nacelle at the rear of the cowling as on the civil DC-3A. Some added a tropical filter that extended the scoop to the forward edge of the cowling. The forward scoop was exclusive to C-47s, but some late ones had long filters aft of the cowlings as on C-47As and Bs. Some C-47s surviving past the end of the war picked up V-prefixes, and at least 11 were converted to C-117C in a rare case of redesignation within the C-class. One C-47 was converted to the XCG-17 glider in 1944.

Army serials for the plain C-47-DLs were 41-7722/7866 (145), 41-18337/18699 (363),

41-19463/19499 (37), 41-38564/38763 (200), 42-5635/5704 (70), 42-32786/32923 (138), and 43-30628/30639 (12).

Because of varying quantities and different contracts, plus equipment changes, the price of C-47 series airplanes varied as much or more than the civil DC-3. The following is a breakdown of C-47-DL price on the second of four separate contracts. Items supplied by the government are included and identified as (GFE):

Airplane	$108,718.00
Airplane Equipment (GFE)	918.00
Engines (GFE)	26,019.00
Propellers (GFE)	4,718.00
Ordnance (GFE)	15.00
Radio (GFE)	8,640.00
Grand Total	$149,028.00

C-47A—The C-47A, or DC-3A-456, differed from the C-47 mainly in having a 24-volt electrical system instead of the original 12-volt. Production was split between Long Beach and Oklahoma City, with 2,954 DLs and 2,300 DKs (Figs. 7-16, 7-17). This total, 5,954, was nearly half of all the military and civil DC-3s built in the U.S.

The block number system was not applied to C-47s until the 200th C-47A was ordered as a C-47A-1-DL. Long Beach models got to -90-DL, but Oklahoma City models only reached -30-DK. It

Fig. 7-6. The troop seats of a C-47 folded down to make room for cargo. Note the absence of cabin insulation and sound-proofing. (Douglas photo)

Fig. 7-7. The C-47 cabin could also be equipped with 24 litters stacked four high for medical evacuation missions. (USAF photo via Douglas)

should be noted that -DL and -DK models with the same block number *were not* identical in the matter of systems and installations. Because of their numbers and longevity, the C-47As picked up about every special-purpose prefix that was ever applied to a C-47 series airplane, plus a lot of one-off and special modifications that were never designated. The Navy received 238 C-47As as R4D-5s, several were converted to amphibians at Army depots following test of the XC-47C, and a few were converted to C-117Cs after the war.

The Army serial numbers for C-47As break down as follows. Block numbers will be found in Appendix F.

C-47A-DL—42-23300/24419 (1120), 42-32924/-32935 (12), 42-100436/101035 (600), 43-15033/161322 (1100).

C-47A-DK—42-92024/93823 (1800), 42-108794/-108993 (200), 43-47963/48262 (300).

C/N Error—In the rush of wartime orders, some C-47s were assigned incorrect C/Ns. For a block of 300 C-47A-DLs, these applied to Army serial numbers 43-47963/48262. The erroneous C/Ns were 13779/14078, corrected to 25224/25523. These are frequently seen in detailed postwar documentation of the C-47s as 13779/25224 for 13779 corrected to 25224 and should not be mistaken for a similar presentation like 13779/14078, indicating a continuous run of numbers such as 13779 through 14078, inclusive.

Total costs for C-47As ranged from a high of $145,117.00 to a low of $115,710.00.

C-47B—The high altitude of the "Hump" run from India into China called for better performance at altitude, so the C-47B (DC-3A-467) was developed. The significant difference from the C-47A was the use of the R-1830-90C engine with two-stage superchargers (Fig. 7-18). This had the same 1200 hp for takeoff, but continuous power was 1000 hp at 2700 rpm from sea level to 6,100 feet. Most of the -90C engines were built by Buick on Navy contracts.

The C-47Bs and some C-117As were the only Army models to use this particular engine. The -90Cs were troublesome, so at war's end, with no further need for such high-altitude operations, the second-stage blower was eliminated and the C-47Bs were redesignated C-47D, a change that took several years to fully accomplish.

Altogether, 3,364 C-47Bs were ordered, but only 3,232 were delivered as such. War-end cancellations and some conversions to C-117 made up the difference. Long Beach built 300 C-47B-1-DLs, the only Bs built there. The other 2,932 were C-47B-1-DK through -50. Of these, 133 were completed at the factory as TC-47B instrument trainers. The Navy got 157 C-47Bs as R4D-6 and the RAF got 894 as Dakota IV. Forty-four TB-47Bs transferred to the Navy became R4D-7. Not all the C-47Bs were delivered as freighters or trainers. Some intermediate block numbers—-2, -6, -8, -11, and -13 to a total of 30—were completed at Omaha as 21-passenger models with airline-type seats, cabin insulation, lavatories, food warmers, and plywood over the metal floor. The three

Fig. 7-8. Those rubber grommets in the center of each C-47 cabin window were to permit aircraft defense by rifle fire—not that the method ever proved to be effective. Note that the troops are all wearing parachutes. (Douglas photo)

Fig. 7-9. A steel-tube mount for glider tow hook was installed on all but the first 200 C-47s. A C-47 could tow one or two troop-carrying Waco CG-4A gliders. (Douglas photo)

Fig. 7-10. C-47s with glider tow hooks used a notably different tail cone than DC-3s and C-53s. After the war, some C-47s were fitted with DC-3 tail cones. Note the fairings on the external cargo door hinges of this C-47B-20-DK. (courtesy Walter M. Jefferies)

C-47B-7s were real luxury liners, with only nine seats but two berths and a galley in addition to the other special features. The last C-47B-50-DK was delivered on October 23, 1945.

Army serial numbers for the C-47Bs, including postwar cancellations, break down as follows:

C-47B-1-DL—43-16133/16432 (300).

C-47B-DK—42-93159 (1), 43-48263/49962 (1700), 44-76195/77294 (1100), 45-876/1139 (264).

C/N Error—All the C-47B-DKs were also given erroneous C/Ns. The incorrect numbers were 14079/17142, corrected to 25524/27223. These of course included all of the TC-47Bs.

Prices for C-47Bs ranged from a high of $101,644.00 to a low of $83,543.

TC-47B—Although the TC-47Bs (Fig. 7-19) were built as such on the Oklahoma City production line instead of being modified as trainers after delivery, they were not built in a solid run. All 133 were scattered at random from the C-47B-5-DK through the C-47B-35-DK blocks. The C-47B dash numbers were retained. The lowest Douglas C/N was 25902 and the highest was 33367, Army serials 43-48641 and 44-77035.

Luxury C-47Bs—A total of 107 C-47Bs in the B-1 through B-25 range were completed in the factory and delivered with 21-passenger cabin seating and furnishings very similar to those of civil DC-3s, including cabin insulation, lavatories, cloak closet, and food warmers. Minor differences in furnishings and military communications equipment resulted in C-47B dash numbers -2, -6, -7, -8, -9, -11, -13, -14, -16, -18, -23, -27, and -28. The three C-47B-7-DKs were notably different in having only nine day passenger seats but two double DST-type berths.

XC-47C—The single XC-47C, 42-5671, was a late C-47-DL, 42-5671, converted by the Edo Aircraft Corporation of College Point, N.Y., to a twin-float amphibian (Fig. 7-20). Edo had built smaller amphibious floats before and during the war, with retractable nosewheels and main wheels behind the step, but the model 28 was by far the biggest ever—then or since.

The float installation increased the maximum gross weight to 34,162 pounds, far above the 31,000 of the other C-47s. Part of this was from extra tankage, an additional 300 gallons in each float. The performance and payload were far below expectations, and there were water handling problems. It could be operated only from smooth water and take-off from land was so sluggish that JATO bottles were tried.

The Army bought 150 sets of Edo 28 floats, but very few were fitted to other C-47s. Of those, only two, 42-92577 and 42-108868, appear in Army records as C-47C. Others retained their original series letters, possibly adding an intermediate block

number. This made more sense than having the series letter C identify the seaplane or amphibian version; the letter would have to change if the plane was reconverted to a standard landplane.

The C-47 amphibians saw limited use in Alaska and the Southwest Pacific but, significantly, none appeared among the postwar civil conversions. **C-47D/C-47Q**—See Chapter 14 for these postwar modifications.

THE XCG-17 GLIDER EXPERIMENT

The most extreme variation of a C-47 was 41-18496, which was converted to the experimental XCG-17 cargo glider and tested in June 1944 (Fig. 7-21). Douglas didn't have anything to do with this; it was strictly an Army project dreamed up at Wright Field. The purpose of the program was

Fig. 7-11. The height of the rear cabin floor of the C-47, with its upward slope that paralleled the ground, was just right for direct loading from Army trucks. This is a C-47 transferred to the Royal Air Force as a Dakota. (courtesy Arthur Pearcy)

Fig. 7-12. Wheeled vehicles could be driven aboard C-47s under their own power with the aid of portable ramps. The Army serial number 41-38614 on this early C-47-DL is yellow against the olive drab camouflage. (USAF photo via Douglas)

Fig. 7-13. A tractor stowed at the front of a C-47 cabin. Note the generous distribution of cargo tiedown rings on the reinforced floor. (USAF photo via Douglas)

Fig. 7-14. When bulk cargo took up most of the cabin floorspace, the C-47 passengers had to ride on top of the boxes. The regulation that required each passenger to have a seat belt was consistently disregarded. (Douglas photo)

Fig. 7-15. The second C-47-DL, 41-7723, with DC-3/C-53 tail cone and no navigator's astrodome. Photographed at the factory January 9, 1942, after the Army serial number was added to the vertical fin. (Douglas photo)

Fig. 7-16. The C-47A differed from the C-47 primarily in use of a 24-volt electrical system. Production was split between Long Beach and Oklahoma City; this is a C-47A-80-DL photographed at the factory March 12, 1944. (Douglas photo)

Fig. 7-17. A C-47A-25-DK built in Oklahoma City photographed at Myitkyna, Burma, in 1944. Note XI Combat Cargo group markings on fin and two-color Army serial number 42-93744. (photo by Kenneth M. Sumney)

Fig. 7-18. The C-47Bs had two-stage supercharged engines, originally identified by the long air scoop over the central portion of the nacelle. This C-47B-45-DK with Russian markings was photographed in Anchorage, Alaska, a stop on the ferry route to Russia. (photo by Logan Coombs)

Fig. 7-19. The TC-47Bs were converted to instrument trainers in the factory before delivery. An easy recognition detail was the three navigators' astrodomes on the top of the fuselage, as on this TC-47B-25-DK. (photo by William T. Larkins)

Fig. 7-20. The single XC-47C was a stock C-47-DL converted by Edo Aircraft, the pontoon builder, to an experimental amphibian. The steps on the right rear float strut are not for access to the cabin but to the wing for aircraft servicing. (USAF photo)

Fig. 7-21. The single XCG-17 was simply a stock C-47-DL with its engines removed and the cabin lengthened forward for increased cargo capacity. It had the flattest glide ratio of any Army cargo glider of the time. (USAF photo via Douglas)

to increase the capacity for supplies carried "Over the Hump" from India to China, not to develop an improved troop glider for combat.

The initial step was to see if a C-47 could be landed like a glider. A long series of power-off landings with pilots of varying experience quickly proved this. The next was to evaluate handling characteristics of a C-47 in tow. The towline was attached to the front of the center section and again performance was satisfactory. The final step was to convert a war-weary C-47 into an actual glider.

The major change was to remove the engines, but the logical drag improvement of eliminating the upper portion of the nacelles and thinning the bot-

Fig. 7-22. A requirement laid down prior to the XCG-17 conversion was that the airframe could be reconverted to a C-47, so the existing firewalls were simply covered with the hemispherical nose cones shown. (photo by Peter M. Bowers)

96

tom was blocked by a requirement for the airframe to be reconvertible to a powerplane (Fig. 7-22). Internally, the cabin was lengthened forward six feet to provide seating for 40 or a payload of 15,000 pounds. Empty weight was reduced from the C-47's 17,865 pounds to 11,000, but normal gross remained at 26,000 pounds.

Because of the clean design, the XCG-17 had the flattest glide—14:1—of any Army cargo glider. The initial advantages seen for the CG-17s were the ready availability of airframes and the much higher tow speeds that could be attained. Some overenthusiastic authors claim the XCG-17 stalled at 35 mph, but official figures say 70.

A single C-47 was not a practical towplane, although one could get the XCG-17 aloft. Taking their cue from the Germans, who used three Ju 52s to tow the giant Messerschmitt 321, two C-47s in tandem could do much better, but usually the job was given to a four-engine B-17 or C-54.

Nothing further was done to convert powerplanes to gliders, but the reverse was accomplished very successfully. The all-metal chase XCG-18, with higher towing speed, was produced with two R-2800 engines as the YC-122 and the chase XCG-20 became the Fairchild C-123 of Vietnam fame when fitted with two R-2800 engines.

The reconvertibility requirement paid off for the government. Instead of being scrapped as a useless glider after the war, the XCG-17 was reconverted to a C-47 and sold surplus. It has had several owners since.

Chapter 8

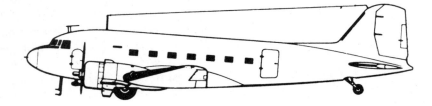

Drafted U.S. Army DCs

As its need for transport planes increased in 1941 and 1942 beyond the factory's ability to supply them, the U.S. Army acquired some DCs the easy way—by drafting 225 existing airliners. Two sources were used here—airliners already serving the airlines and those ordered by airlines but still in the factory.

Although widely used in reference to the civil DC-2s and DC-3s acquired by the Army, the term "drafted" is a misnomer. The owners of the airplanes were paid for them at established market prices on negotiated contracts. The airlines had options to buy the airplanes back later, and many were able to later in the war or soon after.

Many of the airliners retained their passenger seats when used by the Army; others had their interiors stripped for hauling troops and cargo into non-combat areas, often flown by civil airline crews whose airlines contracted to organize and fly transport routes for the Army. A few of the civil DC-3s taken into the army inventory and given army designations were never used by the Army; they were retained by the airlines and continued

to fly as domestic transports in their original airline markings and civil registrations.

Some of the DC-3s drafted while still on the production line did not yet have their full civil furnishings and could be easily modified to military requirements, mainly by the installation of C-47/C-53 type troop seats and military radio.

Both Cyclone and Twin Wasp DC-3s were drafted, but the Army's preference seemed to be for the Cyclone, 152 DC-3s with that engine being acquired compared to 51 Twin Wasp DC-3s.

Unfortunately, photo coverage of all the drafted DC-3 variants is incomplete. There was no requirement, either at Douglas or in the Army, to photograph each different model/series. As established and licensed civil models, the Army put its drafted airliners right to work without sending an example to Wright Field for routine testing. A few tested there to evaluate changes were photographed, however. Some were photographed while in service to illustrate a particular activity, but some of these photos have been lost due to having been misidentified as C-47s or C-53s. Most of

Fig. 8-1. The C-32As were DC-2s drafted from U.S. airlines by the Army. 42-68857, formerly TWA's DC-2-112, NC 13787, was photographed in 1944, still with its original small vertical fin. (photo by Peter M. Bowers)

the available photos of drafted airliners in the C-48 through C-52 series were taken by airplane photo-hobbyists until their activity was shut off by post-Pearl Harbor security restrictions. All military aircraft, regardless of their age, noncombat status, or previous civilian service, were off limits to unauthorized photographers.

C-32A—The C-32As were twenty-two DC2s, mostly -112s and -120s, but all with 740-hp R-1820-F3 Cyclones drafted from widely scattered sources in 1941-42 (Figs. 8-1, 8-2). The Wright engines then became R-1820-33, the same as used in the Martin B-10B. In 1944, two others were acquired in Australia, one a transfer of Royal Australian Air Force (RAAF) A30-10, formerly Eastern Air Lines' NC14969, and the other a civil acquisition that was registered VH-CDZ.

Since these were all given the old C-32 designa-tion, while all the drafted DC-3s got designations from C-48 up, some historians have assumed that the drafted DC-2s were production follow-ons to the XC-32, 36-1. The following Army serial numbers prove otherwise: 42-53527/53532 (6), 57154/57156 (3), 57227, 57228, 58071/58073 (3), 61095, 61096, 65577/65579 (3), 68857, 68858, 70863. Also: 44-83226, 83227.

THE C-48 SERIES

Altogether 36 civil DC-3As were drafted by the Army as C-48s, the common denominator being the DC-3A/DST-A model with the 1200-hp Twin Wasp R-1830-S1C3G engine. Some were taken off the airline routes and others were drafted while still on the production line.

Since these were so similar in airframe and

Fig. 8-2. The U.S. Army did not use all its C-32As. This one, formerly TWA's NC13712, was the second DC-2 built. It was transferred to the Royal Air Force, which leased it to Indian National Airways. The airline operated it under Indian civil registration VT-ARA but also displayed the RAF serial number AX767. (photo by Peter M. Bowers)

powerplant detail to the existing C-41 and C-41A, it is hard to understand why they weren't simply added to that model, becoming C-41B, C-41C, etc., instead of the new model C-48. Surely gear ratios of the engines, one notable difference, would hardly be justification for an entirely new model number, but the right-side passenger door might have had an influence. There is one simplifying saving grace, however; all the C-48s were acquired on the same Air Corps contract, AC-19694.

C-48—The single C-48, Army serial 41-2681, was a 21-seat right-side door DC-3A-197D (ATC-669) intended for United Air Lines as NC25612 (Fig. 8-3). To it belongs the distinction of being the first of the drafted DC-3s, and it was acquired on December 27, 1940. This time, the Army did not give the civil engines an equivalent military designation; they remained R-1830-S1C3Gs even though they were equivalent to the R-1830-92. The principal difference from standard airline configuration was the type and quantity of military radio installed.

In 1943, the C-48 was carried on the Army's books at $159,884. By 1944, the documentation system had been changed to write more of the Government Furnished Equipment costs (GFE) such as engines, propellers, and electronics against the airplane instead of carrying them separately, so it was valued at $168,384.

The C-48 had several different U.S. owners after the war. It crashed July 13, 1958, when under Canadian registration CF-QBD.

C-48A—The three C-48As, 41-7682/7684, were left-side-door DC-3A-368s (ATC-669) taken as a unit from the Douglas production line June/August 1941 (Fig. 8-4). The engines were 1200-hp military R-1830-92s. No previous ownership is known.

The major difference was the cabin arrangement. For use of the General Staff, they had 10 swivel chairs, typewriter desk, clothes closet, and a separate cabinet for parachute stowage, plus military radio. They were by far the lowest-priced of the drafted Army DC-3s; carried on the 1943 books at only $91,000 and on the 1944 books at $134,487.

All three survived the war, first going into non-military government service before finding private owners.

C-48B—Quantity procurement of a single DC-3 variant got underway with the 16 C-48Bs, which were mostly 14-berth DST-A-207Bs, Cs, and Ds (ATC-671) with right-side doors taken from United Air Lines orders. One was a DC-3A-269B taken from Northwest Airlines. The engines appear in Army records as R-1830-S1C3G and as R-1830-51 elsewhere. Since the military -51 is equivalent to the civil R-1830-S1C3G, some later engine changes may have been made. Army documents show the -51 being used in all C-48 models. The C-48Bs are not listed in either the 1943 or 1944 "Unit Cost" documents.

The berthing feature of the ex-UAL C-48Bs suited them for use as aerial ambulances, as well as plush staff transports.

Army serial numbers for the C-48Bs were 42-38324/38326 (3), 42-56089/56091 (3),

Fig. 8-3. The single C-48 was drafted from a United Air Lines DC-3A-197D order while still in the factory. The tail marking identifies Airplane No. 2 of the First Staff Squadron. Note the two-star flag of a Major General. (photo by Peter M. Bowers)

Fig. 8-4. C-48A 41-7682, formerly a DC-3A-368, survived the war and was transferred to the FAA. It still has its military markings but the Army tail number as been replaced by N86 in the government's special block of low civil registration numbers. See Fig. 13-1 for same airplane with registration N1. (photo by Peter M. Bowers)

42-56098/56102 (5), 42-56609/56612 (4), and 42-56629.

C-48C—The C-48C is another 16-plane procurement of 21-passenger DC-3As (Fig. 8-5) and one DST-A with a mix of door locations. One Swiftflite DC-3A-363, NC1000, C/N 3275 with right-hand door, was an oddity—it was originally taken by the Army as C-52D 42-5605 but was redesignated C-48C and given the later serial 42-38260.

Redesignating airplanes was fairly common, obsolete bombers becoming transports (XB-15 to XC-105, B-23 to C-67) and transport types becoming observation (C-21 to OA-3), but they kept their original serial numbers. No such mission changes were involved with the C-52D/C-48C, nor was there an engine change such as made a Curtiss P-1C into the XP-6B. No one switched factory nameplates either; it remained C/N 3275.

C-48C Army serial numbers: 42-38258/38260 (3), 42-38327, 42/78332/38338 (7), 42-78026/78028 (3), 44-52990, and 44-52991.

C-49/C-51 SERIES

The principal difference between the C-48 and the C-49 was the Wright Cyclone engine in the C-49 (ATC-618 for all series except for a few DC-3B-202s on ATC-635). Actually, the C-50 and -51 models also used the Cyclone and most of the planes from C-49 through C-52C were procured on the same ac-

Fig. 8-5. C-48C 42-38327 was ordered by KLM as a DC-3-194H but was completed as a DC-3A with Twin Wasp engines. Photographed at Boeing Field, Seattle, after bringing Army officials to witness the first flight of the Boeing XB-29, September 21, 1942. (photo by Gordon S. Williams)

Fig. 8-6. C-49, 41-7694, was an undelivered eight-window TWA DC-3-362 drafted March 22, 1941. Note last two digits of Army serial number on fin. (Boardman C. Reed photo)

quisition order. With series letters up to K, the C-49 was not only the most varied single model of the drafted DC-3s; it was the most numerous, with 138 airplanes.

C-49—Five of the six C-49s were high-density 24-seat DC-3-384s with left-side doors ordered by TWA but taken right off the production line (Fig. 8-6). The sixth was a DC-3-362, still a TWA order. Engines were initially R-1820-71s, producing 1200 hp at 2500 rpm. This was equivalent to the civil R-1820-G202A. One history says that the six C-49s later had their engines changed to P&W R-1830-51s, which would have made them C-48s or C-52s since the engines still determined the

model number. The 1943 cost for C-49 airframe and engines was only $102,570, later listed as $135,688.

Army serial numbers: 41-7685/7689 (5), 41-7694.

C-49A—The single C-49A, 41-7690, was an undelivered Delta Air Lines left-door DC-3-385, NC28345, acquired by the Army February 23, 1941. The engines were R-1820-71 in Army records and the price was $97,069 in the 1943 book. Acquired February 23, 1941, this one went to the Royal Australian Air Force (RAAF) in 1943 as a Dakota but flew with the civilian call letter VH-CDC instead of a regular RAAF serial. It crashed in the sea at Leyte, the Philippines, November 13, 1945.

Fig. 8-7. This C-49B, Army serial 41-7693, was formerly DC-3-201F of an Eastern Air Lines order. In the absence of unit markings, the last two digits of the Army serial number were used on the fin for airplane identification. (photo by Peter M. Bowers)

102

C-49B—The C-49Bs were three Eastern Air Lines 21-passenger DC-3-201Fs with left-side doors and R-1820-71 engines (Fig. 8-7) taken off the production lines as a unit on February 22, 1941. Civil registrations were to have been NC288386/288388; the Army serial numbers were 41-7691/7693. The first and last went to the RAAF as VH-CDD and CDE, respectively.

C-49C—The two C-49Cs were consecutive left-door DC-3-375As ordered by Delta Air Lines (NC28346, 28347) but were assigned Army serials 41-7715 and 7721 separately (Fig. 8-8). C/Ns were 4814 and 4815. These got a more military treatment than previous draftees, with the airline interior being stripped out and side benches being installed for up to 28 troops. No cabin soundproofing was installed and the airliner floor was protected from the impact of military boots and heavy cargo by a layer of heavy plywood applied over it. The C-49Cs were the first U.S. Army DC-3s to have olive drab and gray warpaint applied. Engines were R-1820-71s and the 1943 price went up to $100,186.

C-49D—The C-49Ds were eleven airplanes acquired from the factory in two batches (Fig. 8-9). The first five were on an Eastern Air Lines DC-3-201G left-door order and were fitted with troop benches like the C-49C. The other six were later random grabs of DC-3B-202, DC-3-201, -210F, -357, and -322B, plus one unidentified (Fig. 8-10). All but the last one had left-side doors. The C-49Ds

were on the 1943 books at $104,882. The engines were listed by the Army as R-1820-71.

Army serial numbers: 41-7716/7720 (5), 42-38256, 42-46324, 42-65583, 42-65584, 42-68860, and 44-52999.

C-49E—The C-49Es were a mixed bag of 22 right-side door DSTs and DC-3s with C/Ns ranging from 1494 to 4132, and not in consecutive order (Fig. 8-11). All were in service with several airlines before being taken into the Army. Engines listed in Army documents as R-1820-G102A. In spite of the mix of day and sleeper cabins, most were fitted out as ambulances with up to 14 stretchers.

Army serial numbers: 42-43619/46323 (5), 42-56092/56097 (6), 42-56103/56107 (5), 42-56617, 42-56618, 42-56625/56627 (3), and 42-56634.

C-49F—The C-49Fs were a mix of DSTs and DC-3s from TWA, Eastern, and Chicago & Southern for a total of nine additional litter carriers, with R-1820-71 engines and some with right-hand doors. 1943 cost was $124,261.

Army serial numbers: 42-56613, 42-56616, 42-56620, 42-56621, 42-56623, 42-56628, 42-56633, 42-56636, and 42-56637.

C-49G—The C-49Gs were eight 21-passenger DC-3-201s taken from Eastern Air Lines. Engines are listed in Army documents as R-1820-G2E, a civil engine that delivered 1000 hp at 2200 rpm. These seemed to differ from other C-49s in having the more common left-side passenger doors. The

Fig. 8-8. One of the two C-49Cs, Delta Air Lines DC-3-375As drafted from the factory. The number 15 on the nacelle could be either the last two digits of Army serial number 41-7715 for the first or the last two digits of the Douglas serial number 4815 for the second. (photo by Peter M. Bowers)

Fig. 8-9. A C-49D photographed in motion at Oakland, California, in October 1941. Absence of tail or nacelle numbers makes individual airplane identification impossible. (photo by Arthur Sutter)

first two were delivered to the Royal Air Force and operated as DC-3s before the RAF name Dakota was assigned.

Army serial numbers: 42-38252, 42-38255, 42-56614, 42-56615, 42-56630/56632 (3), and 42-56635.

C-49H—The C-49Hs were a mixed bag of 19 former airliners from five lines, all 21-passenger DC-3s with R-1820-G102A engines and a broad range of C/Ns from 1941 to 4130. The mix included both right-side and left-side doors. Again, the first

two were delivered to the Royal Air Force (Fig. 8-12).

Army serial numbers: 42-38250, 42-38251, 42-38253, 42-38254, 42-38257, 42-38328/38331 (4), 42-57506, 42-65580/65582 (3), 42-68687/68689 (3), 42-107422, 44-83228, and 44-83229.

C-49I—The letter I was not used as a series suffix in U.S. Army aircraft designations.

C-49J—The biggest single series of C-49s was the C-49J with 34 DC-3-454s and -455s taken from the production line after being started for four different

Fig. 8-10. An indeterminant C-49 series DC-3 photographed at the factory. Wartime releases of this photo misidentified it as both a C-47 and a C-53. (Douglas photo)

Fig. 8-11. A Major General's six-window C-49E late in 1941. Meaning of lettering SEACTC on tail is unknown today. It could be something like South East Air Corps Training Command; such organizations were commanded by Major Generals. (photo by Jack Binder)

airlines. Since all were drafted at once, the Army serial numbers were consecutive, 43-1961/1994, but the C/Ns did not correspond, ranging from 4987 to 6344. The left-side-door airplanes were fitted out as 28-seat troopers with R-1820-G202A engines. 1943 price was up to $137,786, with the 1944 total $148,734.

C-49K—The C-49K was the last variant in the C-49 series, 23 DC-3-455s from American and TWA orders (Fig. 8-13), with consecutive Army serials 43-1995/2017 following right after the Js but preceding some late C-49H procurements. All were left-door 28-seat troopers with R-1820-G202A engines and a price of $147,667.

C-50—The C-50s were four right-side door 21-passenger DC-3-227Ds ordered by American

Airlines, 41-7697/7700 (Fig. 8-14). The engines were R-1820-85, 1100 hp at 2350 rpm and were equivalent to the civil R-1820-G102A. Price was $138,512. 42-7697 and 7698 went to Australia and operated with civil call signs VH- CDK and CDJ. 41-7700 went back to American, then was acquired by Douglas and became the second Super DC-3 prototype in 1949 (see Chapter 12).

C-50A—The C-50As were two DC-3-401s ordered by American Airlines with right-side doors, but were completed with 28 troop seats and R-1820-85 engines. The first, 41-7710, crashed in North Carolina April 21, 1942; the second, 41-7711, crashed at Michigan City December 28, 1946, after being returned to American Airlines.

C-50B—The C-50Bs were three left-side door

Fig. 8-12. C-49H, 42-38250, was drafted from an American Airlines DC-3-277D order and turned over to the RAF, which leased it to Indian National Airways. It then carried both Indian Civil Registration VT-ATB and RAF serial MA925. (photo by Peter M. Bowers)

Fig. 8-13. The next-to-last C-49K, 43-2016, was a former DC-3-455 for Eastern Air Lines fitted with an astrodome and gun grommets in the windows. Here it carries an undersize fuselage star with white rectangles and the short-lived red border of July-August 1943. (photo by William T. Larkins)

DC-3-314Bs ordered by Braniff. Used with airline-type seats, engines were R-1820-81, still similar to the civil GR-1820-G102A. Delivered in June 1941, the first two, 41-7703 and 7704, survived the war and had several different owners and registrations. The third, 41-7705, crashed at Patterson Field in July, 1941.

C-50C—The C-50C was a left-side door DC-3-313B, 41-7695, originally ordered by Pennsylvania Central Airlines but completed as a DC-3-392 with airline-type seats. Engines were R-1820-79, again equivalent to the GR-1820-G102A. Price $126,993. Crashed November 12, 1942, while serving with the 5th Air Force in Australia.

C-50D—The C-50Ds were four DC-3-313Bs, 41-7696, 41-7709, 41-7712, and 41-7713, from a Penn Central order completed as a DC-3-392 and

equipped similarly to the C-50C at a price of $127,623. All survived the war and all but 41-7709 were converted to DC-3As for new owners by change to P & W R-1830 engines.

C-51—The single C-51, 41-7702, was ordered by Canadian Colonial Airlines as DC-3-270C NC34962 with right-side door; the Army made a 28-seat trooper of it (Fig. 8-15). The engines were R-1820-83, similar to the -79 and -85 except for different reduction gear ratios, magnetos, and fuel pump drives that the Army must have thought justified the change of airplane designation. Price was $132,181.

C-52 SERIES

The C-52s were six mixed DC-3A models obtained from three airlines and a private owner in 1941. All used the military R-1830-92 engine,

Fig. 8-14. The first of four C-50s, taken from an American Airlines DC-3-227D order in June 1941. Unlike the C-49Ks, this has neither a navigator's astrodome nor gun grommets in the windows. (Douglas photo)

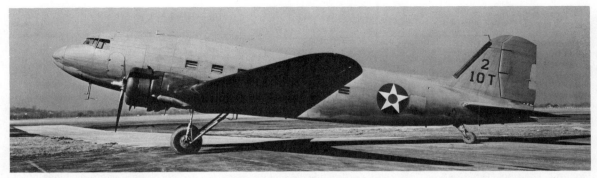

Fig. 8-15. The single C-51 was a former Canadian Colonial Airlines DC-3-270C, reportedly fitted as a trooper. The bars on the windows would indicate that the cabin was used for bulk freight. The unit designator on the fin identifies Airplane No. 2 of the 10th Transport Group. (USAF photo)

equivalent to the civil Pratt & Whitney R-1830-S1C3G. All were equipped as troopers with reinforced floors, some with left-side door, some with right. The 1943 prices for the C-52s ranged from a low of $103,518 for the C-52A to $103,973 for the C-52Bs and C-52C.

C-52—One C-52 was a DC-3A-398, 41-7708, with right-side door ordered by United. It was returned to United after the war but got older DC-3 registration NC15586 instead of the one it was originally assigned, NC34999. 1943 price was $103,824.

C-52A—Another single, the C-52A, 41-7714 was a right-side door DC-3A-394 ordered by Western Air Lines. Returned to Western as NC19387, it has had three other registrations since, N97A, N430SF, and N518DW, plus a modification to left-hand door.

C-52B—A pair of right-side door DC-3A-197Es, were C-52Bs, 41-7706, 7707, ordered by United as NC33648 and 33649 (Fig. 8-16). Both went to Northern Airlines after the war with new registrations NC33326 and 333276, respectively, and then to several subsequent owners.

C-52C—The single C-52C, 41-7701, illustrates a problem in accurately totalling DC-3 vs. DC-3A production. It was started as a DC-3-201G on an Eastern Air Lines order, but was completed as a 28-seat trooper with Twin Wasp engines, making it a DC-3A rather than a DC-3 (Fig. 8-17). Several other DC-3s were completed as DC-3As when the Army drafted them before they were too far along the production line.

C-52D—Army records show the C-52D designa-

Fig. 8-16. The first of two C-52Bs, DC-3A-197Es from a United Air Lines order. Note the oversize Army serial number covering both fin and rudder, typical of applications made in the field after "tail numbers" were adopted in January 1942. The red center was removed from the star on May 15, 1942. (courtesy William T. Larkins)

Fig. 8-17. The single C-52C, 41-7701. Several sources indicate that this was a DC-3-201G on an Eastern Air Lines order. The visible open cowling flaps establish that it was completed and delivered as a DC-3A. (photo by Peter M. Bowers)

tion cancelled, but that was after left-side door DC-3A-363, C/N 3275, ordered by Swiftflight, Inc., was delivered under Army serial 42-6505 on September 6, 1941. It was subsequently redesignated C-48C on March 4, 1942, and given the later Army serial 42-38260. The oddity here is that the airplane was reported by its original serial while serving in India and Africa long after the supposed change. It served two U.S. airlines after the war before going to Indonesia as PK-ZDB in 1968.

ADDITIONAL DRAFTEES

Two more small batches of drafted civil DC-3s were acquired before the final Army production model of the DC-3, the C-117A, was ordered. No verifiable photographs of C-68s or C-84s in Army markings are known to exist.

C-68—Two left-side door DC-3A-414s, 42-14297, 14298, without record of who ordered them, were acquired from the Douglas production line December 31, 1941. These had a 21-passenger interior and R-1830-92 engines, so why they should have gotten a new model number C-68, instead of being added to the C-52s is a mystery. The C-68s were on the 1943 books at $139,966. Both were leased briefly to Pan American, then went to Europe in March and April 1942, the first into the RAF as Dakota LR230 without Mark number while the second served with the U.S. 8th Air Force.

The Dakota was destroyed by a Japanese air

Fig. 8-18. Neither of the two C-68s was photographed as such during the war. This is the survivor, 42-14298, a DC-3A-414, in service with Delta Air Lines after the war, with NC20752 replacing its original registration of NC30005. (photo by Roger Besecker)

Fig. 8-19. The four C-84s were not photographed in military service, either. All survived the war to continue airline service. This is the former 42-57513 after extensive modification in 1965. The "NC" of American civil registrations was changed to plain "N" in 1948. (photo by Roger Besecker)

raid on Myitkyina, Burma, on May 6, 1942, but the 8AF plane returned Stateside after the war and joined the airlines (Fig. 8-18).

C-84—At first glance, it would seem logical to give the four C-84s (42-57157, 42-57511/57513) separate designations from other Cyclone-engined DC-3s since they were the rare DC-3B-202s and one -202A, of which only 10 were built under ATC-635, all for TWA. Dating from 1937-38, the TWA ships were drafted in June 1942. However, the logic does not stand up since all but one of the other ATC-635 ships (it crashed in airline service) were drafted as C-49s—one D, one E, and three Fs.

There was no corresponding separate Douglas letter designation for an equivalent P & W powered semi-sleeper like the DC-3B although there were such airplanes (see C-41A). Army seating was high-density airline type for 28 passengers and engines were civil Wright GR-1820-G202A. Some civil references cite the R-1820-71, which is equivalent to the R-1820-G202A, a slightly different engine.

The C-84s do not appear on the 1943 and 1944 unit cost lists.

All the C-84s were returned to TWA before the end of the war to fly under their original registrations of NC17312, 17314, 17319, and 18953, respectively. They later found a succession of new owners, but only one, NC18953, got a subsequent registration: N139D.

N139D is a puzzle ship. Postwar FAA registration records verify the C/N as 2027, but a photo shows P & W engines, no upper-berth windows, standard main-window spacing, and a right-hand door (Fig. 8-19). These differences cannot be reconciled by the minor DC-3B-202A designation differences, so this particular ship either must have been extensively rebuilt somewhere along the line or someone made a nameplate and registration number switch with another airplane—an illegal but not unheard-of trick of the trade.

Chapter 9

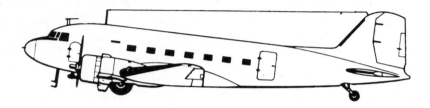

U.S. Navy and British DCs

The U.S. Navy became a customer for Douglas DC-2s before the U.S. Army, and also brought a DC model that the Army skipped, the DC-5. Navy DC-3 procurement began with duplicates of U.S. Army C-47's built under Navy contracts, but most were C-47s diverted from Army contracts. There was also direct purchase of off-the-shelf civil DC-3s and the drafting of other civil DC-3s. The Navy became the only user of "Super DC-3s" (see Chapter 12) and kept them in service several years after retirement of the last Air Force C-47.

British Empire Forces, notably Australia, were the first regular military users of DCs after the U.S. At first, these consisted of secondhand DC-2s; later new airframes were acquired by direct purchase and American Lend-Lease.

U.S. NAVY DESIGNATION SYSTEM

The Navy had an aircraft designating system of its own that differed notably from that of the Army. This also covered the U.S. Marines and the U.S. Coast Guard. It was abandoned in 1962 when the Department of Defense combined the Air Force and Navy designating systems into a single new unified services system. The Navy retained some designations that applied only to its operations, but the DC-3s, which the Navy knew as R4Ds, became C-47s in the USAF's C-for-Cargo series. They did not pick up "old" C-47 designations in spite of being direct equivalents, as the R4D-5s having been built as C-47As with Army serial numbers; the R4D-5s became C-47H. See appropriate R4D writeup for more detail.

A notable exception was the R4D-8 line; R4D-5s, -6s, and -7s rebuilt as "Super DC-3s". In spite of cargo doors and other C-47 features, these became C-117D.

The Navy had originally used the letter T in 1927 to identify transport planes, but since this duplicated the existing T-for-Torpedo plane, it was replaced by the letter R with no phonetic connection. A separate series of letters was used to identify the manufacturer. The first Navy transport sold by Douglas was designated XRD-1—X-for-Experimental, R-for-Transport, and D-for-Douglas.

The -1 identified the initial configuration, and progressed through -2, -3, etc., equivalent to Army/Air force series letters.

The second Navy transport model from Douglas was the R2D-1, a DC-2. There was no need for an X-designated prototype as had been the case with the Army XC-32. Further Douglas Navy transports were R3D for the third, R4D for the fourth, etc.

The Navy was not as quick to assign new designations because of simple things such as an engine change, nor did it use block numbers and factory abbreviations as did the Army. The R4D-1, with Pratt & Whitney Twin Wasp engines and cargo doors, duplicated the Army C-47. The R4D-2, on the other hand, had Wright Cyclone engines and deluxe DC-3 features like the C-49. Yet the significant difference that justified a new model number in the Army rated only a different dash number in the Navy, and in retrospect, the Navy's system was undoubtedly less confusing and more justifiable.

Special-Purpose Suffixes

Special-Purpose Suffixes—The Navy uses only X and Y as status prefixes but identified special-purpose modifications until 1962 with a series of suffix letters equivalent to the Army/Air Force prefix letters. Use of the suffixes was discontinued in 1962 and most of the same letters were then used as prefixes in the new unified services system.

Special-purpose suffixes applied to Navy DC-3 are as follows:

E—Electronic, usually surveillance.

F—Flagship, as used by officers of flag rank. Replaced by Z late in WWII.

L—Cold-weather operations, particularly Arctic and Antarctic. Modified systems, extra heating, etc., but not necessarily skis.

Q—Electronic countermeasures.

R—Normally for other types converted to transports, as PB2Y-3 patrol bomber to -3R. In the case of DC-3 types, conversion from cargo-door R4D-6 to R4D-6R with small door, aft baggage compartment, and other DC-3/C-117A features like airline interior.

S—Anti-submarine search using a variety of electronic equipment and as many or more ran-domes and special antennas than the Q versions.

T—Trainer conversion, usually with extra crew stations for navigator trainees similar to Army TC-47B.

X—An oddity; use of the X-for Experimental as a suffix instead of the customary prefix. Used on only one Navy DC-3, the "Super DC-3" prototype obtained from the USAF as R4D-8X.

Z—Staff Transport or administrative use; replaced F. Sometimes this applied to R4D-5s and -6s that still had cargo doors.

Special-Purpose Prefixes—The new system eliminated the former Navy practice of designating special-purpose airplanes by suffix letter. This was replaced by a system of prefixes, USAF style. Most prefixes applied to the Navy DC-3s matched existing USAF prefixes, but a few were carryovers of Navy suffix letters that now became prefixes. The following prefixes apply to Navy R4Ds that were redesignated C-47 or C-117:

E—Electronics; similar to pre-existing USAF prefix and replacing former E and Q suffixes.

L—Winterized; re-use of former L-suffix as a new prefix.

N—Permanent modification for Special Test; no previous Navy equipment.

S—Search; equivalent to pre-existing USAF prefix and replacing former S-suffix.

T—Trainer; same as USAF, but also Transport, as R4D-6R becoming TC-47J. R4D-7, without a suffix, was always a trainer (ex-TC-47B) and became TC-47K.

V—Staff Transport as USAF, replaced Z-suffix.

Before World War II and during it, the Navy designation was printed on each side of the rudder in three-inch-high block letters. For camouflaged types this was reduced to one-inch figures. After the war, the model designation was relocated on the fuselage near or under the horizontal tail and remains there today.

NAVY SERIAL NUMBER SYSTEM

After several changes from the Navy's first airplane procurement in 1911, the present consecutive-numbering system was adopted in 1917. Navy serial numbers are often referred to as Bureau Numbers (BuNo) because of being assigned by the Navy's Bureau of Aeronautics. When this reached 9999 in 1935 it was started over at 0001. When the rapid buildup preceding WWII ran the numbers in the second series so high that they threatened to duplicate late existing numbers in the 1917-1935 series, the second series was discontinued at 7303 in 1941 and a new five-digit series was started at 00001. Rather than start another after 99999, the third series was allowed to expand to six digits and is still in use. U.S. Navy DCs have been covered by all three of the post-1917 serial number series.

The Navy serial was applied to each side of the vertical fin even with and the same size as the designation on the rudder. During WWII, the serial (or sometimes only the last three or four digits) was sometimes painted on the nose of R4Ds in larger figures.

After the war, the serial was moved to the fuselage beneath the designation and a rather inconsistent practice of adding the serial in large figures, in whole or just the last four or five digits, to the vertical fin for easier identification was adopted.

U.S. NAVY DC-2/5 VARIANTS

The U.S. Navy preceded the U.S. Army in the acquisition of DC-2s but did not parallel Army procurement in DC-2, -3, -4 order; the Navy acquired DC-5s before it bought DC-3s and DC-4s.

R2D-1—Five R2D-1s that were essentially off-the-shelf civil DC-2s were ordered in 1934 (Fig. 9-1). Navy serials were 9620/9622 (DC-2-125) and 9993/9994 (DC-2-142) in the first series; 9621 and 9994 were turned over to the U.S. Marines. These were the first really modern transport monoplanes that the Navy had in numbers, and they served into the early years of World War II. Those not scrapped went to service mechanics' schools as nonflying training aids or to civil schools for the same purpose. One Navy R2D-1, serial 9993, was stricken from the Navy roster in January 1940, but was acquired by North American Aviation and put in service under the DC-2 ATC as a company transport with the civil registration NC39163. Sold in August 1944, it has had several subsequent owners and is believed to be the only DC-2 still flyable in 1985.

R3D-1, 2—After buying DC-2s, the Navy skipped the DC-3 and the experimental DC-4 and bought the DC-5, which was a high-wing transport slightly

Fig. 9-1. The first U.S. Navy DC, a DC-2-125, Navy serial number 9620, used as an executive transport. Note size and location of the U.S. NAVY service identification on the fuselage. (U.S. Navy photo)

Fig. 9-2. The U.S. Navy bought three DC-5s as R3D-1, but one was lost on a test flight before it was delivered. This one, Navy serial No. 1903, was a staff transport assigned to Naval Air Station Anacostia, near Washington, D.C. (photo by A.U. Schmidt)

smaller than the DC-3. The DC-5 had very limited production as an airliner, and the Navy was the principal customer, with three R3D-1s for the Navy (1901/1903 in the second series, Fig. 9-2) and four R3D-2s with cargo doors for the Marines (1904/1907, Fig. 9-3). After Pearl Harbor, the Navy took over the civil prototype as R3D-3 (00805 in the third series). The Army caught up with the Navy DC-5 by drafting the three Dutch East Indies DC-5s that escaped from Java to Australia as C-110s in 1943. Three USMC R3D-2s survived into 1946.

THE R4D SERIES

In a rare example of pre-WWII U.S. Army-Navy cooperation, the two services simultaneously ordered identical cargo versions of the well-established DC-3 to be built on the same production line. The Navy assigned the designation R4D to its DC-3s, with the first examples ordered being duplicates of the still-unbuilt Army C-47. However, higher series numbers were in the air first.

Production of Navy R4D-1s, -5s, -6s, and -7s paralleled Army C-47/C-47B production from the Long Beach and Oklahoma City plants. The R4D-2s vere off-the-shelf airliners and the R4D-3s were

transferred Army C-53s, both from Santa Monica. The R4D-4s were airliners taken over on the Santa Monica production line. The initial R4D-1 contract was placed separately from the Army contract before the Long Beach plant was built, and production, with deliveries beginning in January 1942, was mixed with the early C-47s.

After the initial 66 were built on Navy contracts, all subsequent -1s, -5s, -6s, and -7s were transfers to the Navy of airplanes built on Army contracts with Army serial numbers. The Navy serials were added, sometimes without the Army numbers being deleted. The "Army" influence car-

Fig. 9-3. The U.S. marines obtained four R3D-2s, which were similar to the R3D-1s except for large left-side cargo doors. The Navy procured the Marines' airplanes; hence the use of Navy serial numbers and designations. (photo by Peter M. Bowers)

ried beyond mere Army coloring and equipment standards to the point that some carried the Navy model number with Army block numbers and plant abbreviations, as R4D-6-25-DK on a transferred C-47B-25-DK (Fig. 9-4).

In spite of its use of the C-117D designation after 1962, the Navy did not acquire any of the DC-3s that were built for the Army as C-117A. One Navy R4D-1 was acquired roundabout, a British Dakota I, FD797, obtained from the RAF. Navy procurement of R4Ds did not end with WWII. Some USAF C-47Bs or Ds became Navy R4D-6s as late as 1961.

An interesting reverse transfer occurred in the late 1950s when some R4D-5s and -6s were transferred to the U.S. Army, which had an air arm of its own separate from the USAF. These operated under their Navy designations and serial numbers and were redesignated as the appropriate C-47s in 1962 (see Chapter 14).

The R4D series was not distinguished by extensive modifications that resulted in new model numbers. Most special-purpose alterations were covered simply by adding the appropriate suffix letter to the designation, as an R4D-6Q bristling with antennas and radomes. Even as major a change as the rebuild of standard models to "Super DC-3" configuration was reflected only by a change of dash number to R4D-8.

Other changes were not reflected in the designation at all, as changing R-1870-90C engines to -90D. A similar change in the Army/USAF resulted in C-47Bs becoming C-47Ds. Some R4Ds are known to have undergone "Hi-Per" and "Maximizer" modifications developed by civil organizations in the 1950s, but these revisions did not affect the designation. Modifications for Antarctic operations involved mostly basic aircraft systems and such things as extra heating capacity, engine oil dilution systems, etc., not structural, with an L-suffix as the only indicator. It is not known whether any R4Ds got R-2800 engines, as did the USAF C-47E and EC-47Q.

A characteristic of all R4D cargo plane deliveries was the dispatch of numerous small quantities of airplanes that made up single runs of Navy serial numbers. The planes were not assigned to the Navy in corresponding blocks but were diverted in small batches, often only two at a time, from the larger Army production runs.

R4D-1—The R4D-1s were direct equivalents of the Army C-47, and the Navy got a total of 100; 66 on direct purchase, 33 transferred from the Army, and one from the RAF (Fig. 9-5). A further 30 were cancelled. The Navy serials of the R4D-1s were widely scattered in eight blocks (two in the second series and the rest in the third), and the largest single batch with consecutive C/Ns consisted of 51. Being the oldest cargo DC-3s in Navy service, these had high wartime attrition and the survivors were surplussed soon after the war.

BuNos: 3131/3143 (13), 4692/4706 (15), 01648,

Fig. 9-4. This C-47B-25-DK, 44-76458, was built on a U.S. Army contract and carried full Army markings but was transferred to the Navy and carried the Navy designation R4D-6-25-DK on the rudder and the Navy serial number 50839 on the fin above the Army serial. (photo by Peter M. Bowers)

Fig. 9-5. The second R4D-1 built on the original Navy contract, serial 3132, in Navy rather than Army camouflage and displaying the Navy variation of prewar Army rudder stripes used on camouflaged Navy airplanes from January 5 to May 15, 1942. Only the horizontal red and white stripes were used, not the vertical blue. (Douglas photo)

01649, 01977/01985 (9), 01986/01990 (5), 05051/05072 (22), 12393/12404 (12), 30147, 37660, 37660/37710 (51), and 91104.

R4D-2—Although carrying a later dash number and higher serials than the R4D-1s, the two R4D-2s were the first DC-3s in Navy service. Serial numbers were 4707 and 4708 in the second BuNo series. These were not built to Navy order but were drafted from an Eastern Air Lines contract for DC-3-388s (Fig. 9-6).

The R4D-2s were the only Navy DC-3s built with Wright Cyclone engines (R-1820-71). As VIP transports, they were equivalent to the early Army C-49s. Delivered in February 1941, 4097 was assigned to Anacostia Naval Air Station and 4098 was assigned to Pensacola. Because of their VIP appointments, both were designated R4D-2F when the suffix came into use and became R4D-2Z when

it was dropped.

Both survived the war and found civil owners when declared surplus; 4098 was assigned to a naval attache in South Africa at the time and went on the South African civil register when surplussed in that country.

R4D-3—The 20 R4D-3s were transfers to the Navy from the production C-53 contract and from Army drafts of civil DC-3s (Fig. 9-7). The 17 that the Army drafted were designated C-53C and some sources credit all the R4D-3s as having that designation originally, but it is not so. The Navy serials were in two blocks in the third series, 05073/05084 (12) for the C-53s and 06902/06999 (8) for the C-53Cs, but the airplanes came in widely scattered pairs, with corresponding jumps in original Army serials and factory C/Ns.

The first two R4D-3s were delivered in January

Fig. 9-6. The first Navy DC-3s were a pair of DC-3-388s taken from an Eastern Air Lines order. This is the second, serial 4708, at the factory on March 5, 1941. (Douglas photo)

Fig. 9-7. The Navy R4D-3s were all transfers from Army C-53 contracts. This one is Airplane No. 51 of the Seventh Transport Squadron, VR-7. (U.S. Navy photo courtesy Arthur Pearcy)

1942 and carried Navy coloring, rudder stripes, and stars on both wings. The last delivery from the C-53 contract was on June 22, 1942. The first delivery from the C-53C contract was on November 15, 1942, and the last was early in 1943.

Early R4D-3s carried whatever cargo could get through their airliner doors or into the baggage compartment, but otherwise served mainly as personnel carriers. Engines with the same P & W R-1830-92 used in the C-53s and the C-47/R4D-1s. The R4D-3s were retired from Navy service before the designation change of 1962.

R4D-4—The 12 R4D-4s were more drafted airliners, this time acquired on Navy initiative from a Pan American Airways DC-3A-447 order (Fig. 9-8). The Navy serial numbers were two unknowns and two widely separated batches in the third series, 07000/07003 (4) and 33815/33820 (6). The first was accepted on July 1, 1943, and the last on December 1, 1943. Earlier, seven additional Army C-53Cs drafted from PAA had been transferred to the Navy in December 1942, and appear in some Navy records as R4D-4Rs, serials 33615/33621.

Some R4D-4s served into the late 1940s or early 1950s, but none were in service at the time of the 1962 designation change.

R4D-5—The 238 R4D-5s were Navy equivalents of the Army C-47A and made up the largest single

Fig. 9-8. The sixth R4D-4 still in service in 1947, after the red bars were added to the national insignia. Note serial number 07003 in full on the nose, and the adjacent insignia of the Naval Air Transport Service. (U.S. Navy photo courtesy Arthur Pearcy)

variant of the R4D line (Fig. 9-9). Navy serials were in three batches: 12405/12446 (42), 17092/17248 (150), and 39057/39095 (39). Several were turned back to the Army before delivery. Only 100 R4D-5s were built at Long Beach; the rest were from Oklahoma City.

During the war and afterward, R4D-5s picked up L, Q, R, S, and Z suffixes, plus some civil features (Fig. 9-10). A number were transferred to the Army in the 1950s. The designation was changed to C-47H in 1962, with corresponding prefixes to replace old suffix letters. One new one appeared here: NC-47H on serial 39103. Earlier, 67 had been rebuilt as R4D-8s.

R4D-6—The 147 R4D-6s were originally Army C-47Bs and were assigned three batches of Navy serials: 17249/17291 (43), 39096/39099 (4), and 50740/50839 (100). Deliveries were concurrent with late R4D-5s, and again the batches were small. The largest two were 13 each and most were two-plane pairs. Four more were acquired from the Air Force in 1961 and received Naval serials 150187/150190.

The R4D-6s picked up L, Q, R, S, and Z suffixes (Figs. 9-11, 9-12) and 29 were eventually converted to R4D-8. Those not converted to -8 became C-47J in 1962, with appropriate prefixes replacing old suffixes.

R4D-7—The 44 R4D-7s were all Army TC-47Bs

Fig. 9-9. A Marine Corps R4D-5 with service name and Navy model and serial numbers in the standard wartime position on the fin. By 1945 both C-47s and R4Ds were in service in natural metal finish. (photo by Peter M. Bowers)

Fig. 9-10. A Marine R4D-5Z, the Z-suffix indicating use as a VIP transport. This is unusual in that the cargo doors are retained and there are no curtains in the window or special markings to indicate use by high-ranking officers. (photo by Peter M. Bowers)

built in Oklahoma City (Fig. 9-13). There were two batches of Navy serials, 39099/39110 (10, less 39100), and 99824/99857 (34). All were delivered in lots of two except 39099 and 39110, which were singles. A further 156 of a planned 200 total were cancelled.

The R4D-7s were procured specifically as instrument trainers. Consequently, when the special-purpose suffix T was added to other R4Ds converted for the purpose after the war, it was not added to the R4D-7s. Four were converted to R4D-8 in the early 1950s and the remainder became TC-47K in 1962.

R4D-8—The postwar "Super DC-3." See Chapter 12.

BRITISH COMMONWEALTH DC-2/DC-3 VARIANTS

The first British military DC acquisitions were made by purchasing exiting DC-2 airliners from America. Later DC-3s were acquired by harboring refugee airliners that escaped the invasion of their homelands early in World War II and by drafting others from private owners.

The majority of DC-3s supplied to the RAF and

Fig. 9-11. An R4D-6Q equipped for the postwar training of student radar operators. Note the three-inch insignia red propeller warning stripe around the fuselage in line with the propellers, a postwar addition to all multi-engine U.S. military aircraft. (photo by R.L. Taylor)

Fig. 9-12. A Marine R4D-6R VIP transport modified from cargo configuration to incorporate such civil DC-3 airliner features as small passenger door and rear baggage compartment. (photo by Douglas D. Olson)

other Commonwealth Air Forces were C-47s delivered under the Lend-Lease Act of March 1941.

Royal Air Force DC-2K

The 21 DC-2s acquired by the RAF were identified for the record as DC-2K regardless of Douglas dash number and did not receive the traditional service name (Fig. 9-14). The new RAF serials and the original national registrations and dates of acquisition for the DC-2Ks are presented below:

RAF Serials	Formerly	Acquired
AX755	NC14268 Delta Air Lines	Oct. 1941
AX767	NC13712 TWA (C-32A 42-53527)	July 1941
AX768	NC14966 American Airlines (C-32A 42-58073)	Mar. 1941
AX769	NC14277 American Airlines (C-32A 42-53529)	July 1941
DG468	NC14281 American Airlines	Dec. 1940
DG469	NC14282 American Airlines	Nov. 1940
DG470	NC14283 American Airlines	Nov. 1940
DG471	NC13718 TWA	Feb. 1941
DG473	NC14275 Delta Air Lines	Feb. 1941
DG474	NC14921 Delta Air Lines	Feb. 1941
DG475	NC14924 Delta Air Lines	Feb. 1941
DG476	NC13725 TWA	Feb. 1941
DG477	NC13711 TWA	Feb. 1941
DG478	NC14923 Delta Air Lines	Feb. 1941
DG479	NC13714 TWA	Feb. 1941
HK820	NC14290 Pan American	— 1941
HK821	NC14271 Pan American	April, 1941
HK837	NC14950 Pan American	— 1941
HK847	NC14280 Pan American (C-32A 42-58072)	— —
HK867	NC14278 Pan American	May 1941
—	NC14279 Pan American	May 1941

119

Fig. 9-13. The R4D-7s were TC-47Bs transferred from Army production at Oklahoma City. Easy recognition detail was the trio of astrodomes on top of the fuselage. (photo by Peter M. Bowers)

Fig. 9-14. The DC-2s acquired by the RAF were designated DC-2K. This is DG-478, formerly Delta Air Lines NC14923, photographed in Egypt in 1941 carrying Indian civil registration VT-APA in addition to its RAF serial number and markings. (courtesy Arthur Pearcy)

Fig. 9-15. The first Dakota I, RAF serial FD768, *Windsor Castle*, under test at Farnborough in March 1943. Note the tropical engine air filter used on some C-47s and Dakota Is. (RAF photo courtesy Arthur Pearcy)

All of the DC-2Ks acquired in the U.S. were flown across the South Atlantic to North Africa. Some served there briefly, and most went on to India, with four serving in Iraq. Many were turned over to the government of India for use on Indian National Airlines, where they flew with both their RAF serials and Indian civil registration.

Some of the DC-2Ks were U.S. Army C-32As that the RAF passed on to Indian National Airways, which flew them with Indian civil registrations in addition to their RAF serial numbers.

Royal Air Force Civil DC-3s

Long before the RAF received factory-new C-47s from the U.S. it acquired eight DC-3s from the U.S. Army, which had drafted them in the factory or from the airline routes and assigned Army designations. Two others, never given RAF serials, were Belgian SABENA airliners that escaped from that country in May 1940. These were operated simply as DC-3s before the name Dakota was applied. Five refugee KLM DC-3s and one of the RAF C-49Hs were used by British Overseas Airways Corporation (BOAC) as airliners with civil registrations. The five KLM models were never in the RAF. RAF serials, former registrations, and dates of acquisition are presented below:

All of the ex-U.S. Army DC-3s were sent to India. Most saw service in Burma, and three were sold to Indian National Airways in 1943.

THE RAF DAKOTAS

All of the U.S. Army C-47s supplied to Great Britain as Dakota were turned over under the provisions of the Lend-Lease Act, passed in March 1941.

Under this the U.S. Army and Navy bought and paid for aircraft destined for foreign users, and then "leased" them out. They were supposed to be returned at war's end, and many were, but most were lost through attrition.

As American government property, these planes were all built under Army or Navy serial numbers and carried standard Army or Navy designations, even though they may have been delivered in foreign markings and with foreign serial numbers. Some services adapted U.S. maintenance publications to their own serial numbers while others used the American numbers.

By the time the C-47s were available to foreign users, the North and South Atlantic ferry routes were well established, so it was a simple matter to put extra fuel tanks in the cabin and fly the planes to their destinations rather than ship them.

The principal recipient of the Lend Lease DC-3s was Britain's Royal Air Force (RAF), which received 1,920 C-47s and C-53s in addition to the 10 civil DC-3s that it had acquired earlier. Regardless of actual factory or U.S. Army/Navy designation, all RAF DC-3 types were collectively known as Dakotas of various marks. Other British Commonwealth nations also called them Dakotas.

The 1,920 total is broken down below by U.S. Army designation and RAF serial number shown on next page:

RAF Serial	Formerly	Acquired
LR230	NC30004/C-48 42-14297	Apr. 1942
LR231	NC16094/C-49G 42-38252	Apr. 1942
LR232	NC33675/C-49H 42-38253	Apr. 1942
LR233	NC17313/C-49H 42-38256	Apr. 1942
LR234	NC25623/C-48C 42-38258	Apr. 1942
LR235	NC16082/C-49G 42-38255	Apr. 1942
MA925	NC33653/C-49H 42-38250	May 1942
MA943	NC33655/C-49H 42-38251	July 1942
—	SABENA DC-3-227B 00-AUH	May 1940
—	SABENA DC-3-227B 00-AUI	May 1940

Fig. 9-16. The nine Dakota IIs were former U.S. Army C-53s. This is 42-6457 with RAF serial HK867. Note how the original U.S. star has bled through the RAF roundel that was painted over it. (W.H. Riley photo via Malcolm Stride)

Dakota I (C-47, Fig. 9-15)	53	FD768/818 (51) HK983, HK993
Dakota II (C-53, Fig. 9-16)	9	Serials not on available official lists. Five verified as HK867, MA927, MA928; TJ167, TJ170
Dakota III (C-47A, Fig. 9-17)	962	FD819/967 (149), FL503/652 (150), FZ548/698 (151), KG310/809 (500), TS422/427 (6), TS431/436 (6)
Dakota IV (C-47B, Fig. 9-18)	896	KJ801/999 (199), KK100/220 (121), KN200/701 (502), KP208/279 (72), TP181, TP187

The RAF received its first Dakota I from the Long Beach plant in January 1943, and the first to reach England arrived there by the North Atlantic Ferry route in February. Most subsequent deliveries were direct to the various theatres of operations, the first to reach India arriving in April 1943.

Not all of the Dakotas were retained by the RAF. Many were passed on to Commonwealth nations for their own air forces but, except for

Fig. 9-17. Dakota III KG647 during test at Farnborough, June 1944. The British did not make minor distinctions within series as did the U.S. Army; all C-47As in the RAF were Dakota III regardless of their Army dash numbers. (British Official photo)

122

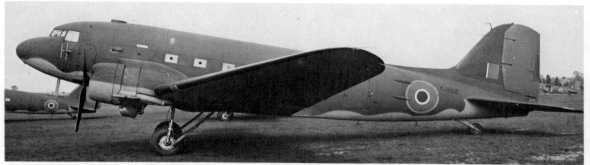

Fig. 9-18. Some Dakotas destined for Britain were given British markings while still in the factory, as this Dakota IV KJ862. Others had roundels painted over American stars after delivery. (British Official photo)

Australia, Canada, and New Zealand, were operated under their original RAF serials.

Most of the Lend-Lease C-47s for Britain were delivered in standard U.S. Army Coloring, but quite a few that went through British depots for incorporation of British items or later overhaul received contemporary British multicolor camouflage. Late in the war, some RAF and other Commonwealth Dakotas were stripped to natural metal finish.

In 1951, the RAF acquired 18 additional Dakotas when airlift was needed to support operations against insurgents in Malaysia. These were all former C-47A and B Dakotas that had been sold as surplus to various British airlines and private owners. All were given the following RAF serials:

WZ984	XF645/649 (5)
WZ985	XF667
XV280	XF746/749 (4)
XB246	XF756
XF619	XF757
XF623	1 Unknown

These were disposed of by sale in 1956.

What is probably the greatest tribute to the unmatched utility of the DC-3 occurred in 1971. The last RAF Dakotas were retired in 1970, but the model proved so indispensible for certain work that the RAF re-acquired two, gave them new serial numbers, and put them to work at the famous Royal Aircraft Establishment in Farnsborough. One, ZK947 (formerly RCAF 661) is still in service at this writing and is expected to serve to the end of this century!

Another Dakota joined the RAF temporarily. In 1980, to commemorate the Berlin Airlift, the Australian government donated a Dakota to the Berlin Museum. However, since Australia no longer had clearance from East Germany to overfly its territory, while England did, the plane was given the late but official RAF serial ZD215 just for that one flight.

AUSTRALIAN DC-2/DC-3 VARIANTS

Australia was actually the first British Commonwealth country to use the DC-3 as a military airplane. Four civil DC-3s were drafted from Australian National Airways in 1939 and early 1940.

The serialization system of the Royal Australian Air Force (RAAF) was unique to that country. Starting in 1921, it identified airplanes with the letter A, followed by a sequential number that identified the particular model, then the actual number of aircraft of that model. The series was started over in 1935.

The four drafted DC-3s, plus 10 DC-2s bought from Eastern Airlines in 1940, were all identified as A30. The DC-3s were A30-1 through A30-4 and the DC-2s were A30-5 through A30-14. The Lend-Lease Dakotas got a different basic number, A65. The 124 Dakotas break down as follows:

Dakota I (C-47)	3	A65-1, -3, -4
Dakota III (C-47A)	56	A-65-2, 5/59
Dakota IV (C-47B)	65	A-65-60/124

Fig. 9-19. An Australian Dakota with the red removed from the roundels and fin flash and radio call letters similar to Australian civil registrations applied to the vertical tail. (courtesy Merwin W. Prime)

Australia also had a mix of 24 C-47s, C-49s, C-50s, and C-53s on loan from the U.S. Army, separate from Lend-Lease, and operated them under their Army serial numbers for a total of 152 military DC-3s. Many Australian Dakotas were repainted in Australia's own dark green shade that was notably darker than American Olive Drab. In addition, many carried Australian radio call letters that resembled the Australian VH-and-three-letters civil registrations. These were painted on each side of the vertical tail (Fig. 9-19). Some U.S. C-47s and other models based in Australia also used these VH call letters. These were in addition to standard U.S. military markings and serials.

CANADIAN DAKOTAS

The Royal Canadian Air Force (RCAF) re-

Fig. 9-20. The Royal Canadian Air Force was late in adopting the change in roundel and fin flash proportions adopted in Britain in June 1942. This RCAF Dakota I, delivered in March 1943, has the old roundel proportions and the full-fin coloring used only briefly by Britain in 1940. (courtesy Arthur Pearcy)

Fig. 9-21. In 1943 New Zealand added U.S.-style white rectangles to each side of its roundels, but unlike the Australians, retained the red centers. The fin flash was made much narrower than the British and Australian standard, as on this Dakota I, NZ3517. (courtesy Arthur Pearcy)

ceived 182 Dakotas, either by direct purchase from the U.S. or indirectly through RAF Lend-Lease channels (Fig. 9-20). Sixty-one were given sequential RCAF serial numbers while 122 carried RAF serials in the FL through KP series. The direct-purchase Dakotas had the sequential serials, while the Lend-Lease models obtained from Britain had the RAF serials.

The RCAF got its first Dakota on March 29, 1943. While RCAF Dakotas towed gliders and made supply and paratroop drops in the invasion of Europe and subsequent campaigns, their most heroic work was done in Southeast Asia. Of two squadrons that had been sent to India, one, the 435th, almost single-handedly supplied the famous "Wingate's Raiders" in their Burma campaign. When it was all over the 435th's Dakotas had racked up 29,873 flight hours and 16,592 sorties. Average daily utilization for the Dakotas was seven hours, an amazing figure for the time. A few RCAF Dakotas were still in service in 1982.

Direct-purchase RCAF Dakota serials:

650/664 (15)
960/994 (35)
1000 (1)

10910/10918 (9)

NEW ZEALAND DAKOTAS

The Royal New Zealand Air Force (RNZAF) had 49 Dakotas of various marks serialled NZ3501/3506 (6) and NZ3516/3558 (43).

An oddity of RNZAF planes during World War II was that they did not follow the RAF and RAAF practice of deleting the red center of the Commonwealth insignia, or roundel, for use in the Southeast Asia and Pacific theatres. This was done because of its similarity to the Japanese "Rising Sun" marking. The RNZAF retained the red center as well as red for the fin flash, but merely made it much smaller than its standard proportion to the rest of the marking (Fig. 9-21).

In mid-1943 the RNZAF added white rectangles to each side of the roundel the way the U.S. added them to its star-in-circle marking. Ordinarily, this did not have the blue border of the U.S. marking, but there were cases with subsequent Lend-Lease aircraft where the RNZAF roundel was simply painted over the U.S. star, with the rectangles left as they were. The last RNZAF Dakota was retired in November 1977.

125

Chapter 10

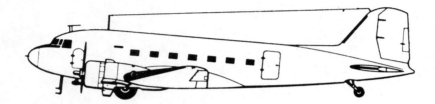

The DC-3 in World War II

World War II was the event that changed the image of the DC-3 from a simple peaceful airliner to one of the most versatile airplanes ever built, and created a demand for its global services that made it the most-produced transport plane in history.

CIVIL OPERATIONS

Civil operations were affected first, even before hostilities broke out in September 1939. Germany had acquired DC-2s and DC-3s with the annexation of Czechoslovakia and put several into military service with the Luftwaffe. Even earlier, several secondhand DC-2s and the single DC-1 had served the Loyalist forces in the Spanish Civil War of 1936-1939. While most carried civil registrations, they were so controlled by the military that civil and military roles became indistinguishable. On one occasion, a Spanish DC-2 with reduced fuel load carried 35 armed troops in a cabin that normally accommodated 14 passengers. The Loyalist DC-2s often crossed rebel territory with impunity because they could outrun Franco's fighters.

The same was true for other nations as the big war began to affect them. After September 1939, neutral nations tried to conduct business as usual, but with difficulty. European neutrals such as Holland, Denmark, and Sweden took to painting the name of the country in very large letters on their airliners to distinguish them from similar models used by the warring nations (Fig. 10-1). Later, to increase their visibility, the planes were painted overall International Orange (Fig. 10-2). United States airliners operating outside the country retained normal airline markings but applied large American flags to fuselages, tails, and wings (Fig. 10-3).

In Europe, occupied countries of course had no airline activity but the airlines of the major belligerents carried on internal and foreign operations under tight military control. This sometimes resulted in the odd situation of German and British DC-3s being parked side-by-side on the ramps of neutral nations such as Spain.

In England, a total of 82 Lend-Lease U.S. Army C-47As, one U.S. Army C-49H, and five refugee

Fig. 10-1. The neutral nationality of this DC-3A-214 was prominently proclaimed by large lettering on the upper fuselage and wing and Swedish flag on the tail. It escaped the German invasion of May 1940, returned to Sweden after the war, and was sold to Finland in 1954. (courtesy John Stroud)

KLM DC-3-G102As were turned over to British Overseas Airways Corporation (BOAC) by the British government for airline use. These were all given civil registrations but also carried standard military camouflage (Fig. 10-4). In Australia, some U.S. Army airplanes were turned over to civil airlines serving the military and operated with a mix of U.S. Army and Australian civil markings (Fig. 10-5).

The operation of unarmed civil aircraft in or near combat zones was not without hazard. Several European DC-3s were shot down over the open sea

Fig. 10-2. To increase their visibility, some neutral airliners near the war zone, such as this Belgian DC-3-227B, were painted overall international orange. OO-AUH escaped the German invasion and continued to operate commercially out of England. It was interned by Vichy France in August 1940, when it landed in Algiers, and was turned over to the Luftwaffe. (courtesy John Stroud)

127

Fig. 10-3. American airliners operating outside the U.S. proclaimed their nationality with large American flags. This is U.S. Army C-53, 42-68693, used with civil registration NC30093 on Pan American's South American routes. (PAA photo)

on international flights. In China, a DC-3 of China National Aviation Corporation was bombed while on the ground at Suifu, China. One bomb hit the right wing of the DC-3, destroying it (Fig. 10-6). The rest of the plane was undamaged except for shrapnel holes but the only way it could be salvaged was to fly it out of the plowed field in which it had landed to avoid the Japanese raiders.

In an effort that was widely publicized at the time, a replacement wing from a DC-2 (*not* a DC-3) was ferried to the site lashed to the belly of another DC-3 and was installed in the field. The resulting

"DC-2 1/2" was safely returned to its base in Hong Kong (Fig. 10-7).

Amazing as this feat was at the time, it became almost routine in the Southwest Pacific/Asiatic areas, when spare wings were needed for other DC-3/C-47s or smaller models. The panels were simply lashed under a C-47 and flown to where they were needed (Fig. 10-8).

In 1941 the U.S. airline fleet was greatly reduced when the Army took airliners—mostly DC-3s—right off the airline routes and requisitioned others ordered by the airlines but still in the fac-

Fig. 10-4. British civil registrations were applied to Dakotas turned over to British Overseas Airways Corporation by the RAF. For overseas operation, the registration letters were underlined in red, white, and blue, and the military fin flash was retained, as on this Dakota IV G-AGKN. (courtesy Arthur Pearcy).

Fig. 10-5. In Australia, some airlines operated military aircraft in both civil and military markings, as this C-50, 41-7697, of Guinea Airways, on loan from the U.S. Army. (courtesy Merwin W. Prime)

Fig. 10-6. This CNAC DC-3 was caught on the ground by Japanese warplanes and was bombed and strafed. A bomb blast shattered the right wing as shown. (Douglas photo)

Fig. 10-7. The damaged CNAC DC-3 became a true "DC-2 1/2" when it was fitted with the shorter right wing of a DC-2 and successfully flown back to its base. (Douglas photo)

tory. After Pearl Harbor the U.S. public could still buy tickets as in peacetime, but ran the risk of being "bumped" by military personnel or important civilians travelling on priorities. A story is told of a civilian who was to fly from Washington, DC, to New York to give a lecture. At the airport he was bumped by a military man with a priority who, it turned out, was flying to New York to *attend* the lecture!

After Pearl Harbor, all nonessential civil fly-

Fig. 10-8. After the success of the CNAC "DC-2 1/2" operation, the ferrying of spare DC-3 and C-47 wings to places where they were needed became commonplace, as demonstrated by this C-47 in the South Pacific theatre. (Douglas photo)

ing was banned in areas up to 150 miles inland from the coastline, and what civil flying was done was under tight military control with lots of associated paperwork. As a result of this, one special DC-3A-408, the Douglas Company's own demonstrator and executive plane, NC30000, C/N 4809, joined the Army under unusual circumstances (Fig. 10-9). By the time the necessary approvals could be obtained for a short executive flight from the Santa Monica plant, the personnel could often have made the trip by surface transportation. The paperwork delays so reduced the utility of the plane that Douglas got the Army to take title to it. It was given the designation of plain C-53 and serial number 43-36600 in a special reserved block 43-36600/36608. Douglas then continued to use it under a Bailment contract since as a military plane it did not have its former civil clearance problems. It went to Hawaiian Airlines as NC33649 after the war.

Another oddity of U.S. airline travel during the war years was that cabin window curtains were drawn while on and in the vicinity of airports that had major defense plants or military installations nearby.

Some of the drafted U.S. airliners were retained by the airlines and continued to serve the routes in their original airline markings but as government property. Others went into warpaint and were operated by the Army in various transport roles. Many, carrying military markings and camouflage, were operated by airline crews under Army/airline contracts. Some flew scheduled cargo routes while others flew cargo and personnel to all parts of the world as directed by the Army (Figs. 10-10, 10-11).

The Army turned some C-53s over to the airlines for military contract operations and Pan American got some for civil operations by China National Airlines (CNAC) in China (Fig. 10-12).

MILITARY OPERATIONS

In World War II the DC-3/C-47 was put to every conceivable mission that an unarmed, unarmored, and supposedly non-aggressive airplane

Fig. 10-9. Douglas' own executive DC-3A-408, NC30000, with the large letters U.S. on the fuselage that were decreed for all civil aircraft operating in the West Coast Defense Zone after Pearl Harbor. Paperwork problems so reduced the utility of the airplane that Douglas got the Army to take it as a special C-53, 43-36600, then turn it back on a bailment contract. (Douglas photo)

Fig. 10-10. Some U.S. airliners flew for the U.S. Army without being drafted. This eight-window United Air Lines DC-3A-197E, NC33647, carries Army camouflage and markings, but the number on the fin is the factory serial number of the airplane, *not* an Army serial or a civil registration. (courtesy Joseph P. Juptner)

could be assigned to. As a straight cargo plane, it was treated like a truck, meaning that it was expected to carry everything that could be crammed into the cabin regardless of the niceties of weight and balance control. Further, the C-47 did not always have to land to unload its cargo; military supplies were parachuted to ground troops by the simple expedient of kicking them out the side door (Fig. 10-13). For some low-level operations, packaged cargo was dropped without benefit of par-achute (Fig. 10-14). To speed up this procedure, roller systems were devised that eliminated the need to manhandle cargo from the front of the cabin to the rear. Further hauling capacity, plus faster delivery, was obtained by hanging up to six cargo packs under the center section like bombs for delivery by parachute (Fig. 10-15). There were limitations to the truck analogy, however; excess passengers did not ride on top, but stowaways were discovered in wheel wells (fortunately before take-

Fig. 10-11. Another civil airliner operating in military markings, including Air Transport Command insignia on the fuselage. This is American Airlines' DC-3-277B, NC25664, with the factory serial number on the fin for identification. (USAF photo)

United Air Lines DC-3A-197B NC18942 was delivered in April 1938. Here it displays the distinctive red, white, and blue trim used by United from 1940 through 1949. The NC prefix to the registration number was changed to plain N in 1949. (photo by James A. Morrow)

The second DC-3D completed from cancelled C-117A airframes was delivered to Pacific Northern Airlines in January 1946. Here is NC37465 over rugged and spectacular Alaskan terrain. (courtesy Douglas Aircraft Co.)

This DC-3C, N31 of the FAA, was formerly Navy R4D-6R 5077B. When photographed in 1957 it carried a special "Day-Glo" orange and white color scheme also used by some R4Ds transferred to the U.S. Army. (photo by Victor D. Seely)

This R4D-6Q, 50776, has a white top to the fuselage to reduce solar heating of the cabin but the rest of the airframe has been painted a silvery-gray. Note the additional antennas and radomes in this late 1950s photo. (photo by James A. Morrow)

C-47A-30-DK 43-48160 displays fuselage decoration that made many Air Force DC-3s resemble civil airliners in the 1950s and 1960s. (Tom Cuddy photo via Dustin Carter)

The U.S. Navy's exhibition parachute team, "The Chuting Stars," was transported in this specially painted R4D-8, 50762. (1961 photo by Clay Jansson)

This orange and white DC-3C, N645, was originally R4D-6/C-47J 50779 before being transferred to the U.S. Department of the Interior in 1965. (photo by Victor D. Seely)

This Navy C-47J landing at North Island Naval Air Station in May 1963 shows the sometimes extensive use of high visibility conspicuity markings at the time. (photo by Dustin Carter)

This DC-3C, formerly R4D-6 50819, displays the standardized orange and white coloring used by FAA DC-3s from the mid-1960s until retirement. (photo by James A. Morrow)

LC-47J 50776 of the Navy's Arctic Research Laboratory at Barrow, Alaska, displays the unique dark gray and orange color scheme used by many R4D/C-47s modified for arctic and antarctic operations. (1967 photo by James A. Morrow)

An Air Force C-47A-20-DK, 42-93005, displays standard arctic markings at Elmendorf Air Force Base, Alaska, in June 1967. Note natural metal areas around lettering and the use of O-prefix to serial number to indicate an Air Force airplane over 10 years old. (photo by Norman Taylor)

Since the orange "Day-Glo" coloring adopted for increased visibility faded badly, it was replaced by regular non-fluorescent orange in the late 1960s as shown on this C-117D. Note use of last three digits of Navy serial 50782 on nose and four digits on tail. (Peter M. Bowers collection)

When North Central Airlines donated DC-3-201B N21728 to the Ford Museum in 1975, it had more flying time than any other airplane in the world—83,454 hours. (1968 photo by James A. Morrow)

This EC-47P-30-DK, converted from a C-47B, displays the new multicolored camouflage scheme adopted by the U.S. Air Force during the Vietnam War. (photo by Norman Taylor)

DC-3C N148Z of the U.S. Forest Service, photographed at Boise, Idaho, in April 1974, was originally C-47A-90-DL 43-15957 and spent its entire postwar career in government service. (photo by Arthur P. Dowd)

This DC-3C has spray booms under the wings for mosquito control in New Orleans. It was originally C-47A-20-DK 42-93040 before becoming a C-117C. (photo by James A. Morrow)

A 1939 DC-3-277, modified with nine cabin windows and cowling flaps, but with its original registration number, takes off in front of the Douglas Santa Monica plant during the 40th anniversary celebration of the DC-3 in December 1975. (courtesy Douglas Aircraft Co.)

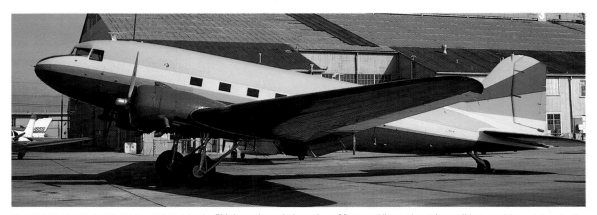

The two-inch-high registration letters allowed by the FAA for antique airplanes (over 30 years old) are almost impossible to read beyond the wingtips of this 1940 DC-3-201C, a former Eastern airliner. It was registered N20TW when photographed at Oakland, California, in January 1976. (photo by Arthur P. Dowd)

This colorful former C-53, 41-20094, is representative of many worn-out DC-3s that have been parked out in the weeds and gradually cannibalized to keep other DC-3s flying. This photo was taken in 1978 but the registration was not cancelled until 1982. (photo by Arthur P. Dowd)

This French Navy C-47D (note the anchor superimposed on the fuselage cocarde) carries the former USAF designation C-47D and the USAF serial number on the rear fuselage beneath the horizontal tail. (1979 photo courtesy James A. Morrow)

The only scheduled airline in the U.S. using DC-3s in 1985 is Provincetown-Boston Airlines of Hyannis, Mass., which operates a mixed fleet of 12 prewar-II DC-3s and DC-3As in addition to smaller models. DC-3A N33PB was photographed in October 1985. (photo by James A. Morrow)

For ceremonies concerning the rollout of its first Douglas DC-10 in 1970, American Airlines leased this DC-3A-453 and painted it with prewar-II American Airlines markings. The only unauthentic details are the latter-day application or registration N999Z to the rudder and the fact that the airplane is a DC-3A with left-hand door; American used DC-3s with right-hand doors. (courtesy Douglas Aircraft Co.)

This 1939 American Airlines photo shows the airline's unique markings of the time, with color on the trailing edges of wings and tail. The American Airlines' house pennant is visible above the copilot's side of the cockpit. (courtesy American Airlines)

Fig. 10-12. Several of the C-53s that the U.S. Army turned over to Pan American Airways were sent to China for use on Pan Am's affiliate, China National Aviation Corporation. Note the absence of a standard Chinese civil registration. (photo by Peter M. Bowers)

Fig. 10-13. One of the major wartime activities of the C-47 was as a paratrooper. Here C-47s, some with their landing gear lowered to achieve minimum airspeed, make a low-level supply drop after paratroopers landed to recapture the island of Corregidor from the Japanese. (USAF photo via Douglas)

Fig. 10-14. Some low-level supply drops were made with parachutes, some without. These C-47s are dropping supplies both ways at Mandalay, Burma. (USAF photo)

Fig. 10-15. To increase their capacity and permit quicker dropping of supplies, some C-47s such as 41-38592 with both British fin flash and U.S. flag on the tail, were fitted with up to six external cargo packs, two of which are still in place here. (USAF photo)

Fig. 10-16. When paratroopers jumped from airplanes, their parachutes were opened by static lines attached to the airplane, as demonstrated by this RAF Dakota IV KK138. (courtesy Don Wallace)

off) and inside the fuselage.

For successful operation of unarmed cargo planes over enemy territory, total control of the local airspace was absolutely essential. Large formations of slow-moving troopers and towplane/glider combinations were highly vulnerable to enemy fighters and it was the job of escorting fighters to keep intercepting fighters away. Actually, most C-47s and other cargo planes lost in such operations fell to ground-based antiaircraft fire—*Fleigerabwehrkanon,* or "flak," than to enemy interceptors. The cargo planes were far more vulnerable to this than the heavy bombers because of their low operating altitudes—around 2000 feet compared to 30,000 or more for the bombers.

Paratroops

The delivery of paratroops was a primary mission of both C-47s and C-53s and required no post-delivery modifications. A normal paratroop load for a C-47 was 27 fully armed men. They jumped under the guidance of a jumpmaster, who got his signal from the pilot when the airplane was over the proper point. Normal jumps were with static lines attached to the airplanes; these opened the parachutes as soon as the jumpers were clear of the plane and remained attached to it (Fig. 10-16). The lines could be pulled back into the cabin prior to landing.

For C-47s, the normal formation for a paratroop operation was a stream of nine-plane elements consisting of three tight three-plane vee-formations in a "vee of vees" (Fig. 10-17).

Normally, the paratroops slept, sang, or otherwise killed time during the cruise to the drop zone. Then they received a 20-minute warning and prepared to jump. Close to the release point the jumpmaster gave the command "Stand up." Next came the command "Hook up," and each man snapped his static line to an overhead cable that ran the length of the cabin. When a red light over the door came on, the first trooper stood ready to jump. When the green light came on, he jumped—usually after a hearty slap on the back by the jumpmaster—and was followed as quickly as possi-

135

ble by the rest of the troops.

Glider Tug

Another special role taken on by the C-47 was the towing of troop gliders, mostly the 15-place Waco CG-4A. With a wingspan of 83 feet 8 inches, the CG-4A was nearly as large as the C-47 (Fig. 10-18), but because of its high drag and light construction limited the cruising speed of a one-to-one C-47/CG-4A combination to 120 mph.

Normal operations called for a C-47 to tow one CG-4A at the end of a nylon line with the glider in the traditional "high tow" position, just above the towplane's slipstream. In some cases, two CG-4As were towed by a single C-47, with each glider pilot flying between 20 and 30 degrees to one side of the towplane by application of rudder trim. For one of the pair, the towline was 75 feet longer so that the gliders would not collide if they happened to get too close to the centerline due to turbulence or other reasons.

Normal formation for cruising and approach to the glider release area was a right echelon, with each C-47 approximately 200 feet to one side of the one ahead and approximately 25 feet behind it (Fig. 10-19). Double tows used the same airplane formation but with over 300 feet lateral spacing and 160 longitudinal (Fig. 10-20).

For the mass takeoffs of gliders in major operations, the CG-4As and C-47s were grouped tightly

Fig. 10-17. When dropping paratroops over wide areas, the C-47s flew in a long column made up of "vee-of-vees" formations three Vs wide. (USAF photo)

Fig. 10-18. C-47s towing single Waco CG-4A gliders used nylon tow ropes 350 feet long. This combination is taking off from England for the airborne invasion of Holland, September 18, 1944. (USAF photo)

at the downwind end of the runway, often with a double row of C-47s in the middle and the gliders offset to the outer sides for single tows (Fig. 10-21). For double tows, two gliders were parked side-by-side behind each C-47.

In the major glider operations, many of the gliders were damaged on landing and were hardly worth salvaging. Others were dismantled for return to their starting point or to a new base in captured territory.

For glider retrieval from areas too small for a conventional towed takeoff, the U.S. Army developed a "snatch pickup" system. In this the towplane flew over the glider while trailing a hook

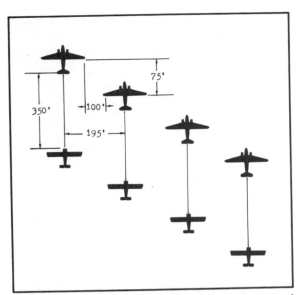

Fig. 10-19. C-47s towing single CG-4As flew in elements of four, with right echelon formation and spacing as shown here.

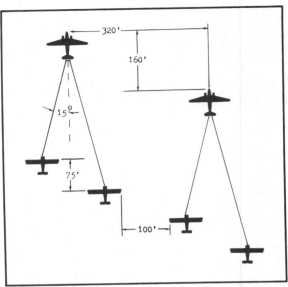

Fig. 10-20. For double tows, the tow ropes were of different lengths to avoid the risk of glider collision and the right echelon formation was spaced as shown.

Fig. 10-21. Gliders and towplanes were grouped tightly at the starting end of the runway so that rapid sequential takeoffs could be made. The gliders and towplanes had to be hooked together on the runway; they could not taxi into takeoff position individually as could airplanes alone. (USAF photo)

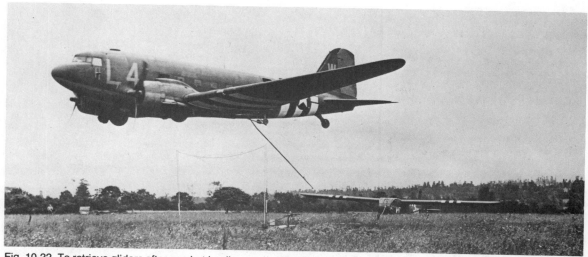

Fig. 10-22. To retrieve gliders after combat landings, a "snatch" system was developed whereby a motionless glider could be snatched into the air by an airborne C-47. This is the first such recovery of a CG-4A from France after the invasion of June 6, 1944. (USAF photo)

that engaged the towline, the free end of which was elevated on a pair of poles (Fig. 10-22). To reduce the shock of accelerating a 7500-pound mass from zero to 100 mph in a few seconds, an inertia reel in the towplane wound out a cable against increasing drag.

Most large-scale glider operations were over relatively short distances—up to 300 miles. In some smaller operations to supply remote outposts, guerrilla operations, and detachments behind enemy lines as in Southeast Asia, longer tows were undertaken. In July 1943, an all-time record tow was made by a Canadian Dakota towing a CG-4A (which the RAF designated Hadrian) from Canada across the North Atlantic to Britain, a distance of 3220 miles, in 28 hours. This proved only that it *could* be done; it did *not* become standard practice.

Miscellaneous Activity

The C-47 adapted easily to all climates and types of terrain. The Russians made great use of their Lend-Lease C-47s and their own Li-2s in their frozen territory (Fig. 10-23). The U.S. had less occasion for such operations, but developed a combination ski-wheel arrangement that permitted flight from either snow or hard ground (Fig. 10-24). The amphibious version of the C-47 was a disap-

pointment, and only a few other than the XC-47C were used, mainly in the Southwest Pacific and Alaska (Fig. 10-25).

Some C-47s acquired additional military equipment, such as search radar used for leading paratroop formations to the target area and for aerial search for aircraft ditched at sea. This was carried in a retractable radome under the rear of the cabin (Fig. 10-26).

The military DC-3s flew into some tight areas that such large planes would normally pass up. Some ran off the usable areas of such fields and had to be retrieved by local manpower (Fig. 10-27). In most cases, C-47s could fly out of any field they could get into, but on occasions it was necessary to install solid-propellant rocket motors (called JATO for Jet Assisted Takeoff) under the center section.

In most areas where permanent airbases with paved runways were not available, the airplanes operated from runways and hardstands surfaced with pierced steel planking, or PSP. These were sections of perforated sheet steel that could be pinned together and laid over soft or muddy ground (Fig. 10-28).

The transports were not safe from enemy action when on the ground, especially in advance

Fig. 10-23. A Russian-marked C-47B-25-DK in typical cold weather setting. Dog teams and their sleds were often transported by air. (H.J. Nowarra collection)

Fig. 10-24. Skis with open centers to accommodate airplane wheels were developed to permit operation from either snow or hard ground without having to change from one to the other as in previous practice. Note the horizontal stabilizing fins projecting from the rear of the skis, which lay flat against the engine nacelles when the wheels were retracted. (USAF photo)

Fig. 10-25. At least two C-47s with amphibious floats appeared after the XC-47C. This is the second subsequent conversion, former C-47A-10-DK, seen in Alaska. (courtesy Alwyn T. Lloyd)

areas. C-47s supplying Allied troops struggling for Guadalcanal late in 1942 were not only attacked by raiding Japanese bombers and fighters, but were subject to ground fire from nearby Japanese troops just outside the perimeter of the airfield. In France, airfields seized in the invasion of June 6, 1944, operated while under fire from nearby German artillery (Fig. 10-29).

Even the Japanese "Tabbys" were at hazard on the ground in areas subject to the Allied advance. In the face of overwhelming air power, the Japanese went to great lengths to hide their rapidly diminishing aircraft when they were on the ground (Fig. 10-30). For their few aircraft that were allowed

to fly during the surrender negotiations, the Japanese replaced their "meatball" insignia with large green crosses on a white background (Fig. 10-31).

Ingenious American mechanics did some prodigious jobs of salvage and repair of C-47s and other military aircraft that by all standards should have been scrapped. In some cases, they actually did assemble complete new airplanes from scrapped components and put them back in service, sometimes quite unofficially (Fig. 10-32).

MAJOR CAMPAIGNS

It is impossible in a book of this size to detail the World War II campaigns in which the C-47 and

Fig. 10-26. Some C-47s, like this C-47A-20-DK, 42-93255, were fitted with search radar in a retractable belly radome to lead paratroop formations to the drop zone. (USAF photo)

141

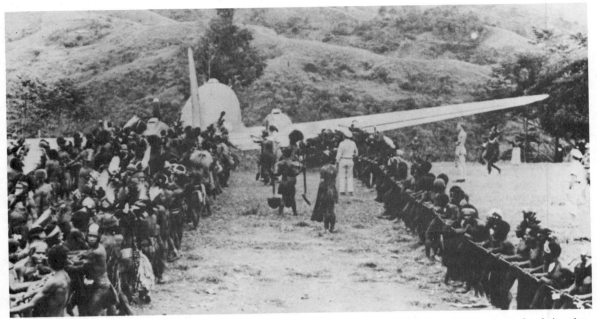

Fig. 10-27. Some C-47s, like this one in New Guinea, got into situations from which they could be extracted only by plentiful manpower. (USAF photo via Douglas)

Fig. 10-28. C-47s in a joint Army/Navy medical evacuation operation somewhere in the South Pacific. Note that the airplanes and ambulances are parked on pierced steel planking, or PSP. The airplane marked 3111 is C-47A-20-DK 42-9311. (USAF photo via Douglas)

Fig. 10-29. A C-47 carrying search radar and black and white "invasion stripes" operating from a newly established airfield in France that is still under German artillery fire, June 1944. Note the barrage balloons intended to interfere with low-flying attack planes. (USAF photo)

the Dakota played major roles. Major campaigns will be listed here only in brief. Needless to say, the C-47 was the mainstay of every Allied campaign that involved the mass use of paratroopers and glider tugs. A later equivalent design with an earlier designation, the Curtiss-Wright C-46 Commando,

Fig. 10-30. This grounded Japanese Tabby was hidden under camouflage when U.S. forces captured a Japanese air base in the Philippines. (U.S. Army photo)

143

Fig. 10-31. This prewar DC-3A, found in Japan during the occupation, carries the green cross marking that was used by Japanese airplanes allowed to fly during the surrender negotiations. The Tabby in the background is ready for scrapping. (courtesy Arthur Pearcy)

entered service in 1943 but was never a serious threat to the C-47 either in quantity, reliability, or versatility (Fig. 10-33). The place of the C-47 in World War II was emphasized by General Dwight D. Eisenhower, Commander in Chief of the Allied Forces in Europe in 1943-45:

"... four other pieces of equipment that most senior officers came to regard as among the most vital to our success in Africa and Europe were the bulldozer, the jeep, the 2 1/2 ton truck, and the C-47 airplane. Curiously, none of these is designed for combat."

When the Allies went on the offensive in the Southwest Pacific with the invasion of Guadalcanal in August 1942, the U.S. Navy got the troops and their initial equipment ashore. The defending fighters flew in, but because of interference by the Japanese fleet, the Navy could not maintain open supply lines. The fighters were almost out of action from fuel and ammunition shortages. It fell to the Army and the RAAF to bring in those essential items by air, a 1300-mile round trip from the Allied-held island of Espiritu Santo. The C-47s had to fly the whole trip on one fueling since they could not refuel on Guadalcanal's Henderson Field.

Guadalcanal was an early and prime example of a major military operation succeeding in the face of determined opposition largely because of the airlift of essential materials. Another was the aerial supply of China from India over the famous "Hump," the Himalaya Mountains, highest in the world and home of some of its worst flying weather. After the Japanese closed the Burma Road, the one remaining gateway to China, in 1942, that country could be supplied only by air, and the C-47 was the

Fig. 10-32. Mechanics of the 5th Bomb Group, 13th Air Force, stationed in the Philippines assembled these four C-47s from junked parts, one for use as a "hack" by each squadron in the group. Each was painted like a civil airliner and carried the marking BOMBER BARONS AIRLINER above the cabin windows. Note B-25 and A-24 (Army SBD Dauntless) in unusual natural metal finish at far right. (courtesy Frederick A. Johnsen)

144

Fig. 10-33. The Curtiss-Wright C-46, developed from the CW-20 airliner, had an earlier Army designation than the C-47, but teething troubles kept it out of significant service until late in the war. This is a C-46D-15-CU with paratroop doors on both sides of the fuselage. (Curtiss-Wright photo courtesy F.H. Dean)

mainstay of the Air Transport Command operation that took over the task in December 1942. The distance from Dinjan, in India, to Kumming, China, was only 500 miles, but the route quickly came to be regarded as the world's most hazardous one.

The C-47s were supplemented by C-46s in 1943, but that model had been rushed into production and on into service too quickly. The early series were highly unreliable, and not until late 1944 were the C-46s sufficiently debugged to provide reliable airlift. From a meager 85 tons of supplies airlifted into China in July 1942, airborne supplies had reached a total of 71,042 tons a month by July 1945. The C-47 was the mainstay of this operation through its three full years as the only source of imported military and civil necessities for war-torn China.

The first American paratroop operation was practically a theatrical comedy of errors, fortunately with minimal casualties. In connection with Operation *Torch*, the invasion of French North Africa in November 1942, 39 C-47s carrying paratroopers were dispatched on a 1250-mile nonstop flight from England to Morocco. There were last-minute changes of plan, and not all units got the word, so did the wrong things on arrival. Some were fired on while flying over neutral Spain; others landed in Spanish, rather than French, Morocco and were interned.

C-47s and Dakotas performed major supply roles during the Allied advance westward in North Africa from Egypt early in 1943. At times, the advancing forces were as much as 700 miles ahead of their supply sources and could be supplied in essential time only by air.

Paratroop operations still had problems of communication and identification as proved by Operation *Husky*, the invasion of Sicily in July 1943. In addition to dropping some of the troops in the wrong area, the 109 C-47s suffered severe casualties when they were fired upon by their own ground and naval forces. In September, 2500 paratroopers participated in the invasion of Italy.

Things were better organized in time for Operation *Overlord*, the invasion of France from England in June 1944. This involved over 900 C-47s, C-53s, and Dakotas and over 100 gliders that delivered 17,000 troops to the continent. This was followed in September by Operation *Dragon*, the invasion of Southern France, which is hardly noted by historians. Some 400 C-47s and C-53s delivered paratroopers into the area, who secured airfields for the next-day arrival of over 400 troop and supply gliders.

The airborne invasion of Holland in September 1944, Operation *Market Basket*, involved more C-47s, gliders, and paratroops than did *Overlord* and *Dragon* but was a near-disaster from an overall military standpoint. By month's end, a total of 20,000 paratroops had been delivered, plus another 13,700 by glider. Approximately 1000 others landed by airplane on airstrips prepared by their predecessors. In addition, 5,230 tons of equipment, including 1927 vehicles and 568 pieces of artillery, were delivered on a total of 7800 sorties. Unfortunately, due to strong German defenses pinning down the invaders, many of these essential supplies fell into enemy hands.

The greatest airborne invasion of all time, was Operation *Varsity*, the advance across the Rhine River into the heartland of Germany that began on March 24, 1945. The DC-3 was represented by 903 C-47s and C-53s towing 897 CG-4As. Other transports, plus British airplanes and gliders, made *Varsity* highly successful. The tragedy of *Market Basket* was avoided this time as the aerial operation was closely coordinated with the advance of strong ground forces.

Perhaps the most unique airborne troop/supply operation of World War II was Operation *Thursday*. In this, started in March 1944, 12,000 troops, or two full divisions, were to be placed far behind Japanese lines in Burma. This was possible only in the absence of significant fighter opposition. Troops, supplies, and bulldozing equipment were all carried by C-47s, Dakotas, and an initial 67 CG-4As. After airstrips were built, additional supplies could be flown in, casualties carried out. Some of the gliders were retrieved by the "snatch" method.

Although it received virtually no publicity for the role, the C-47 also performed a major service in the return of battle casualties to rear-area hospitals. Usually, the C-47s picked up the wounded from secure airfields to which they had been delivered by surface transport or light aircraft. In others, particularly in Southeast Asia and the Pacific, the C-47s were under enemy fire while loading. In the first six months, over 50,000 casualties from the battles for the liberation of Burma were evacuated by air, principally in the C-47 and Dakota.

Chapter 11

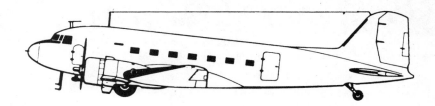

Postwar Civil Operations

The airlines of the world quickly returned to normal after the end of World War II and were able to capitalize on two significant wartime developments. The first was the building of hundreds of airfields throughout the world, which enabled air service to be provided to areas that previously had none. The other was a generous supply of cheap surplus military transports, mainly DC-3/C-47s, that could be put into commercial service as fully licensed civil aircraft with no costly modifications. Both U.S. and foreign airlines were quick to buy surplus DC-3s at prices between $8000 and $15,000. Many that were overseas at war's end were collected at various locations and sold by the government without being returned to the States first. Even some of the prewar DC-3s confiscated by Germany were "liberated" and returned to their original owners or found new ones.

Surviving DC-3s in Japan did not fare so well; both American- and Japanese-made versions were scrapped rather than being put to use. A few "Tabbys" in China at the time of the surrender were confiscated by the Chinese Air Force.

Russian-built Li-2s and Lend-Lease C-47s, none of which were returned to the U.S. government, were used by the Russian state airline Aeroflot and by air forces and airlines of countries under Russian influence.

CONTINUED PRODUCTION

In the U.S., Douglas sought to fulfil the demand for DC-3s equipped to full civil standards in two ways—first by converting surplus C-47s and second by building new DC-3s.

DC-3C—The initial postwar DC-3Cs were 21 former C-47s modified by Douglas at Santa Monica to prewar airline standards, with 21-passenger seating, the cargo door replaced by a hinge-down type, and a DC-3 left-side baggage door installed. Douglas applied new C/Ns to these rebuilds, 43073/43092 and 43154, and they were licensed under the prewar DC-3A Type Certificate A-669. The first, formerly C-47A-DL 43-30674 (C/N 13825), was used briefly as a company demonstrator before being sold (Fig. 11-1). While

Fig. 11-1. The first DC-3C, converted by the Douglas Santa Monica plant as a demonstrator from C-47A-DL, 43-30674. This was Douglas' second use of the registration number NC30000. (photo by Peter M. Bowers)

at Douglas it made the second use of the NC30000 registration first used on the DC-3A demonstrator C/N 4122 that the Army took as a C-53 in 1942.

The other C-47s, counted in the thousands, were converted mostly by small independent shops that had lower overhead than giant Douglas and could do the work to Douglas-approved drawings at less cost. In some cases, airlines did the work in their own shops at a cost of approximately $10,000. Following conversion, the DC-3Cs got supplementary nameplates issued by the converting agency giving the new designation, the shop's name, and the date. The original nameplate was retained and the original C/N was used in all subsequent paperwork. Surplus C-53s converted to airliners required less modification and were

licensed as DC-3As under ATC-A-669 (Fig. 11-2).

There was no standardization of doors, seats, or windows among the non-Douglas DC-3C conversions. Many retained their cargo doors even though used for passenger work. Others used smaller DC-3 type doors modified to hinge downward to serve as stairs for simplified passenger entry. Some modified for high density passenger work were provided with eight cabin windows to a side (Fig. 11-3). Many former C-47s were fitted with standard DC-3 tail cones but others did not bother with them. Those used primarily for cargo work retained their cargo doors, tilted rear floor, and the six port (left) and seven starboard (right) windows. None of these variations, nor subsequent changes, affected approval under ATC A-669.

Fig. 11-2. Surplus C-53s in postwar civilian service were registered as DC-3As since they did not require as much modification as C-47s converted to DC-3Cs. NC18600 of Western Air Lines is former C-53, 41-20130, acquired by the airline in August 1949. (Western Air Lines photo)

Fig. 11-3. One of a variety of non-Douglas DC-3C conversions. This former C-47-DL, 41-18362, has eight left-side cabin windows, the cargo doors have been replaced by a hinge-down door with built-in steps, and a DC-3 baggage compartment and tail cone have been added. (photo by Peter M. Bowers)

DC-3D—In the Oklahoma City plant, Douglas completed 28 C-117A airframes as civil DC-3Ds (Fig. 11-4). These differed little from their original military configuration and continued the run of C-47B/C-117A C/Ns, 42954/42981. Again, licensing was under ATC A-669. The DC-3Ds were the last of 10,655 DC-3s built, with the last one being delivered May 6, 1946. Several of the DC-3Ds were photographed by Douglas, but apparently no one had the historical foresight to photograph C/N 42981, NC1624, the last DC-3 built.

SUBSEQUENT MODIFICATIONS

In the first two postwar decades, many minor improvements were made to DC-3s, both prewar civil models and former C-47s, to improve their performance or utility. For passenger and executive planes, the easiest speed-enhancing changes were faster landing gear retraction mechanism to reduce drag and improve performance immediately after takeoff. Other refinements were the addition of doors and fairings to enclose the projecting halves of the landing wheels when they were retracted. Sometimes these were all combined with new tight-fitting engine cowlings and propeller spinners that further reduced aerodynamic drag (Fig. 11-5). Some corporations used DC-3s not only as executive transports but for research and development of new equipment, such as electronics (Fig. 11-6). Goodyear used one to test a new crosswind landing gear that it had developed.

A more major change was to install larger 1450-hp Pratt & Whitney R-2000 engines as used in the DC-4/C-54 for increased takeoff and altitude

Fig. 11-4. The second DC-3D, NC37465, completed by the Douglas Oklahoma City plant from cancelled C-117A airframes. Externally, this is distinguishable from prewar DC-3As only by the C-47B style carburetor air intake above the nacelle. (Douglas photo)

149

Fig. 11-5. This former C-47A-15-DK, 42-92835, displays most of the external modifications visible on postwar DC-3Cs, including tight engine cowlings, propeller spinners, wheel well doors, modified windshields, some enlarged cabin windows, and a sharper nose cone. (photo by Peter M. Bowers, 1962)

performance. The slightly longer engines fitted under the same cowling as the R-1830 Twin Wasp, but the propeller was a few inches farther ahead of the cowling lip (Fig. 11-7). A more common and less costly engine change was to replace the Wright Cyclone engines of prewar DC-3s with the Pratt & Whitney Twin Wasps, converting them to DC-3As under ATC A-669.

Such modifications did not affect ATC A-669; they were made on Supplemental Type Certificates (STCs) to A-669 as worked out by the modifying organizations and approved by the government. Other changes were relatively minor, such as clos-

ing off the right-side doors of some prewar DC-3As and installing C-47 cargo doors on the left side (Fig. 11-8), enlarging cabin windows on some deluxe executive models (Fig. 11-9), and replacing the exhaust-muff cabin heating system with separate gasoline-burning combustion heaters (Fig. 11-10).

There were also conversions of DC-3 to turbine power. See Chapter 15.

POSTWAR U.S. AIRLINE USE

The airlines of the U.S. began replenishing their DC-3 fleets even before war's end when the

Fig. 11-6. This former C-47A-60-DL, 42-68702, used by Bendix, is unusual in being fitted with a right-side hinge-down door. Note the extended nose cone for experimental airborne radar. (photo by Peter M. Bowers)

Fig. 11-7. A prewar DC-3-201A modified in 1951 for TV personality Arthur Godfrey with Pratt & Whitney R-2000 engines, giving it the unofficial designation DC-3A-R2000. Note how much farther the propellers are ahead of the cowling than on R-1830 engines. This plane later became the private transport of the Governor of South Carolina. (photo by Peter M. Bowers)

Army began to return some of the drafted airliners. However, this act generated some unforeseen problems. The lines did not always get the same DC-3s back that they had given up. This led to problems at the terminal when a line using left-side-door airplanes found itself with some right-side-door versions. When the line operated a mix, the pilots sometimes forgot which side the door was on for the particular plane they were flying and put the wrong side of the airplane toward the terminal. The pilots of one airline took care of this problem by pasting paper cutouts of a paper fist on the instru-

ment panel with a projecting thumb pointing to the side of the airplane the door was on.

DC-3s with the wrong engines were a more serious problem from operational and maintenance standpoints, and the airlines sometimes changed DC-3s from one engine to the other in their own shops.

When surplus C-47s and C-53s came on the market in quantity, the airlines quickly added many to their existing DC-3 fleets. The life of the DC-3s on the major trunk lines was short, however; they were replaced by the new four-engine equipment,

Fig. 11-8. Prewar DST-A-207D, NC33642, of United Air Lines, modified in postwar years with clipped wingtips, C-47 cargo door replacing original right-side door, upper berth windows deleted, and cabin interior lined with sheet fiberglass to protect structure from bulk cargo. (photo by Peter M. Bowers)

Fig. 11-9. This prewar DC-3-454 became C-49J, 43-1963. After postwar airline use it was modified as an executive transport with deluxe interior, enlarged cabin windows, and upgraded Wright Cyclone engines, which required cooling flaps. (photo by Peter M. Bowers)

Douglas DC-4/C-54s and Lockheed Constellation/C-69s that the airlines had ordered before Pearl Harbor but were taken over by the military. The DC-3s were then relegated to the shorter "feeder" routes and remained in the service of the major U.S. airlines well into the 1950s (Fig. 11-11).

Not all of the C-47s adapted to airline use or freighter were owned by the lines or their bankers. Some were on loan from the Army (Air Force after 1947), which permitted the amount of modification needed to convert a C-47 to DC-3C and airline standards. When returned to the Air Force, some of these reflected their passenger configuration by being designated VC-47. Others had departed so far from the C-47 configuration that they were redesignated C-117C.

Cashing in on their wartime experience in carrying freight for the Army in DC-3s, some airlines used specialized DC-3s for a new postwar phase of their business—all-freight flights on regular schedules. Some of these were prewar DC-3s adapted for the purpose (Fig. 11-12), while others were war-surplus C-47s.

As the DC-3s phased out of the trunk airline routes they became the mainstays of a new type of airline—the regional carrier. These were lines that served the smaller cities off of the trunk routes and covered only relatively small sections of the country (Fig. 11-13). Low cost and fast turnaround

were hallmarks of their operation, and their terminals at some of the smaller cities were tiny one-man operations with no maintenance or fueling facilities. The hinge-down doors with built-in steps were assets here—there was no need to roll loading steps up to the airliner. For brief stops, it became common practice to shut down only the engine on the passenger-loading side of the airplane. While most of the DC-3s still operating in the U.S. today are freighters, one regional airline, Boston-Provincetown, still operates them on scheduled passenger service in 1985.

DC-2 AND B-18

The DC-2 had been almost entirely replaced on U.S. airlines by DC-3s prior to Pearl Harbor, but a few saw postwar service with the non-skeds and crop dusters after the war, including some surplus Army C-39s and a Navy R2D-1 licensed under the DC-2 ATC A-540 (Fig. 11-14). There were only six DC-2s on the U.S. civil register in 1947 and only one—the former R2D-1—is still airworthy at this writing. It was borrowed by the Dutch airline KLM and refurbished for a 50th Anniversary re-enactment of the famous 1934 England-to-Australia air race, painted in the markings of the KLM DC-2 that placed second to a specialized racer.

Some surplus B-18s also made it onto the postwar civil register, initially as freighters (Fig.

Fig. 11-10. Closeups of original (top) and modified DC-3A/C engine cowlings. Exhaust system at the top has a hot air muff around the exhaust stack (below) for cabin heating. Shorter stack at right has no muff; the cabin is warmed by separate combustion heaters. (photos by Peter M. Bowers)

Fig. 11-11. This DC-3C, formerly C-47-DL, 42-5681, is a rare example of a scheduled airliner operating on skis. Note that the N-prefix to the registration number was not moved to the right when the letter C was removed after 1948. (photo by Norman E. Taylor)

Fig. 11-12. This United Air Lines DC-3A Cargoliner, photographed in February 1946, was originally a DC-3-454 that became C-49J, 43-1979. After leasing it from the government in July 1945, the airline converted it to a DC-3A by engine change and used it as a freighter, finally purchasing it in 1949. (photo by Peter M. Bowers)

Fig. 11-13. A DC-3C of West Coast Airlines, formerly C-47A-10-DK, 42-92704, photographed in a typical feeder-line operation at Yakima, Washington, in 1954. (photo by Peter M. Bowers)

154

Fig. 11-14. The only DC-2 still flying in the U.S. in 1985 is this former Navy R2D-1, Navy serial 1404. Note the postwar addition of a DC-3 dorsal fin. (photo by Dustin W. Carter, 1956)

11-15). Eighteen were on the register, licensed under Category-2 certificate 2-577, issued March 31, 1947.

THE NON-SKEDS

Right after the war a new type of airline operation appeared in the U.S., the non-scheduled freight carrier, or "non-sked." This was an example of personal initiative and free enterprise at its best and demonstrated all the advantages and disadvantages of the system. Some of the non-skeds were adequately financed and started with significant fleets of planes, mostly DC-3Cs (Fig. 11-16). Others were one-airplane operations manned by a few discharged service pilots and mechanics. They flew whenever they could obtain a load and took it to wherever its stateside destination was. As closely

as can be determined by aviation historian William T. Larkins, there were 187 such independent non-sked operators.

Some of these one-plane operations were conducted under the highest standards of operations and maintenance while others got by with a minimum expenditure of maintenance funds and questionable crew qualifications.

The small non-sked operators took advantage of seasonal demand for agricultural products, as for example flying early California strawberries to the Northwest. The following is an example of an extreme comedy of errors:

An independent non-sked DC-3C was loaded with strawberries for delivery to Boeing Field in Seattle, Washington. When it reached the area, Boeing Field was fogged in so the DC-3C had to

Fig. 11-15. A surplus B-18 used as a freighter by Veteran's Air Cargo. The fuselage door of the B-18 was slightly larger than that of the DC-3. (photo by Peter M. Bowers, 1947)

Fig. 11-16. When former 14th Air Force pilots formed the Flying Tiger Line after the war, they decorated their DC-3Cs with the famous "sharkmouth" marking of their wartime fighters. This is former C-47-DL, 41-38660. (photo by A.U. Schmidt)

divert to Ellensburg, Washington, 90 miles away on the east side of the Cascade Mountains, an area with an entirely different climate.

The landing brought one immediate problem—the cabin was so packed with berries that the crew had to exit the plane via a ladder put up to the forward baggage door. The next day, as the crew was preparing to leave for Seattle, a government inspector happened to visit the airport and asked to see the crew's papers, a spot check that he was authorized to perform.

It turned out that the pilot's medical certificate, which validates his license, had expired, and it fur-

ther turned out that the copilot was not rated for the DC-3. No local doctor was authorized to give pilot medical examinations so the pilot had to take surface transportation to another city to get his physical. By the time he got back, the Seattle weather had shut Boeing Field down again, so the berry-laden DC-3 sat in the broiling eastern Washington sun. The crew gave crates of berries away to local personnel, but most of them remained in the plane—cooking.

Finally the smell got so bad that the airport manager had to have the plane towed to a remote downwind corner of the field.

Fig. 11-17. A DC-3C used as an agricultural spray plane. Note the full-span spray rails and the large external chemical tank under the center section. Other DC-3 sprayers utilized tanks in the cabin. (Douglas photo)

Fig. 11-18. An eight-window DC-3C, formerly C-47A-35-DL, 43-23803, based at Renton, Washington, for spraying fog-dispensing chemicals when nearby Seattle-Tacoma airport is fogged in. Note the cloth covers on wings and horizontal tail to avoid takeoff delays due to removal of snow or frost. (photo by Peter M. Bowers)

Some DC-3s were used for crop and forest spraying (Fig. 11-17). At least one was used for the unique task of fog dispersal. Based at Renton, Washington, it was under contract to spray fog-dispensing chemicals over nearby Seattle-Tacoma International Airport (Fig. 11-18). (When the author, who lives directly under the approach to SeaTac, used to hear a DC-3 over the house at 5:00

Fig. 11-19. Three DC-3Cs were modified as borate bombers, but only one was actually used in firefighting operations. Here N62874 salvos its full 875-gallon load of water-borate mixture in a demonstration. (photo by Milo Peltzer)

A.M. in the 1970s, he knew it was a foggy day without having to get up and look out of the window.)

Although it was a successful sprayer, the DC-3 was, surprisingly, not a success at the related task of "Borate Bombing," dropping an 875-gallon mixture of water and fire-retardant chemicals on forest fires. The same tanks used to contain spray were fitted with dump valves so that the water could be dropped all at once or in train like bombs (Fig. 11-19). Three DC-3s were fitted out as borate bombers by separate organizations between 1964 and 1970, but only one was actually used as a firefighter, for three seasons in 1970-72.

GOVERNMENT USE

One non-airline user of a DC-3 fleet, mostly DC-3Cs converted from C-47s and R4Ds transferred directly from military surplus, was the U.S. government's aviation regulatory branch, the FAA, which used over 40 from 1946 to the late 1970s. This organization kept its uniquely painted orange-and-white DC-3s (Fig. 11-20) at major airports throughout the country that housed FAA regional offices. Many were used for the specialized task of checking airways radio beams as well as for transportation. All of these carried civil registrations under 100 in the special block of low numbers (to over 200) reserved for government-owned aircraft. These are hard for historians to keep track of because their low registration numbers were of-

ten reassigned; one particular DC-3C might have carried three or more different numbers at different times in its FAA career.

Other government agencies such as the U.S. Forest Service, Coast and Geodetic Survey, etc., also used low-number DC-3s. Some of the Forest Service DC-3s, plus others leased from private operators, were used for a very specialized and hazardous job—dropping "smoke jumpers" from low altitudes to fight forest fires, usually in mountainous terrain. Normal load was 12 to 16 jumpers and their equipment. The Forest Service retired its DC-3s in the late 1970s.

The National Advisory Committee for Aeronautics (NACA, later NASA for National Aeronautics and Space Administration) had its own under-1000 fleet numbers for DC-3s and other planes with the suffix letters NA added to the fleet number as civil registrations (Fig. 11-21).

FOREIGN AIRLINE USE

Airlines throughout the world were quick to acquire surplus C-47s and to put "liberated" prewar DC-3s back to work. As in the U.S., conversions ranged from full airline configuration to bare minimum work that retained most of the military features including the C-47 cargo doors and astrodomes. The Europeans also had small one- and two-plane non-sked and charter operations (Fig. 11-22).

Fig. 11-20. A pair of low-number FAA DC-3s based at Boeing Field, Seattle, in 1967. Note five main cabin windows and one new elongated window behind the cockpit. The heavy outline around the door was a mid-1960s FAA requirement that transport plane doors be outlined in a color contrasting with the aircraft coloring for outside assistance in case of a crash. (photo by Peter M. Bowers)

Fig. 11-21. A DC-3C, still with C-47 astrodome and tail cone, marked as Airplane No. 817 in the NASA fleet. Note that the letters NA have been appended to the fleet number to make the civil registration N817NA. (photo by Victor D. Seely)

As an example of the DC-3s matchless versatility, the German airline Lufthansa which had long since retired its DC-3s, leased one from a Dutch charter operator for a very special service. The airport at Stuttgart had been shut down temporarily for repaving in 1963. Rather than pass up this important passenger terminal even briefly, the airline flew its leased DC-3 from an airport taxiway instead of the wide runway.

Countries behind the so-called "Iron Curtain," those under Russian influence and Russia itself, also used surplus Lend-Lease C-47s as well as Russian-built Li-2s for civil and military purposes (Fig. 11-23).

The low price and ready availability of DC-3s on the secondhand market made them attractive to airlines established in many of the newly emerged nations of the 1960s and 1970s. These countries were usually former colonies in which airline service had been provided by the "home" country. For at least six, a DC-3 was the first airplane to appear on the new country's civil register, with the new national identify symbol preceding the letters AAA.

In some countries, the use of DC-3s and other airliners was shared jointly by the civil and military sectors, with civil registration and military markings being carried on the same airplane (Fig. 11-24).

BEGINNING OF THE END

As the aging DC-3s were replaced by later models in the passenger field, more and more of them gravitated to the heavy hauling business.

Fig. 11-22. This surplus C-47A-20-DL, 42-23548, was also Dakota III FD864 before picking up four different postwar civil registrations under three nationalities. Here it carriers Dutch registration PH-DAC for a Dutch charter operator, 1963-1967. (courtesy The Aviation Bookshop, London)

159

Fig. 11-23. Although Lend-Lease aircraft were supposed to be returned to the U.S. after World War II, Russia retained all that it had. This C-47B, with extra cabin windows and a DC-3 tailcone, was photographed in the markings of Aeroflot, the Russian National airline, at Helsinki, Finland, in 1949. (courtesy John Stroud)

Some C-47s that had been converted to passenger DC-3C configuration were refitted with cargo doors for freight (Fig. 11-25).

The low price of nearly worn-out DC-3s made them attractive as expendable vehicles for such one-time missions as smuggling narcotics into the U.S. Sometimes landings were made in such small remote-area airstrips that the DC-3 could not take off again or was damaged by overrunning the runway on landing, so was simply abandoned after being unloaded.

One factor contributing to the demise of the DC-3 in many remote parts of the world was not a lack of spares for the airframes and engines but a shortage of 100/130-Octane aviation gasoline. With the great increase in the number of jet aircraft throughout the world, many airports stopped stocking fuel for the larger reciprocating engines.

While many retired DC-3s have been preserved as static or flying museum pieces (see Chapter 16), the majority have either been scrapped out completely or stripped of useful parts and pushed out behind the hangar to rot away in the weeds (Fig. 11-26).

MOVIE CAREER

The DC-3 began to appear in motion pictures soon after it went into airline service. The publicity departments of the major airlines provided the studios with takeoff and landing scenes showing their markings for routine use in depicting departures and arrivals of the actors in the scenarios. This practice is still followed for today's jetliners.

Since DC-3s were not expendable in their trunk airline days, much of the dirty-weather flight scenes and the crashes were staged with models of vary-

Fig. 11-24. This prewar DC-3A-279A of Panagra was acquired by the Peruvian Air Force in 1950 and flew subsequently with civil and military Peruvian markings simultaneously. (photo by Gordon S. Williams)

Fig. 11-25. The FAA retired most of its DC-3 fleet in the late 1970s. New owners applied for new registration numbers and some of the DC-3s to be used as freighters had C-47 cargo doors reinstalled. Note the new metal of the door and the old FAA paint on this 1980 conversion. This former R4D-5, Navy serial 12429, had FAA registrations N58 and N78 before becoming N78125. Compare with Fig. 11-20 on p. 158. (photo by Peter M. Bowers)

ing accuracy. In recent years, with worn-out DC-3's readily available at scrap prices, the real thing has often been used for some spectacular but carefully controlled crash scenes. In the old days, the model crashed and the passengers crawled out of a mockup. Today, the battered fuselage is more apt to be that of a real DC-3 (Fig. 11-27).

Although appearing many times in movies and TV, the DC-3 has always played (and still plays) the role of a bit player or extra—never the star as in the case of the many shows built around the

glamorous B-17. Not all of these roles are in aviation movies as such. Often an airline flight in a DC-3 is merely a means of getting a diverse group of people together. After the principal characters have been established, the plane crashes in the first or second reel and the survival adventure—the real subject of the picture—begins. Specific movie and TV presentations are too numerous to list here, but some should be mentioned:

In the original 1937 version of the movie *Lost Horizon,* a DC-2 was used to abduct the hero and

Fig. 11-26. The fate of many a worn-out DC-3—stripped of useful parts and pushed out behind the hangar to rust away. This is former C-47A-90-DL, 43-15728, in August 1984. (photo by Peter M. Bowers)

Fig. 11-27. This crashed DC-3C, formerly C-47A-80-DL 43-15196, was carefully set up for the 1977 movie *Tarantulas: The Deadly Cargo*. Like other movie wrecks, it carried fictional organizational markings but used the last of its several U.S. civil registrations, N208R. (courtesy Ace Photo Service)

his companions to Shangri-La. The 1973 remake featured much more airwork—spectacular mountain flying by Frank Tallman in a DC-3. The TV series *Black Sheep Squadron*, built around the World War II operations of the U.S. Marine Corps F4U Corsair squadron in the South Pacific, made frequent use of a civil DC-3C that masqueraded as the R4D supply plane, complete with drop-down air-liner door and a highly unauthentic color scheme. Other movies featuring World War II operations over Europe have paid much more attention to authenticity of color, markings, and other details.

DC-3 aficionados can be assured that their favorite airplane will be seen in its established role for many years to come in movies and TV shows yet to be made.

Chapter 12

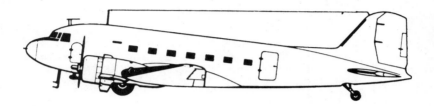

The Super DC-3

After the departure of the DC-3 from the trunk routes of the major airlines was hastened by the use of new four-engine equipment, two other new postwar models speeded its departure from the shorter routes. These were the Consolidated Vultee, or ConVair, 240 (Fig. 12-1) and the Martin 2-0-2 (Fig. 12-2).

Both were publicized as DC-3 replacements, but in fact were not. Very similar in size, power, capacity, and performance to each other, they had less wingspan than the DC-3 but were far heavier at gross weights approaching 43,000 pounds. Powerplants were 2400-hp Pratt & Whitney R-2800 Double Wasp engines. These produced cruising speeds in the area of 290 mph with passenger loads of 32-40 passengers. Of course, these had the latest features, such as tricycle landing gear and cabin pressurization. The ConVair received ATC A-793 in December 1948, while the Martin got the later A-795 in August 1947. Price tags were $316,000 to $498,000 for the ConVair and approximately the same for the Martin.

For all their higher performance and modern

conveniences, the ConVair/Martin twins could not match the performance of the DC-3 at the low end of the speed scale, or its ability to get in and out of small fields. They displaced the DC-3 from many areas that it served but neither they nor any other twin-engine transport has ever fully replaced the DC-3.

At war's end, both Lockheed and Boeing designed new high-wing twin-engine models specifically for the feeder market. The Lockheed prototype reached flight stage but was scrapped, while the Boeing was never finished.

Douglas did not enter the twin-engine airliner field at all after the war with its own version of a DC-3 replacement. Instead, it concentrated on continued production of the C-54/DC-4 and development of the stretched version that emerged as the DC-6 and the DC-7. However, a need for a twin with less speed and capacity than the ConVairs and Martins and better short-field capability was quite apparent. Douglas then came to the conclusion that the only replacement for a DC-3 was another DC-3. Since there were many shortcomings to the existing

Fig. 12-1. One intended postwar replacement for the DC-3 was the ConVair 240, a 32 to 40 passenger pressurized airliner with 2000-hp engines. The built-in airstairs could be installed on either the right or left side according to airline preference, and some had alternate tail-loading stairs like the Martin 2-0-2. (photo by Peter M. Bowers)

DC-3 by postwar standards, there was no point in reopening production lines to build more 1935 model airliners. Instead, existing DC-3s could be upgraded with new features that would increase their performance and comply with the new regulations. Preliminary design work began in 1947.

At first, this idea was similar to the original DC-2/DC-3 relationship, with a few relatively simple changes to the basic DC-3. As it turned out, more changes had to be made to meet new regulations and requirements, so the revised and original DC-3s were more like the final DC-2/DC-3 relationship, with very little commonality of parts and equipment.

ENTER THE DC-3S

As completed from existing DC-3 airframes, the two DC-3S prototypes, called "Super DC-3s," were virtually new airplane designs. The original fuselage was stretched 3 feet 3 inches to provide 30 to 38 passenger seating with eight windows to

Fig. 12-2. The Martin 2-0-2, with tail-loading ramp, was very similar to the contemporary ConVair 240 in size, capacity, and performance, but was no more successful as a DC-3 replacement. (photo by Logan Coombs)

a side. This was accomplished by inserting a "plug" in the constant cross-section area of the fuselage ahead of the wing and inaugurated a practice that was to be followed by many subsequent designs that were "stretched" to increase their capacity.

The center section remained the same but the all-new outer wing panels were shortened for a span of 90 feet (reduced from 95) and an area reduced to 969 square feet from 986. The wingtips were squared off and the leading edge sweep-back was increased to 19.5 degrees while the formerly straight trailing edge was now swept back 4 degrees. A significant increase in wing strength resulted from use of the new 75ST aluminum alloy in place of the original 24ST. New nacelles housed 1475-hp Wright R-1820-C9HE Cyclone engines in the first prototype and 1450-hp Pratt & Whitney R-2000-D7 Twin Wasps in the second. The nacelles were deep enough to completely enclose the wheels when they were retracted and the tailwheel was made retractable.

The increased gross weight of 31,000 pounds and the increased power called for redesigned and enlarged tail surfaces. These were extreme departures from previous DC-3 configurations, being roughly trapezoidal with an enlarged dorsal fin ahead of the vertical fin. The new horizontal tail had a greater span than the original by 11 feet 4 inches. The civil prototypes used left-side hinge-down air-stair passenger doors in the standard DC-3 position.

The top speed increased to 270 mph, and the cruising speed to 251 mph at some loss of short-field capability in spite of the power increase.

The first prototype DC-3S (Figs. 12-3, 12-4) was produced at Santa Monica. It was a former C-47-DL, 41-18656, C/N 6017, that Douglas bought from Western Airlines. This was given a new C/N, 43158, and Douglas' third use of registration N30000, the DC-3C demonstrator that had carried it in 1946 having been sold and given a new registration. First flight on June 23, 1949, was very successful and raised Douglas' hopes for good reception of the DC-3S by the airlines, but such was not to be.

The second prototype, with P & W engines (Fig. 12-5) was converted from an older DC-3-277D. This was originally C/N 4122, drafted out of the factory as C-50 41-7700. It was bought from American Airlines and given new C/N 43159 and the registration originally assigned to it before it was drafted—N15579. Later, this number was to be replaced by N30000 for Douglas' fourth use of the number after the first DC-3S was sold to the U.S. Air force.

Following testing, the Cyclone-powered version of the DC-3S was awarded ATC 6A-2 on July 24, 1950. At this time, the procedure for issuing ATCs was being revised. Instead of all certificates being issued sequentially from Washington, DC, they were now issued by FAA offices in separate FAA administrative regions throughout the country. The DC-3S was the second design certificated in then FAA Region Six that covered the western states.

For the airlines, the plan was to have the air-

Fig. 12-3. The first DC-3S, or "Super DC-3," was converted from C-47-DL, 41-18656, and carried Douglas's third application of registration N30000. (photo by E.M. Sommerich)

Fig. 12-4. Flight view of the first DC-3S, showing the completely enclosed wheels and the special color scheme while used as a Douglas demonstrator. (Douglas photo)

line supply an airworthy DC-3 airframe, which Douglas would then convert to DC-3S configuration. Unfortunately, all the new parts drove the price up to unacceptable levels—more than the cost of an original prewar DC-3 plus the turned-in airplane.

Civil sales of the DC-3S were killed by the venerable DC-3 itself; the regulations that were expected to drive the stock DC-3s off the airlines that still used them were waived for these models. The small lines that were expected to be the major customers for the DC-3S were able to retain their old models and could not justify the greater cost

of a DC-3S in spite of its considerably improved payload and performance.

Only three DC-3s beside the second prototype were sold to airlines—all to Capital Airlines, which did not retain them for long. These were prewar American Airlines DC-3-178s with original C/Ns 1557, 1554, and 1548 and registrations NC 16019, 16016, and 16012, respectively. They were given new C/Ns 43191/43193 and reregistered as N540S/542S (Fig. 12-6). N542S was given new registrations N11SA, N156WC, and N156PM by subsequent owners and was eventually converted to turbine power (see Chapter 15).

Fig. 12-5. The second DC-3S, converted from a prewar DC-3-277D, was similar to the first except for using Pratt & Whitney R-2000 engines. After the first DC-3S was sold to the U.S. Air Force, its N30000 registration was transferred to N15579. (photo by Edgar Wischnowski)

Fig. 12-6. After a short airline career, the Super DC-3s found new owners. This is N540S being used as an executive transport in 1970. (photo by Peter M. Bowers)

MILITARY SALES

Since the DC-3S didn't fare well in the civil market, Douglas modified the first prototype for military missions and offered it to the U.S. Air Force. Following its tests by the Air Force and the Navy, the airframe became the most redesignated and renumbered DC-3 ever. It had two Douglas C/Ns, three Army/Air Force designations, two Army/Air Force serial numbers, and two Navy designations and serial numbers.

The military changes consisted of replacing the single-wheel landing gear legs with two-wheel legs for operation from soft fields (Fig. 12-7), provision for the attachment of JATO bottles for short-field and overload takeoffs (Fig. 12-8), and restoration of the C-47 cabin doors for cargo.

YC-129—The original designation assigned by the Air Force was YC-129, indicating the service test version of a new model. The serial number was also new, 51-3817. Former military serials were not restored when ex-military aircraft were re-acquired for service use. The YC-129 designation was soon replaced by one more indicative of the airframe's C-47 origins; YC-47F. The new 51-3817 serial was retained.

After evaluation, the Air Force decided that the YC-47F was not enough of an improvement over the existing C-47s, now mostly C-47Ds, and did not order any further Super DC-3s. The single YC-47C was then sold to the U.S. Navy.

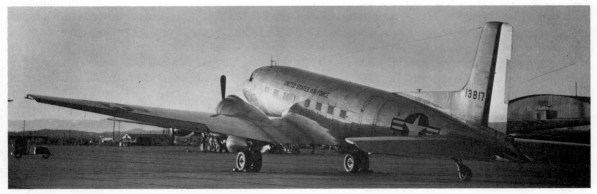

Fig. 12-7. The first DC-3S was modified to military standards, including C-47 cargo doors and dual landing wheels, and offered to the U.S. Air Force as YC-129 before being sold as the single YC-47F with new USAF serial number 51-3817. (Douglas photo)

Fig. 12-8. To improve short-field takeoffs at high gross weights, Douglas fitted the YC-47F with detachable solid-fuel rocket boosters, as had been used on some C-47s during World War II. (Douglas photo)

R4D-8X—Douglas made minor changes to the former YC-47F for the Navy, the most notable externally being a return to single-wheel landing gear units and nine windows on the right side of the cabin. The Navy assigned the designation R4D-8X, with the oddity of the X being used as a suffix rather than a prefix (Fig. 12-9). The Navy serial number was 138659, changed to 138820 upon completion of testing and redesignation as plain R4D-8 (Fig. 12-10). It was redesignated C-117D in 1962.

R4D-8—The Navy was more receptive to the Super DC-3 prototype than was the Army and ordered 100 conversions after testing the R4D-8X. These were made from a random batch of R4D-5s, -6s, and -7s with Navy serials ranging from 17103 through 99845. Although the R4D-8s got new Douglas C/Ns 43301/43400, they retained their original wartime Navy serials, which were not in sequence relative to the new C/Ns (Fig. 12-11).

The R4D-8s were well suited to the Navy's long-range missions and saw service worldwide. They also became mainstays of the Navy's operations in Antarctica, easily making the nonstop flight from New Zealand to the Antarctic continent until replaced by four-turboprop Lockheed C-130s in the late 1950s. Because of their range, demonstrated reliability, and performance on one engine, R4D-8s were the only twin-engine landplanes that the Navy used for passenger service between the U.S. and Hawaii.

Although the R4D-8s were used for a variety of missions they received only three special-purpose suffixes—L, T, and Z. None of the R4D-8Ts were former R4D-7 instrument trainers. All of the R4D-8s were redesignated C-117D in the revised designation system of 1962. The R4D-8Ls became LC-117D, the R4D-8Ts became TC-117D, and the R4D-8Zs became VC-117Ds (Fig. 12-12).

Fig. 12-9. After the USAF lost interest in the YC-47F it was sold to the U.S. Navy, which assigned serial number 138659 and the designation R4D-8X. (Douglas photo)

Fig. 12-10. Upon completion of its Navy tests, the R4D-8X dropped its X-designation and was issued new Navy serial number 138820. Here it displays the designation C-117D that replaced R4D-8 in 1962. (photo by Robert Esposito)

Fig. 12-11. The 100 "production" R4D-8s were all conversions from existing Navy R4Ds. Note the nine right-side cabin windows on the R4D-8, converted from R4D-7, 39104, but retaining the original Navy serial number. (U.S. Navy photo)

Fig. 12-12. A U.S. Marine Corps VC-117D based at Washington, D.C., in 1967, and displaying the white fuselage top adopted for Navy passenger planes in 1953 to reduce solar heating of the cabin. The rest of the aluminum skin has been painted light gray. (photo by Roger Besecker)

Fig. 12-13. Some of the R4D-8/C-117Ds assigned to overseas Embassy use carried the lettering UNITED STATES OF AMERICA instead of the standard Navy or Marine designation. (photo by Robert F. Dorr via Jim Sullivan)

Fig. 12-14. Douglas sold only four Super DC-3s to civil customers, but more got into private hands after the U.S. Navy surplused C-117Ds in the late 1970s. C-GDOG was photographed at Malton, Quebec, Canada, on September 3, 1985. (photo by K.M. Molson)

The C-117Ds were the last DC-3s in U.S. military service, with a few assigned to overseas stations and embassies surveying into the early 1980s (Fig. 12-13). Quite a few were sold surplus and have considerably confused the identity situation. Two surplus C-117Ds appear on the civil register as DC-3S, along with one of the original airliners. Three others appear as "Super DC-3" in company with another ex-airliner. Eight appear as "Super R4D-8" in spite of the R4D-8 designation having been dropped more than 15 years before such airplanes became surplus, and nine C-117Ds are in the register under that designation. Other surplus C-117Ds have found new owners in Canada (Fig. 12-14).

Chapter 13

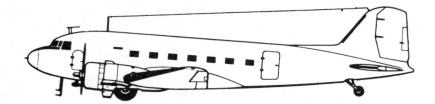

Condemned and Reprieved

In view of the new high-performance four-engine airliners that the lines ordered in 1940/41 (but did not get until 1946 because of the military takeover), it was readily apparent by 1942 that there would be new regulations in effect after the war and that the now-venerable DC-3 would not be able to comply with them. The FAA had stated in 1942 that it expected to revoke the airworthiness certificates of DC-3s in 1948. This fact, plus new technology, was responsible for the drive to develop a DC-3 replacement, essayed but not satisfactorily performed by the ConVair 240 and the Martin 2-0-2.

LEGISLATED INTO OBSOLESENCE

The revised postwar regulations as they applied to Air Carrier aircraft, meaning scheduled airliners and other revenue operations, did indeed discriminate against the 1935 technology of the DC-3. It looked like the old bird would be grounded as unsafe. Fortunately, this disastrous order was not issued.

The DC-3 had proven itself a safe and depen-

dable carrier for some 12 years of war and peace under all imaginable conditions of weather, minimum maintenance, and overload operations. None except a few early accidents, their causes quickly corrected, could be blamed on specific shortcomings of the airplane.

A sober analysis of the civil aviation scene in the late 1940s revealed that grounding of the DC-3 fleet would have drastic scheduling and financial impact on the air transport industry. The major airlines still had significant numbers in service and of course they were the mainstay of the independent freighters and regional airlines. Since no suitable substitute models were on hand to replace the DC-3s and allow business to carry on at the same level, it became essential to postpone the demise of the DC-3.

There was obvious economic justification for this, and some technical precedent. Back in 1937, a widespread revision of aircraft certification requirements made certain features in common use to that time illegal for subsequent production. These included single-ignition engines, 3/32" control cable, fuselage fabric extending forward to the engine compartment, and certain performance parameters.

SAVED BY GRANDFATHER

To avoid grounding a major portion of the existing general aviation fleet that operated the affected designs, a "Grandfather Clause" was written into the regulations to permit the continued licensing and operation of those designs given ATCs prior to the adoption of the new rules. However, if a pre-1937 design that was using a single-ignition engine was to continue in production, it had to adopt a twin-ignition engine and pick up what other new details were required.

This proved to be the case for the DC-3. Although out of production, it was no less an airplane because of the new regulations. Operating within its obvious limitations relative to later designs, it could do as good a job as ever and in many cases do jobs that later designs could not equal. It was now more obvious than ever that the only replacement for a DC-3 was another DC-3.

In view of these obvious realities, the FAA dropped action against the DC-3 and declared in 1953 that its Airworthiness Certificate was "Good until it wore out"! (It is noteworthy that the FAA acquired its first DC-3, a DC-3-348, in April 1941, and retained it as NC14 until August 1945. Its second was a DC-3A-368, formerly C-48A 41-7682, acquired in August 1946, and retained until 1975 (Fig. 13-1). Some 40 other DC-3s converted from C-47s and R4Ds were acquired in the interim.)

OPERATING CATEGORIES

As mentioned, DC-3s did not remain on the trunk routes as Air Carrier aircraft past the early 1950s. However, a few still serve a regional line in scheduled passenger service in 1985 (Fig. 13-2). DC-3s that are not in "Experimental" or "Restricted" categories presently operate with "Standard Licenses," i.e., airworthiness certificates, under four separate parts of the Federal Aviation Regulations, or FARs. When a particular DC-3 is referred to as a "Part 135 Airplane," the words mean that it is licensed to operate under that numbered part of the FARs. In some cases, DC-3s that would normally operate in one FAR part because of the nature of their business are granted waivers that allow them to operate in another part that has less stringent requirements for maintenance programs, crew training and qualifications, safety equipment, etc.

Part 91 covers General Aviation operations, meaning mostly private flying, but a few DC-3s are found here, including some used by private businesses to haul their own product from source to market or transport their own personnel. Some privately owned DC-3s are found here, as well as some owned by museums and foundations that fly

Fig. 13-1. This FAA DC-3A-368 was C-48A, 41-7682, acquired in August 1946. It was first registered N86, then became N1 for use of the FAA Administrator. When replaced by later equipment, it was reregistered as N6 and survived until 1975. (William T. Larkins photo via Harry Gann)

Fig. 13-2. Only one scheduled U.S. passenger airline still uses DC-3s in 1986. N136PB of Provincetown-Boston Airlines is a DC-3-201 built in October, 1937, and became C-49G 42-56630. It was later converted to DC-3A standard and is presently the world's highest-time airplane, with over 87,000 flight hours. Note the unusual relocation of the baggage compartment door to the right side of the fuselage. (Photo by Jeffrey Magnet)

them in non-revenue operations as flying museum pieces. Associated maintenance and crew qualification requirements are minimal.

Part 121 is for scheduled air carrier passenger service and has the highest standards for crew qualification and aircraft maintenance programs. Very few DC-3s operate in Part 121 today.

Part 125 covers certain commercial operations of "large" aircraft (20 or more passengers or 6000 pounds payload). Crew and maintenance standards are not as high as for Part 121, and the commercial operators cannot publicly advertise their services.

Part 135 covers air taxi services and scheduled air freight lines (Fig. 13-3). Crew and maintenance standards are not as high as for Part 121, but are higher than for Part 125. This is the FAR part under which most working DC-3s operate today.

Fig. 13-3. This special DC-3A freighter with most cabin windows removed and protective bars over the others is former C-53, 42-15876. Lining the cabin walls with sheet fiberglass and barring the windows is common practice for DC-3s carrying heavy freight. (photo by E.M. Sommerich)

LICENSE CATEGORIES

Several different types of license (actually FAA Airworthiness Certificates) apply to U.S. civil aircraft. These affect their operation, crew requirements, and even their earnings.

Standard licenses are issued to aircraft that meet the full requirements of their approved Type Certificates, and allow them to be used commercially for revenue purposes, fly out of the country, and perform all operations permitted provided the certificate is kept current according to FAA inspection requirements.

Experimental licenses are issued to aircraft used for purely experimental work such as testing new developments or for exhibition. The latter are licensed in the "Exhibition" subcategory of the Experimental category. Often an airplane operating on a Standard license will be put on "Experimental" briefly while some new item of equipment is being tested.

Experimental status is highly restrictive as to when and where the airplane can fly, and only essential crew can be carried in non-revenue operation.

Restricted licenses are issued in cases where the installed equipment (such as tanks and spray rails on a sprayer), although proven, makes the plane unsuitable for normal commercial service. Many DC-3 sprayers and special-purpose modifications are found in this category.

VISIBLE LICENSE STATUS

Until the end of 1948, the license status of U.S.-registered aircraft was proclaimed in the aircraft registration figures carried on the upper right wing, the lower left wing, and both sides of the rudder. The actual number assigned was preceded by two letters—N, the international identification assigned to the U.S., and a second letter that identified the type of license in effect. NC identified a full commercial license, NX designated Experimental, NR designated Restricted, and NS identified government-owned (either federal or state, usually with numbers under 100).

Sometimes a Standard-License airplane will be licensed Experimental for a short time to prove out new equipment or undergo a temporary modification such as the installation of ferry tanks. The change of status used to be indicated by changing the NC to NX, often by merely placing an X over the C with masking tape. Photos show many DC-3s with such temporary marking changes (Fig. 13-4).

After 1948, the second letter was deleted. Airplanes with Experimental and Restricted certificates then had to proclaim their status with the appropriate words painted in two-inch high block figures adjacent to the entry door. The term "NC License" remained in verbal use for several more years before being replaced by "Standard License."

Starting with the advent of Air Defense Identification Zones (ADIZ) in coastal areas of the U.S. during the Korean War, it became advisable to add the registration in figures at least 12 inches high to each side of the fuselage or vertical tail. In 1966 the side registrations became mandatory and the wing registrations were no longer required.

In the absence of the second letters, aircraft registrations are now referred to as "N-numbers."

PRESENT VALUE

For airframes that are all over 40 years old, the prices for airworthy DC-3s are amazingly high. There is no established "Blue Book" value for used airplanes as there is for used cars, based on year of manufacture. Cost is determined by a great number of variables, such as total airframe flight hours, engine model and hours since overhaul, modifications (such as cargo door, Maximizer kit and heavy landing gear, combustion heaters), and, most important of all, the record of compliance with mandatory Airworthiness Directives (ADs) issued by the FAA.

ADs are inspections for condition and/or structural fixes that past performance of that particular model has shown to be necessary within a certain number of flight hours. In order to retain its airworthiness certificate, the airplane must show compliance with the AD in its maintenance records. Often, a Douglas Service Bulletin is issued in conjunction with an AD or to head off an AD to show the operator how to accomplish the necessary work, list the required parts, etc.

Fig. 13-4. United Air Lines DC-3A-197 with its standard NC license temporarily changed to NX in 1941 while being used to test engine modifications. (photo by Peter M. Bowers)

For its half-century of operation the DC-3 has accumulated only 26 ADs—a *remarkably* low total compared to many later and supposedly better-engineered designs. The most significant ADs against the DC-3 are a pair involving the wings, 63-21-01 and 66-18-02, issued in 1963 and 1966, respectively. These call for inspection of the outer wing attach angles for cracks within the first 50 flight hours after issuance of the AD and at 450-hour intervals thereafter. Also, all outer lower wing skin doublers must be replaced with new heavier doublers.

AD 66-18-02 also requires removal of the outer wing panels after the accumulation of 7500 hours of flight time but before 8000 hours, for inspection. Wing panel removal is required periodically thereafter to minimums of 4000 hours or greater intervals depending on previous modifications. A recent "wing pull," indication that a DC-3 on the market has plenty of flying time ahead of it before recurrence of the major expense of another wing pull (somewhere between $12,000 and $18,000), is an important factor in the asking price. At an average daily utilization of four hours, 4000 flight hours add up to over three calendar years of operation.

The electronic equipment installed in the DC-3 also affects the price, and some of it is pretty expensive. No DC-3, regardless of age or condition, can operate today with its original communications and navigation equipment. The low-frequency radio ranges and tower communications were replaced by very high frequency types soon after World War II, and there are all sorts of new radio and radar systems in use that did not exist when the last DC-3 was built.

The following four classified advertisements were selected from eight that offered used DC-3s for sale in a July 1985, issue of *Trade-A-Plane News*, a widely distributed newspaper serving the used airplane community. Note the emphasis on engine time and wing pull, and the wide price range.

☐ DELUXE C47 CONVERT., 170/680 on -92 engines, recent wing pull, only 12,300 since brand new!! Full deicing, light weight radios, cargo door, cargo floor, 26,900 gross, 18,312 mp. Beautiful condition. 26 easily removable seats. Ready to go!! $159,500. Trades invited.

☐ C47J, TT15,394, 263/767 on 90D's, 340 since wing pull, OH props, radar nose, cargo door, heavy gear, metal cargo floor, just completed heavy inspection, lot of work done, no corrosion, licensed, ready to fly. $95,000.

☐ C-47, CARGO DOOR, METAL floor, 1000 SMOH (-92's), located overseas, good cond., best offer. Call for details.

☐ DC-3 AIRLINER, 30 PASSENGER, just off Part 121 Kardex maintenance program. New Imron paint. Recent wing pull, TTAF 21850, PW1830-96, LE350 SMOH, RE990

SMOH by Piedmont. Deice boots. Must sell ASAP. Great condition, $127,900, owner DC-3 rating, manuals included. Back-up DC-3 in camouflage paint off 135, $80,000.

While most latter-day DC-3 sales are initiated through published advertisements like those above or through established aircraft brokers, and prices are in a recognized range, some are picked up at bargain prices. These are at Sheriff's sales, usually the result of the bankruptcy of a previous operator, or the sale of DC-3s confiscated from smugglers or other haulers of illicit cargo.

MODIFICATIONS

The extended life of the DC-3 has seen the appearance of many modifications not originated by Douglas. Various individuals and airline shops that have reason to modify a DC-3 (or any other certificated aircraft) to improve performance or capacity, replace original equipment no longer available, or to increase user convenience or safety can work out their own modifications without Douglas' consent. However, these changes must be approved by the FAA, and while they are being tested the airplane must go on "Experimental" status with attendant restrictions.

Once the modification has been approved, the airplane can return to "Standard" category and revenue service. The originator is then issued either a "One-Time" or a "Multiple" Supplemental Type Certificate (STC) in his name. This allows the airplane to operate under its original ATC—say a DC-3 under ATC A-669—with the STC change incorporated. A "One-Time" STC can be awarded from relatively crude prototype drawings. A "Multiple" STC that allows the originator to make that modification available for any other DC-3A or DC-3C operators from drawings, kits, and licenses must make finished drawings and instructions available that any mechanic can work from. STCs are specific as to which DC-3 series can use them.

In many cases, several different individuals came up with essentially the same modification or improvement, such as one-piece birdproof windshields or wheel well closure doors, available to all DC-3 users on multiple STCs. Examples of one-time STCs are Rolls-Royce "Dart" turboprop engines in a DC-3S airframe and the conversion of DC-3 outer wing panels to "wet" wings containing 550 gallons of fuel. However, in spite of any new designation assigned to the modified DC-3 by the holder of the STC, as DC-3-TP for a DC-3 powered with Pratt & Whitney PT6A turboprops, the FAA usually, but not always, recognizes the airplane only by its ATC designation, in this case a DC-3C.

Some commercially-originated DC-3 modifications resulting in STCs have been incorporated in U.S. military C-47s and R4Ds without affecting the designation via a prefix or suffix letter (Fig. 13-5). Altogether, 175 STCs have been issued for the DC-3 through April 1984.

ATC CHANGES

In many cases, DC-3s and DSTs built under one ATC have undergone such modifications as a change of engine model that remove them from the configuration of their original ATC and qualify them for another, as a DC-3 with Wright Cyclone engines built under ATC A-618 having them replaced by Pratt & Whitney Twin Wasps covered by ATC A-669.

Although the converted DC-3 may now be mechanically and outwardly identical to a DC-3A, it is still a DC-3. The FAA does not allow changes to be made to the original nameplate. Major modifications such as different engines or the conversion of C-47s to DC-3Cs are identified by the installation of a supplemental nameplate. In FAA records, a DC-3 converted to Twin Wasp engines is a modified DC-3, not a DC-3A (or vice versa, Fig. 13-6). This fact is very disturbing to aviation enthusiasts who photograph various DC-3s without having access to the interiors to check the nameplates. In such cases, a DC-3 appearing to be a DC-3A can only be verified as such by working backward through registration records to the original configuration and designation.

In less extreme examples, DC-3As built under ATC A-619 qualify, still appearing as DC-3As, for ATC A-669 following minor changes made to update their original Twin Wasp engines or to use

Fig. 13-5. U.S. Army white-and-orange C-47Js incorporating such commercially originated modifications as one-piece windshields, larger pilots' side windows, the tight engine cowlings of a "Maximizer" kit, and wheel well closure doors.

later-series Twin Wasps approved for ATC A-669. Engine upgrade approval dates for all DC-3 ATCs are listed in Appendix C.

In the case of the DC-3, the FAA has not held rigidly to its practice of registering the airplanes only by their original ATC designations. Because of many modifications, reregistrations, loss of paperwork, and the building up of "new" airplanes from scrap, many DC-3s have been registered with non-ATC designations. Altogether, the 1985 U.S. Civil Register lists 33 different designations for DC-3s (see Appendix D).

Some DC-3Cs and Ds have their designations expanded by addition of several variations of the R-1830 engine, and others are registered by their former military designations. In a few cases, the former military serial number, rather than the Douglas C/N, is used in the FAA paperwork.

A MODERN OPERATION

The commercial operators that use DC-3 fleets today are not necessarily long-established firms that are simply keeping old and fully-depreciated equipment in service. Some are quite new and operate at a profit by capitalizing on the DC-3's still-unmatched combination of economics and capability for short-haul heavy-load markets. At today's prices, a new airplane with the 7500-pound payload of the DC-3 and only a little more speed can cost about four million dollars, while a DC-3

Fig. 13-6. A rare example of a Twin Wasp-powered DC-3A or C having its engines changed to Wright Cyclones. This former C-47A-70-DL, 43-15250, is still a DC-3C in FAA records. It has 1450-hp R-1820-C9HD Cyclone engines as used in the DC-3s with cooling flaps, modified windshields, wheel well closure doors, and square instead of rectangular cabin windows.

in good condition can be acquired for well under $200,000.

Salair, Inc., is a good example of a "new" DC-3 operator. It was founded in May 1980, with a single DC-3 being used to haul fish in Alaska. It has since expanded to a fleet of 12 DC-3s, with six based at Seattle-Tacoma (Sea-Tac) airport in Seattle, Washington, two in Portland, Oregon, two in Sacramento, California, and two in Anchorage, Alaska.

The Sea-Tac operation, conducted under FAR Part 135, is typical. Salair contracts with large-volume long-distance freight carriers such as Flying Tiger and Emery Air Freight, which bring cargo to Seattle in large jet cargoplanes like Douglas DC-8s and Boeing 727s. Salair distributes some of this freight to other major Northwest cities over short distances that cannot be served economically by jets with the necessary capacity.

The major Salair operation from Sea-Tac does not consist of out-and-back runs to single cities. Rather, it flies a roughly rectangular route with Sea-Tac at one corner. Flights are all one-way around the route, with an average daily utilization of approximately three hours per airplane.

FACTORY SUPPORT FOR THE DC-3

In a situation unique in the industry, Douglas still provides factory support for the DC-3 half a century after its introduction.

This is engineering assistance only, such as solutions to technical problems, data for compliance with ADs, help in relicensing rebuilt airframes, replacing manuals, etc. Operators requiring replacement hardware or structural items are expected to obtain them on the secondhand market, from salvage yards, or to repair or build components in accordance with factory and FAA-approved drawings.

As an example of "new" engineering assistance to the DC-3, Douglas called an all-operator's meeting in November 1985. This introduced new inspection procedures and a manual developed to detect corrosion and correct structural deterioration problems in high-time DC-3 airframes. This is the result of experience with the jet airliner fleet, some examples of which encountered corrosion problems and even structural failure as they greatly exceeded the flight hours and calendar time that they had been designed for. Considering the numbers of over-40 DC-3s still in service, Douglas felt that preventive and corrective procedures similar to those developed for the jets would be appropriate for the venerable DC-3.

STILL IRREPLACEABLE

The world's aircraft industry has introduced many new transport-category airplanes since the end of World War II, some of them intended to be DC-3 replacements. However, none has been able to combine the operating costs, payload, and small-airport capability of the DC-3. Early in 1962 then-chairman of the Civil Aeronautics Board Alan S. Boyd summed up the requirements for a DC-3 replacement as follows:

- ☐ Seat up to 24 passengers.
- ☐ Carry 1000 pounds of cargo in addition to passenger's baggage.
- ☐ Operate from runways 4000 feet or shorter and possibly include vertical takeoff and landing (VTOL) capability.
- ☐ Operate over 80 to 100-mile stages of a 500-mile route with only one fueling.
- ☐ Cost $500,000 or less.
- ☐ Operate at an airplane-mile cost of 60 cents or less.

The absence of such an airplane 50 years after the introduction of the DC-3 proves that:

"The only replacement for a DC-3 is another DC-3."

Chapter 14

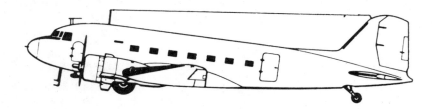

The Old Soldier Carries On

When World War II ended in 1945, the various DC-3 variants were the second-oldest design in the U.S. Army and Navy inventories. The Boeing B-17, the prototype of which flew in July 1935, preceded the DC-3 by only five months.

As with any military model of such vintage, it was logical to assume that the military DC3 would quietly phase out by being downgraded to utility and hack work as new designs took over its prime missions. This assumption became only partly true.

Most of the prewar DC-3s and drafted airliners were out of the Army and Navy inventories by 1946, but a few C-48s and C-49s that were in VIP use were retained. A few C-53s converted to VC-53s (Fig. 14-1) remained in service until 1961, leaving the C-47 and C-117 as the only DC-3s in the USAF inventory (Fig. 14-2).

As in the war years, identification of the various DC-3 variants from a distance was difficult. Late in 1945 a system of "buzz numbers" was adopted for visual identification from the ground to permit reporting of unauthorized low flying, or "buzzing," by Army airplanes. Two letters and three numbers made up the marking, carried on each side of the fuselage and under the left wing (Fig. 14-3). For DC-3s, the first letter, C, identified the airplane as an Army/Air Force C-type. The second letter identified the model within the C-type, as follows:

CE	C-47
CF	C-48
CG	C-49
CH	C-53
CU	C-117

The three numbers were the last three digits of the airplane's Army/Air Force serial number, so the "buzz numbers" for C-47B-40-DK 44-77277 appeared on the airplane as CE-277.

The C-47 (to use the single designation for both services) did give up one of its major World War II missions, glider-towing, but carried on in all others and even developed new missions. It served as a guinea pig for many tests of new equipment and mechanical features (Fig. 14-4), soldiered on in several subsequent official and unofficial wars,

Fig. 14-1. VC-53, 41-20088, in the overall silver lacquer finish used by some passenger C-47s and C-53s in late 1940s and early 1950s. The right-side hinge-down door was added during early postwar lease of the airplane to an airline. (photo by E.M. Sommerich)

Fig. 14-2. The rear cargo door section of VC-47D, 43-49260, has been sealed and the inner door of the forward cargo door section has been converted to hinge-down airstairs. Nose and rear fuselage are banded with Day-Glo orange for high visibility. (photo by Peter M. Bowers, 1961)

Fig. 14-3. SC-47B-45-DK, 45-1012, displaying "buzz number" CE-012 on the fuselage and high-visibility yellow Air Rescue markings over fading wartime camouflage. (photo by William T. Larkins)

Fig. 14-4. C-47A-35-DL, 42-23918, was used in conjunction with a manned Culver PQ-14B target plane to develop a system whereby short-range jet fighters could be towed by their wingtips on long-range missions for the defence of ConVair B-36 bombers. (courtesy Joseph V. Mizrahi)

and—most surprising of all for an allegedly obsolete 30-year-old airliner—became a highly effective multi-gun attack plane! The Coast Guard, normally a branch of the U.S. Treasury Department but taken over by the Navy during World War II, used R4Ds in the postwar years and C-47s became the mainstays of the National Guard as later Air National Guard troop carrier squadrons.

The Navy made extensive use of R4Ds in its postwar Antarctic expeditions, even launching some from aircraft carriers (Fig. 14-5). An R4D-5 named *Que Sera Sera* made the first landing at the South Pole (Fig. 14-6). A USAF C-47D made the first North Pole landing on May 3, 1952. When they became available, R4D-8 "Super DC-3s" replaced the older R4D-5s and -6s in the Antarctic (Fig. 14-7).

After V-J Day, surplus U.S. and British C-47s and Dakotas became available to former Allies, former enemies, and a host of newly emerging nations. Altogether, nearly 100 recognized Air Forces of the world, plus various guerilla forces, have used the C-47 or other DC-3 variants including Li-2s. As late as 1983, 67 Air Forces were still using them as transports.

ADDITIONAL DESIGNATIONS

The first peacetime year, 1946, brought further series designations to both U.S. Army/Air Force and U.S. Navy C-47s as indicated below:

POSTWAR U.S. ARMY/AIR FORCE

New series designations for Army/Air Force C-47s resulted from minor equipment changes, use of larger engines, and changes of mission, with series letters reaching C-47Q in 1965.

Fig. 14-5. R4D-5 serial 17237 was one of six used on the Navy's Antarctic expedition of 1946-47. Here it takes off from the aircraft carrier *Philippine Sea* with the aid of JATO, January 29, 1947. The black-bordered orange band around the fuselage is for increased visibility against the snow. (U.S. Navy photo)

Fig. 14-6. R4D-5s in Antarctica. Serial 12418, right, named *Que Sera Sera*, made the first landing at the South Pole on October 31, 1956. Note JATO bottles and ski-wheels. Rear portion painted orange for visibility, top of fuselage white, and remainder of fuselage light gray. (U.S. Navy photo via Douglas)

Fig. 14-7. R4D-5s replaced R4D-5s in Antarctica in 1957. Serial 17219 is seen in flight with the landing gear extended due to emergency repairs being made after damage was sustained in a remote-area landing. (U.S. Navy photo)

C-47D—The C-47Bs in service after WWII were all converted to C-47D over a period of several years by deleting the high blower from the R-1830-90C engines, making them R-1830-90Ds. Continuous output remained 1100 hp at 2550 rpm at sea level. This change had no effect on the outward appearance of the engine nacelle or the particular airscoop/filter combination.

The C-47Ds carried on all the previous missions of the Bs except the high-altitude work, and took on new missions as the need arose. Some of these are obvious from the prefix writeup, but "A" deserves separate discussion.

AC-47D (1)—The original application of A to the C-47D was in 1953 when 26 Ds were modified by Hayes Industries for the Airways and Air Communication Service of the Military Air Transport Service (MATS). These were used for checking the electronic navigation aids on the MATS routes. They were redesignated EC-47D in 1965 when a new use for the A-prefix appeared. The notable external feature of the original AC-47D/EC-47D was the extended nose housing additional electronics (Fig. 14-8).

AC-47D (2)—The second AC-47D (originally to have been FC-47D) featured one of the most unusual armament installations fitted to that time on any combat airplane. This was even more unusual in that the heavy firepower was installed in a slow, obsolescent transport over 30 years old

instead of in a newer, more rugged, higher-performance airframe. It was the C-47's very antiquity and low-speed performance that suited it so well to the mission, which was called Tactical Support but was widely understood to mean A-for-Attack. This mission gave the old Gooney Bird a new name—"Puff, the Magic Dragon," after a popular children's song of the time. Another nickname given to the armed AC-47D was "Spooky," its Southeast Asia call sign. The AC-47D story rates a complete book of its own, but here it is in brief:

To increase the time that machine guns could be held on a target, a technique was worked out whereby the fixed guns were mounted laterally in the plane. The pilot then flew an "on-pylon" turn around the target instead of making the usual fast straight-on pass. The guns were something new to fixed-wing aircraft—six-barrel General Electrical 7.62mm miniguns with revolving barrels much like the old Civil War-era Gatling guns.

A battery of three or four of these rapid-fire weapons, presided over by an armorer, was used. Sometimes up to three fired out of the rear windows on the left side, with another in the open door (Figs. 14-9, 14-10). Firing was usually in sequence, controlled by the pilot—a three-second burst from the first, then the second, etc.—or all could be fired at once. The ground target got a near-continuous hosing, but the 7.62mm ammunition didn't have much

Fig. 14-8. AC-47D-5-DK, 43-48783, of Military Air Transport Service (note insignia) with extended radar nose. White fuselage top to reduce solar heating ends above window line; on some other C-47s the white was carried below the windows. Note the border. (William J. Balogh photo via David W. Menard)

Fig. 14-9. Closeup of second use of the AC-47D designation, a gunship in Vietnam. This is a former TC-47B (note old astrodome mounts) with miniguns projecting from the cabin windows. New style of tail serial on camouflage does not check out with last digits of known TC-47B serials. (photo by Robert C. Mikesh)

penetrating power. Normal altitude for this operation was about 1000 feet, which left the slow "Puff" or "Spooky" pretty vulnerable to return fire from protected ground guns. Four squadrons of AC-47Ds were used by the USAF in Vietnam from mid-1965 into 1969, after which these ancient "new" weapons were turned over to the Vietnamese forces, the Air Force opting for bigger AC-130 gunships with 20mm and 40mm guns in addition to the 7.62mm miniguns.

Other special-mission prefixes applied to C-47Ds were E, H, R, S, T, and V, plus J and N for experimental and test conversions.

C-47E—The C-47E designation was also assigned twice:

C-47E (1)—The originally planned use of the C-47E designation was for planned early postwar conversions of C-47s to use 1475-hp Wright R-1820-80 Cyclone engines. The use of such a different engine justified the use of a new series letter (just a few years earlier it would have justified a whole new model number). However, the change was not made.

C-47E (2)—Another engine change resulted in adoption of the C-47E designation in 1953, when Pan American Airways modified eight C-47As and Bs for MATS as airways checkers. Larger Pratt & Whitney R-2000-4 engines out of Douglas C-54s were used, not so much for the increase to 1290 hp, but because the increased generator capacity was needed to run all the electrical equipment. In a few cases, other C-47s were fitted with R-2000 engines without changing the series letter.

Since the C-47Es were created for the airways mission alone, there was no need for a special-purpose prefix.

The R-2000 engine fitted under the same cowlings used for the R-1830s, and C-47Es could be identified visually only by the fact that the propellers were now a few inches farther forward (Fig. 14-11). This change was sometimes reflected by moving the red warning stripe on the fuselage a corresponding distance forward.

YC-47F—The "Super DC3," originally given the

USAF designation YC-129, is covered in Chapter 12.

C-47G—Designation not used.

C-47H—See U.S. Navy designations which follow.

C-47I—The suffix letter I is not used in U.S. Army/Air Force designations.

C-47J through **C-47M**—U.S. Navy designations. See Navy designations below.

C-47N (EC-47N)—The Ns were special electronic countermeasure conversions of C-47As for use in Vietnam (Fig. 14-12). Some of the missions accomplished by these slow unarmed aircraft over enemy territory are still on the secret list.

C-47O—The letter O is not used in U.S. Army/Air Force designations.

C-47P (EC-47P)—The P was an electronic countermeasures conversion of the C-47D similar to that of the EC-47N (Fig. 14-13).

C-47Q (EC-47Q)—The Q is the highest designation assigned to a USAF C-47, and applies to electronic countermeasures conversions similar to the EC-47N and EC-47P (Fig. 14-14). It made no difference whether the airframe had previously been a C-47A or a C-47D; a change to R-2000-4 or -7 engines for their increased electrical output was the controlling factor. Some of each ended up as EC-47Qs.

As on C-47Es, the longer propeller shaft and gearboxes of the R-2000 engines were the only external identifying features, especially when the

Fig. 14-10. Interior view of an AC-47D in Vietnam, showing the rigid mounts of the multi-barrel miniguns that fire through the windows and the open door. (Douglas photo)

Fig. 14-11. C-47E, 43-48906 (note only last five digits of serial), was formerly a C-47B-6-DK, here assigned to diplomatic work. The lettering UNITED STATES AIR MISSION TO THE REPUBLIC OF ECQUADOR is spelled out in both English and Spanish above the windows. Note crossed flags, Day-Glo orange bands on nose and fuselage, and relocation of the red propeller warning stripe farther forward to align with propeller on larger R-2000 engine. (photo by Harry Gann)

designation was eliminated, as was often the case.

POSTWAR U.S. NAVY DESIGNATIONS

In 1962 the U.S. Department of Defense combined the existing U.S. Army/Air Force and U.S. Navy aircraft designations into a new single tri-service system. Where U.S. Navy models duplicated airplanes and missions of the Air Force, the Navy models were given corresponding Air Force designations but with higher series letters. This overlooked the fact that some Navy models were duplicates of existing Air Force models that had simply been given Navy designations (C-47A to R4D-5, etc.).

Navy R4Ds through R4D-7 currently in service received C-47 designations to C-47K. Then the Navy made further modifications on its own that added suffix letters through C-47R. The R4D-8 "Super DC-3s," in spite of their C-47/R4D origins, were redesignated C-117D as detailed in Chapter 12.
C-47H—The C-47Hs were former R4D-5s, with R4D-5Qs becoming EC-47H, R4D-5Ls becoming LC-47H, and R4D-5Zs becoming VC-47H (Fig. 14-15).

Fig. 14-12. An EC-47N, formerly C-47A-70-DL, 42-100665, used for electronic countermeasures in Vietnam. Note new camouflage style and reduced size of star-and-bar insignia on fuselage. (photo by Norman E. Taylor, December 1970)

Fig. 14-13. The EC-47Ps were similar to EC-47Ns except that they were converted from C-47Bs. This is former TC-47B-30-DK, 44-76668. (photo by Norman E. Taylor, April 1971)

Fig. 14-14. This view of EC-47Q-10-DK, 43-49208, shows the extended propeller shafts used on the Pratt & Whitney R-2000 engines that determined the Q series letter. (photo by David W. Menard)

Fig. 14-15. LC-47H serial 17221 redesignated from R4D-5L in Christchurch, New Zealand, after return from Antarctica, December 1967. Top of fuselage is dark gray to absorb solar heat; wings from ailerons outboard and tail section are orange for increased visibility. Fabric surfaces are silver, and remainder of airframe is light gray. (courtesy Jim Sullivan)

Fig. 14-16. R4D-6s like serial 50817 were redesignated C-47J following the designation changes of 1962. (photo by Douglas D. Olson)

C-47J—The C-47Js were former R4D-6s (Fig. 14-16), with the following conversions of Navy suffix letters to new special-purpose prefixes:

R4D-6Q	EC-47J
R4D-6L	LC-47J
R4D-6S	SC-47J
R4D-6R	TC-47J
R4D-6Z	VC-47J

C-47K (TC-47K)—Since the R4D-7s were instrument trainers only, they were designated TC-47K under the new system (Fig. 14-17).

C-47L (EC-47L)—Information is sketchy and contradictory on the C-47Ls. One source ways that these were electronic conversions of R4D-5s and -6s (or C-47H and J) for service in Vietnam, but photos show a lack of antennas and other electronic features while showing markings of planes assigned

Fig. 14-17. The U.S. Navy R4D-7s, formerly Army TC-47Bs, were redesignated TC-47K. Serial 39107 has the original three astrodomes on top of the fuselage and an extended nose cone for airborne radar. Note absence of a black border to the white fuselage coloring. (courtesy Jim Sullivan)

Fig. 14-18. C-47L, 50747, formerly an R4D-6, displaying the American flag used on the tails of U.S. military aircraft assigned to overseas diplomatic service. (Bude Donato photo via Harry Gann)

to diplomatic service. It could be that the electronics were removed and the planes reconverted to transports without changing the designation (Fig. 14-18).

C-47M (EC-47M)—The C-47M is a situation similar to that of the C-47L, with the only available photos showing diplomatic markings rather than electronic details (Fig. 14-19).

C-47R—One C-47M, Navy serial number 99830, was fitted with R-2000-6 engines and redesignated C-47R for naval missions from the high-altitude airfields of Equador.

U.S. ARMY USE

After the U.S. Army Air Forces became the new U.S. Air Force in September 1947, the Army maintained a separate Air Force of its own strictly in support of ground operations. This fleet included some 40 C-47s. However, these were not leavings from the new U.S. Air Force, but were acquired from both the Air Force and the Navy between 1963 and 1972. One, with the highest Army/Air Force serial number assigned to any DC-3, 66-8836, was a former civil-registered DC-3C (ex-Navy R4D-5 serial 1720s) purchased from the U.S. Department of Immigration and Naturalization. Oddly, the former R4D-s obtained from the Navy as C-47H and J retained their Navy serial numbers instead of readopting their original Army serials (Fig. 14-20).

The last U.S. Army C-47H, Navy serial number 12436, was retired to the U.S. Army Museum at

Fig. 14-19. C-47M, 17214, formerly an R4D-5, assigned to diplomatic service in Brazil. Note the erroneous flag application; it should trail to the rear. The mission lettering appears in English and Portuguese on the nose. (photo by Duane Kasulka)

190

Fig. 14-20. This U.S. Army NC-47J was formerly Navy R4D-6 16277, but retained its Navy serial number after transfer. Color is overall white with orange trim. (photo by Robert Esposito)

Ft. Rucker, Alabama, in 1982, making it the last DC-3 to fly for the U.S. armed services.

MISCELLANEOUS MODIFICATIONS

Some modifications were made to individual U.S. and foreign C-47s and Dakotas that did not affect their designations. Some were simple passenger conveniences like enlarged cabin windows and drop-down doors with built-in steps. Others were the aerodynamic refinement kits used by some civil DC-3s, wheel well enclosures, tight engine cowlings, and one-piece windshields. Some carried various blisters, antennae, and external electronics packages, including the extended noses of the original AC-47Ds, for special purposes (Fig. 14-21).

A really odd modification—again without designation change—was the fitting of the radar nose structure of the Lockheed F-104 Starfighter to the nose of C-47s used by the RCAF, the Belgian Air Force, and the new Luftwaffe (Fig. 14-22). This nose contained the target-seeking radar of the F-104. It was connected to the C-47s control system and its presence in a C-47 permitted supervised pilot training in its use. Other radar developed for fighter use was flight-tested in an RAF Dakota (Fig. 14-23).

MAJOR POSTWAR OPERATIONS

The combat life of the C-47 did not end with V-J Day. It soldiered on in other wars, both the shooting kind that brought it under enemy fire, and "cold war" operations in which food and essential survival supplies were the weapons. Some of these are mentioned briefly here:

Fig. 14-21. A C-117D used by the Naval Arctic Research Laboratory under civil registration number N722NR (for Naval Research). Note side-looking radar (SLAR) under the belly. Nose, tail, and wingtips painted orange; top of cabin white, remainder light gray. (photo by Peter M. Bowers, 1977)

Fig. 14-22. A pair of Canadian Forces (changed from RCAF) Dakota IVs fitted with the radar noses of Lockheed F-104 Starfighters for training purposes. Dakotas with such noses were nicknamed "Pinocchio." (Douglas photo)

Berlin Airlift

This was the most prodigious airlift operation of all time, dwarfing the massive "Hump" service to China of 1942-1945.

The three western sectors of the German city of Berlin are associated with West Germany and its allies, but the city is located deep inside Communist East Germany. By treaty, three ground routes were open to the city through East German territory. In a political maneuver of the ongoing "cold war" between the so-called "Western World" and the East European block of Russian-dominated nations behind the Iron Curtain, ground access to West Berlin was cut off on June 26, 1948. No personnel could move into or out of the city except by

air, and essential supplies—including coal as well as foodstuffs—could be brought in only by air. No one, particularly the Russians, believed that a major city could be supported for any length of time, much less the 15 months that passed before the second Battle of Berlin was won. The blockade was lifted September 1, 1949, after the amazing airlift overflew it.

When the need for large-scale airlift became apparent, the job was given to the U.S. Air Force and the RAF. Both services hastily mobilized cargo planes, mostly C-47s and Dakotas, that were in service or storage in Europe, (Fig. 14-24). The USAF started Operation *Vittles* from Weisbaden in the U.S. zone of Germany and the RAF started with *Knicker*, later *Carter Paterson,* and finally *Plainfare*

Fig. 14-23. RAF Dakota III TS423 as a flying test bed for the nose-mounted radar of the British English Electric Lightning fighter. (courtesy Arthur Pearcy)

Fig. 14-24. A mix of camouflaged and natural metal C-47s on the curved ramp of Temple Hof Aerodrome early in the Berlin Airlift. (USAF photo via Douglas)

from the British zone. Altogether, some 105 USAF C-47s and 40 RAF Dakotas were used. The C-47s were soon replaced as faster and greater-capacity C-54s became available, but the Dakotas, although supplemented by larger models, served to the very end and actually carried the last official load into the city.

Korea

The invasion of South Korea by Communist North Korean troops on June 25, 1950, was resisted not only by South Korea but by several other countries of the United Nations (UN) organization in what was called a "Police Action," not a war. The

U.S. was the principal outside participant. This action put the C-47s and R4Ds back in combat in a small-scale continuation of most of their World War II activities. Supply of frontline troops and medical evacuation were major missions, but both the Air Force and the Navy put their unarmed C-47s and R4Ds over enemy territory on paratrooping and leaflet-dropping missions plus flare-drops in support of nighttime ground operations (Fig. 14-25). New missions also emerged with the use of the old Gooney Bird for electronic detection of enemy activity. The USAF also supplied C-47s to the Republic of Korea (ROK) Air Force (Fig. 14-26).

The Korean War ended in June 1953, but the C-47 soldiered on. No suitable direct replacement

Fig. 14-25. A Marine Corps R4D-8 with undersides painted black for night operations over enemy territory in Korea. (photo by Charles N. Trask)

for it was yet available.

French Indochina

During World War II the Japanese occupied all of French Indochina. This territory returned to French control after the war but there was constant trouble with Communist factions and independence movements. French military forces were sent in to deal with them, and C-47s were a mainstay of air operations. When the number available from French stocks was inadequate in 1954, more were obtained on loan from U.S. Air Force bases in the Philippines. In spite of this and other help, the

French forces were defeated; C-47s did heroic work in evacuating wounded and endangered troops from the battle zones (Fig. 14-27).

The French loss resulted in the formation of three new countries—Laos, Cambodia, and Vietnam. The division of Vietnam into two zones—the Communist North and the democratic South, sowed the seeds for a later "unofficial" war involving the C-47.

Malaysia

Britain likewise had troubles in some of its territories that had been occupied by Japan during the

Fig. 14-26. A former USAF VC-47D turned over to the Republic of Korea Air Force but still using its original U.S. serial number, 43-48301. (photo by Charles N. Trask)

Fig. 14-27. C-47D-20-DK, 43-49723, in postwar service with the French Air Force. Some USAF C-47s based in the Philippines were loaned to France for use in Indochina in 1953-54. (courtesy Alain Pelletier)

war. Communist and insurgent activity in Malaysia was serious in 1948, and Dakotas played a major role in the air operations. Some activities were repeats of World War II supply-drop missions and flights into small forward-area airstrips. Also, a new role emerged—the broadcast of voice messages to the insurgents on the ground through loudspeakers installed under slow-flying Dakotas (Fig. 14-28). This operation was so successful that a special flight was formed just for it. Later designs were tried for the work, but none could match the Dakota's performance.

To meet its needs for Dakotas in Malaysia, the RAF acquired 36 DC-3s from the civil register in 1951, issued new RAF serials, and retained these

until 1956. The Malaysian hostilities ended in 1960, with Dakotas active to the end.

Vietnam

In 1962 Communist North Vietnam invaded South Vietnam, and as in Korea, the United Nations rallied to resist. The major role fell to the U.S., however, and again the C-47, plus the civil DC-3, was involved in combat.

Although a 30-year-old design seemingly had no business in a latter-day war, the C-47 not only performed its traditional military role, it took on new ones. In a continuation of some Korean and Malaysian missions, USAF C-47s dropped propaganda leaflets over enemy-held territory (Fig.

Fig. 14-28. An RAF Dakota IV, serial KP277, in postwar coloring fitted with loudspeakers under the center section for broadcasting voice messages to Malaysian insurgents in the early 1950s. (courtesy Arthur Pearcy)

195

14-29). Electronic surveillance with various EC-47s continued, but some were used for electronic countermeasures, jamming enemy radar or providing false targets to enable other aircraft to operate undetected. Some were equipped with infrared cameras and detectors for night photography and reconnaissance.

In Vietnam the C-47 (and the Fairchild C-123) adapted one of its postwar-II civil activities—large-area spraying—to a new form of tactical warfare. The tanks of the C-47 spray planes, which did not receive special-purpose prefixes for the mission, were filled with a defoliating chemical known as Agent Orange. This was sprayed on trees and other vegetation that gave cover to infiltrating Viet Cong guerrillas to strip them of their leaves. This became a very controversial procedure; the Viet Cong accused the U.S. of engaging in chemical warfare but that did not stop the practice. Some U.S. soldiers who came in contact with the chemical are suffering ill effects from it 20 years later and are suing the U.S. government over its use.

By far the most surprising mission given to a 30-year-old unarmed transport was that of a heavily armed attack plane—the AC-47D. After tests in the U.S., the AC-47 was introduced in Vietnam early in 1965 and proved highly successful. An eventual total of 53 was used until the USAF transferred the mission to the South Vietnamese Air Force in 1969, after they were finally replaced by later model Fairchild AC-119s and four-turboprop Lockheed AC-130s. Originally nicknamed "Puff, the Magic Dragon," the AC-47 soon earned the additional nickname (and operational call sign) of "Spooky" because its use of tracer ammunition on night missions, plus its unusual sound, created a very "spooky" effect.

One civil DC-3 set the all-time record for passengers carried when it evacuated 98 orphan children, plus five adult attendants and a crew of three, from DuLat to Saigon on March 23, 1975, as the war was ending.

The USAF provided many aircraft, including C-47s, to the South Vietnamese Air Force throughout the 1962-1975 war. Some of these escaped to neighboring countries during the final advance of the Viet Cong, but many, including intact USAF C-47s, were abandoned to the enemy during the retreat and evacuation.

REARMING FORMER ENEMIES

In an oddity of history, former major enemies of World War II became staunch allies of the U.S.,

Fig. 14-29. A USAF C-47D in the new camouflage adopted during the Vietnam war dropping propaganda leaflets over Viet Cong territory. The leaflets are dispensed through chutes in the side of the fuselage rather than being dumped out an open door as in previous practice. Note absence of fuselage star and use of very small (15-inch) star on upper left wing. (USAF photo)

Fig. 14-30. The new German Luftwaffe of 1956 made good use of C-47s and Dakotas supplied by former enemies. This is C-47D-20-DK, 43-49728, in new Luftwaffe camouflage. The controlling Allies decreed that the new German cross marking should not duplicate those of either World Wars I or II. (courtesy Georg Fischbach)

Britain, and other United Nations in early postwar years. Russia, on the other hand, became a "cold war" adversary.

It soon behooved the victors to lift the initial postwar restrictions on military forces and activities in Germany and Japan. In 1956 Germany was allowed a new Luftwaffe, and among the aircraft supplied by Britain and the U.S. were 20 C-47s and Dakotas. Some of the C-47s were actually former Lend-Lease Dakotas that had been refurbished in British depots in 1954 and returned to U.S. jurisdiction for use in Europe. The new Luftwaffe retained its C-47s and Dakotas until March 1976 (Fig. 14-30).

Similarly, Japan received a mix of C-47s and R4Ds starting in 1958 (Fig. 14-31). These remained in service into 1974.

Fig. 14-31. A rearmed Japan also received DC-3s; both C-47s and R4Ds from the U.S. This is a former R4D-6 painted light gray with orange nose cone, wing and tail tips. (courtesy Hideya Ando)

Fig. 14-32. A United Nations C-47B or Dakota IV in the all-white color scheme used for United Nations mercy flights into militarily unsettled regions. (courtesy Arthur Pearcy)

UNITED NATIONS

While not an actual nation, nor maintaining an air force as such, the United Nations organization (UN) used aircraft in many relief missions to drought-stricken areas of the Third World and to assist in the evacuation of refugees in areas of revolution and political takeover. Many DC-3s and C-47s were used for this work, starting in 1948 and continuing into the late 1950s. These were usually painted overall white with prominent U.N. markings (Fig. 14-32). They were not owned by the UN, but were mostly loaned by the U.S., Britain,

Fig. 14-33. A former RCAF Dakota IV currently used by Britain's Royal Aircraft Establishment at Farnborough. The RCAF serial was used briefly, erroneously prefixed with KG in the belief that it was an original RAF serial. The current RAF serial ZA947 has since been applied. (courtesy Arthur Pearcy)

Italy, and other member nations as needed.

THE IRREPLACEABLE DAKOTA

While the C-47s, and Dakotas ceased to serve in quantity in the major air forces of the world during the 1970s, a few examples carried on in odd jobs to which they were well suited and which other models could not do as well. After the U.S. Navy retired its C-117Ds from stateside service, a few were retained overseas for use by naval attachés and embassy personnel.

A unique example of the indispensability of the C-47/Dakota is a pair used by Britain's Royal Aircraft Establishment (RAE) at Farnborough. After the Dakota was retired from RAF service in 1970,

the RAE had need for two aircraft with its unique capabilities. None were available for transfer from the RAF, so two were purchased from other sources in 1971. One was a Dakota III, formerly TS423, which regained its former RAF serial number. The other was a former RCAF Dakota III, formerly USAAF C-47A-60-DL 42-24338. This had RCAF serial number 661, which was mistakenly applied as KG661 in the belief that it was KG661 of a batch supplied to Canada by Britain (Fig. 14-33). A new RAF serial, ZA947, was soon issued.

ZA947 is now the only military DC-3 operating in Britain, sister ship TS423 having been sold, but it is expected to remain in RAE service until the year 2000.

Chapter 15

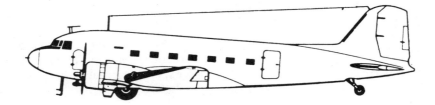

Turboprop DC-3s

Early in World War II, a new type of aircraft powerplant was introduced which reached significant production and combat status by mid-1944. This was the gas turbine, called turbojet or plain "jet" in its aircraft application. Thrust was provided by the high-speed exhaust of low-grade fuel—essentially kerosene—out the tailpipe.

However, jets were most efficient at high speed and required specially designed airframes in which to attain optimum performance. They could not be used as direct substitutes for piston engines in existing aircraft. The gas turbines were made viable for existing aircraft in the speed range of contemporary transports—180 to 250 mph—by gearing the turbine down to drive a conventional propeller. The resulting turbine/propeller combination was called a "turboprop." In some installations, the exhaust could be directed aft to contribute jet thrust. For example, the Rolls-Royce Dart Mark 532 delivers 2108 shaft horsepower through the propeller, plus 496 pounds of jet thrust. One pound of thrust is equivalent to one horsepower at 375 mph, more above that speed and less below.

BRITISH EXPERIMENTS

Two of the leading turboprop manufacturers in the early postwar years were Armstrong-Siddeley and Rolls-Royce, both in England. New airliners designed to use turboprops were on the drawing boards, but none were yet available as test beds for the engines. In order to test their turboprops in flight, both firms resorted to the simple expedient of removing the P & W Twin Wasps from DC-3s and substituting the new turboprops. It should be emphasized here that these conversions were made simply to provide flying test beds for new engines, *not* attempts to improve the DC-3.

Armstong-Siddeley

Armstrong-Siddeley leased a Dakota IV, KJ839, from the RAF and installed two 1400-eshp (equivalent shaft horsepower) Mamba engines in August 1949 (Fig. 15-1). Because the Mamba was so much lighter than the Twin Wasp (approximately 1000 pounds compared to 1450 pounds), it was necessary to install the turboprop considerably

Fig. 15-1. The first turboprop DC-3 was this Dakota IV, KJ839, leased from the RAF in 1949 by Armstrong-Siddeley to use as a flying test bed for the Mamba turboprop engine. Note how much farther forward the turboprops are mounted relative to the standard P & W R-1830s.

farther ahead of the wing than the R-1830 in order to maintain the proper longitudinal balance of the airplane without the need for excessive ballast in the nose. Development of the Mamba for civil use was discontinued but was continued as a military powerplant. KJ839 was soon reconverted to standard configuration.

Rolls-Royce

Rolls-Royce leased another Dakota IV, KJ829, for test of the 1400-eshp Dart turboprop in March 1950. The Darts were installed even farther forward on the airframe than the Mambas, putting the propellers ahead of the cockpit instead of even with it as the Mambas were.

The Dart proved to be eminently successful as a commercial powerplant. It is still in production at this writing (September 1985) and has worked up to 3000 eshp. The early Dart was the intended powerplant for the new Vickers Viscount four-engine 40-59 passenger transports ordered by British European Airways (BEA). To give its pilots

and maintenance personnel experience in turboprop operations before delivery of the Viscounts, BEA got Rolls-Royce to convert two civil Dakota IVs, G-AMDB and G-ALXN, to Dart power (Fig. 15-2). These were used on scheduled BEA services between England and the continent for over two years. Because of their experimental nature, they did not carry passengers. Both were eventually reconverted to piston power.

Rolls-Royce, meanwhile, bought KJ829 from the RAF for further use as a Dart test bed. It received registration G-37-1, the "B" registration given to experimental aircraft. This was later replaced by the normal registration G-AOXI, still with Darts. It was retired in April 1963 without engines and was used as a source of spare parts for other DC-3s.

AMERICAN EXPERIMENTS

John Conroy Projects

The first attempt to use turboprops to improve the performance of the DC-3 was an American ef-

Fig. 15-2. Rolls-Royce also leased a Dakota IV from the RAF to flight test the Dart turboprop engine and later converted two civil-registered IVs for British European Airways to use for crew and maintenance training in an airline environment. Note that the propellers are farther forward than on the Mamba conversion. (courtesy F.G. Swanborough)

fort by John M. Conroy, who was no stranger to surprising aircraft modifications. It was he who developed the huge fuselage modifications to Boeing Stratocruiser airliners to create the Pregnant Guppy and other Guppy oversize cargo carriers.

The Turbo-Three

In January 1968, Conroy, operating under his own company name of Conroy Aircraft Corporation of Santa Barbara, California, obtained former C-53

41-20133, which had been used by TWA as NC44783 and had flown under new registrations N2001 and N700CC subsequently. Conroy acquired still another registration for it, N4700C (C for Conroy). He then bought four 1650-hp Rolls-Royce Dart Mark 510 engines from a retired Vickers Viscount and installed them in N4700C to drive four-bladed propellers (Fig. 15-3).

The Conroy Turbo-Three was far more than a simple engine change on a DC-3. Conroy an-

Fig. 15-3. The first American turboprop DC-3 was the Conroy Turbo-Three of 1968 that used Rolls-Royce Dart engines from a surplus Vickers Viscount airliner in a deliberate effort to improve the performance and service life of the DC-3. N4700C is a former C-53, 41-20133. Note that the propellers are ahead of the cockpit. (photo by Don Downie)

ticipated a gross weight increase to 32,000 pounds. This required the installation of a new "heavy" landing gear required for DC-3s operating with maximum landing weights above 26,900 pounds. Since the takeoff weight was more than 105 percent of the approved maximum landing weight, it was necessary to add a fuel jettison system. To give the Turbo-Three transoceanic range, Conroy increased the fuel capacity from 822 U.S. gallons to a maximum of 1922 by the addition of tanks in the outer wing panels.

Although Conroy hoped to get the Turbo-Three approved for 1600-hp engines, initial testing was done with the Darts derated to 1350 hp to stay within existing DC-3 operating limits. One important detail dictated by the FAA was that the propellers could not be in line with the crew or the cockpit controls, as they were on the Mamba installation. The propellers on the Turbo-Three were ahead of the cockpit, as on the British Dart installations.

It was intended that the Dart conversion for DC-3s would be available at the Conroy plant or by kit for conversion in the owner's own shop. Estimated conversion time was 30 days.

The first flight of the Turbo-Three was on May 13, 1969, and after a relatively short checkout period was flown to the Paris Air Show. The performance increase was impressive—a cruising speed of 215 mph at a gross weight of 32,000 pounds. Range with the normal fuel load of 822 gallons was 940 miles; with 1922 gallons it was 2250 miles.

In spite of an intensive 23-country sales campaign and the promise of an improved-performance DC-3 at reasonable cost that could be certificated under a supplement to ATC A-669, neither the airlines nor the FAA took a favorable view of a 1935-technology airliner with 1949 engines in 1969. The Turbo-Three was never certificated and no similar conversions were sold. However, the airframe was to undergo further turbine experiments as the Tri Turbo-Three in later years.

Super Turbo-Three

The next Conroy turboprop DC-3 effort was

undertaken on behalf of a potential customer, the Western Company of North America. The third production DC-3S Super DC-3, C/N 43193, was obtained from its third postwar owner as a DC-3S (previous registrations as DC-3S were N16012, N5425, and N111SA before becoming N156WC for Western Company). The DC-3S airframe was left largely intact, with the installation of 1742 eshp Dart Mark 510 engines. Because of the existing nose stretch of the DC-3S airframe, the propellers were located well aft of the cockpit, practically in the standard DC-3 position relative to the crew (Fig. 15-4).

In addition to the 800 gallons in the four center section tanks, there was one 210 gallon tank and one 200 gallon tank in each outer wing panel. Gross weight for takeoff was 31,900 pounds and for landing was 30,400 pounds.

This time the Super Turbo-Three was certificated on a one-only basis under Supplemental Type Certificate (STC) SA3241WE awarded August 18, 1976 to DC-3S ATC 6A2. One-Time certifications are for conversions made from what are in effect prototype drawings. For the STC to be approved for conversions of the basic airframe by others, the drawings have to be available in ready-to-use form. On September 8, 1978, STC 3241WE was amended in the name of later owner Pilgrim Airlines to allow a change to 2108 eshp Dart Mark 532-2L engines. In FAA records the Super Turbo-Three is only a modified DC-3S.

The Super Turbo-Three was sold to Pilgrim Aviation, operators of Pilgrim Airlines, and the registration was changed to N156PM. There is no record of N165PM's use by the airline or any subsequent owner.

Tri-Turbo-3

By 1976 John Conroy had a new firm, the Specialized Aircraft Company, located at Camarillo, California. His next turbine DC-3 effort was the conversion of the original Turbo-Three airframe to a trimotor, with new 1174 eshp Pratt & Whitney of Canada PT6A-45 Turboprops, two in the conventional nacelles and the third in an extended nose. This time the side propellers, now with five blades,

Fig. 15-4. The third DC-3S, or "Super DC-3," was also converted to Dart turboprops by Conroy and received a Supplemental Type Certificate for commercial operation. Note that the propellers are aft of the cockpit because of the longer DC-3S nose. In spite of being designated Super Turbo-Three by Conroy, this airplane was simply a modified DC-3S in FAA records. (photo by William T. Larkins)

Fig. 15-5. In 1977 John Conroy converted the former Turbo-Three to the Tri-Turbo-3 trimotor with new Pratt & Whitney of Canada PT-6A turboprops, but tried in vain to sell it as a maritime patrol and rescue plane. Note the extended nose and the short nacelles that keep the side propellers aft of the cockpit. (photo by John W. Underwood)

were located aft of the cockpit. The registration was changed to N23SA, for Specialized Aircraft (Fig. 15-5).

The use of three engines was not intended to be a steady-state condition; the center engine would be used for takeoff, climb, and high-speed cruise, but would be shut down with the propeller feathered for extended cruising. The weight saved by the lighter engines allowed a payload increase to 12,000 pounds. Cruising speed on three engines was 220 mph at 5000 feet and 230 mph at 10,000 feet. On two engines the cruise was 180 mph. Range on three engines at normal cruising speed was 1135 miles and on two was 1395. Extended ranges were 2700 miles and 3200 miles for three and two engines, respectively.

First flight of the Tri-Turbo-3 was on November 2, 1977. An intensive sales campaign to sell the airplane for maritime search and rescue missions was unsuccessful even though it was demonstrated at the Paris Air Show. Most of the world's air forces were retiring their DC-3s from major missions and were not interested in refurbished DC-3s as first-line equipment, nor were the airlines.

The Tri-Turbo-3 was never certificated. Getting approval for a change to a different type of engine in an airplane was a fairly straightforward procedure. Getting approval for a change in the *number* of engines as well involved a whole new set of rules. Extra engines mean high stress concen-trations in areas not previously designed for them. Major structural changes have to be made and verified by analysis and test. Further, changes in the location of thrust lines could have serious effects on airplane trim that control surfaces designed for a different arrangement might not be able to handle.

Although uncertificated, the Tri-Turbo-3 was sold to Santa Barbara Polair, Inc., on August 20, 1979, but has not been put to any regular use (Fig. 15-6). It appears in FAA records as a modified DC-3A-SIC3G.

DC-3 Turbo Express

The most recent—and most successful—DC-3 turbo conversion is the DC-3 Turbo Express (sometimes called DC-3-TP), produced in 1982 by the United States Aircraft Corporation (USAC) of Van Nuys, California. USAC took former RCAF Dakota IV KK160 for conversion. This had carried postwar U.S. civil registration N502PA but was reregistered N300TX by USAC.

In order to maintain balance with the lighter 1254-eshp P & W of Canada PT6A-45R turboprops, the DC-3 Turbo Express was fitted with a plug in the forward fuselage just ahead of the wing that extended the nose by 40 inches (Fig. 15-7). This kept the propellers well aft of the cockpit as on Super DC-3s.

Other changes included an entirely new electrical system with 300-ampere starter-generators,

Fig. 15-6. The Tri-Turbo-3 was never certificated for commercial operation but was sold to Santa Barbara Polair Corporation in 1979 and has continued to fly on an Experimental license. (photo by Peter M. Bowers)

Fig. 15-7. The latest turbine conversion of the DC-3 is the DC-3 Turbo Express, or DC-3-TP, developed by the United States Aircraft Corporation in 1983. A 40-inch nose extension overcomes the balance problems of the lightweight PT6A engines and allows the propellers to be positioned aft of the cockpit. (courtesy *The Western Flyer*)

modified wing leading edges, squared-off wingtips *a la* DC-3S, enlarged and squared-off horizontal tail, modified hydraulic system, new solid-state elec-

tronics, and improved instrumentation (Fig. 15-8).

With the fuselage extension, the interior length of the cabin was increased but passenger seating

Fig. 15-8. Flight view of the DC-3 Turbo Express, a former Dakota IV, shows off the squared wingtips and the extended horizontal tail. Although it was the second turboprop DC-3 to receive an STC for commercial operation, it was the first to be used for revenue passenger service. (courtesy *The Western Flyer*)

was limited to 30. The C-47 cargo door was retained. STC SA2221NM was issued as a supplement to ATC A-669 on December 1, 1983, on a "one airplane only" basis. Gross weight remains at 26,900 pounds and the usable fuel at 741.0 gallons in the 800-gallon tank total. With wing structure reinforcement, the fast-range cruising speed is 236 mph. The DC-3-TP appears in FAA records as a modified C-47B.

The prototype DC-3-TP was sold to Harold's Air Service of Fairbanks, Alaska, and has been put in revenue passenger service, the first for a turbine-powered DC-3. Harold's Air Service is scheduled at this writing to receive the second DC-3-TP, after which the STC should be available for other DC-3 operators.

Chapter 16

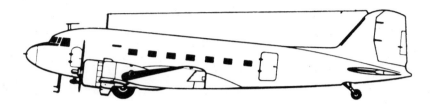

DC-3 Monuments
and Museum Pieces

In the second postwar-II decade, when the historical significance of the DC-3 was really beginning to be appreciated, concerned individuals and organizations began serious efforts to preserve some of the still readily available examples for posterity. Over succeeding years, these preserved DC-3s have been seen in three principal places—established civil or military museums, park or airport displays, and as the property of organizations that maintain them in flying condition for appearance at air shows.

MUSEUMS

Established museums are by far the safest havens for retired DC-3s, since many are either displayed indoors or are parked outdoors in sheltered areas that protect them from violent windstorms. Vandalism is greatly reduced for such enclosed or close-in exhibits, and outdoor exhibits are usually kept clean.

The most highly visible DC-3 in the world is a retired Eastern Air Lines DC-3-201, N18124. This was delivered to Eastern on December 7, 1937, and remained with the airline until its retirement with 56,782 flight hours in September 1952. It was donated to the Smithsonian Institution in May 1953.

Since July 1976, with the opening of the National Air and Space Museum (NASM) on the Mall in Washington, it has hung in the Air Transportation Gallery in the company of other notable transports (Fig. 16-1). The NASM is the most popular tourist attraction in Washington, being visited by some 15 million people a year.

In 1975, a U.S. regional airline, North Central, donated what was then the world's highest-time airplane to the Ford Museum at Dearborn, Michigan (Fig. 16-2). A former Eastern Air Lines DC-3-201B, NC21728, later passed to Wisconsin Central and then to North Central, had accumulated 83,454 flying hours to its retirement.

In May 1966, a DC-3C, N56589 (formerly C-47A-85-DL 43-15512), was donated to the Oregon Museum of Science and Industry (OMSI) in Portland by West Coast Airlines. The plane had a total of 32,181 flight hours to its retirement in 1963

Fig. 16-1. An Eastern Air Lines DC-3-201, N18124, suspended in the Air Transportation Gallery of the National Air & Space Museum in company with such other famous airliners as the Ford Trimotor and the Boeing 247D. (National Air & Space Museum photo courtesy Jay Spenser)

Fig. 16-2. At the time it was donated to the Ford Museum in 1975, North Central Airlines' DC-3-201B had more flying time than any airplane in the world—83,454 hours. Cowling flaps for Cyclone engine are a postwar addition, along with windshield, window, and door modifications. (North Central Airlines photo courtesy Kent Kistler)

and had seen service with the 89th Troop Carrier Command in the invasion of Normandy.

In a unique arrangement, this plane actually became a room of the museum. It was parked alongside the main building, and an enclosed brick passageway was built from the building to the cabin door (Fig. 16-3). A fence on the ground protects the plane from external vandalism.

Getting the DC-3C to the museum was a major task; it was not simply towed on its own wheels to the facility from a nearby airport as was the case with the Eastern/NASM DC-3 and others. The West Coast DC-3C was dismantled at Boeing Field, Seattle, Washington, some 140 road miles away. The fuselage was taken off of the center section and loaded on a long trailer for the highway trip.

By 1982 the old DC-3C with its West Coast markings had become quite weather-worn, so OMSI asked Hughes Air West, which was a successor organization to West Coast, if it could provide a new paint job. This it did, so the DC-3 now displays Hughes Air West markings—colors that it never carried in its flying days.

Another DC-3, Union Oil Company of California's N760, had a dual museum career. Formerly TWA's DC-3-362 from 1941-1950, it was owned by Union for the next 31 years. In its last few, with Union paying the cost, it was loaned to the California Museum of Science and Industry in Los Angeles. The Museum used it for six field trips a year, bringing museum exhibits to schoolchildren in remote parts of the state. When Union retired N760 in July, 1982, it was donated to the museum. Mindful of how fabric deteriorates when left in the open, Union weatherproofed the plane by replacing the fabric with sheet aluminum and applied a weather-resistant new paint job. The DC-3 was then towed on its own wheels to the museum site 28 miles from its Burbank hangar (Fig. 16-4). After reassembly in the Denney Air and Space Garden, the 43-year-old airplane was ceremoniously dedicated as a museum exhibit on July 12, 1984.

Another unique delivery problem was encountered by the Royal Australian Air Force (RAAF) Dakota that the Australian government donated to the Berlin museum as a memorial to the 1948-49 Berlin Air Lift. Since the RAAF no longer had permission to fly the controlled corridors into Berlin through Communist-dominated territory, the Dakota was repainted with temporary RAF markings and given a new RAF serial number, ZD215, just for its one final flight (Fig. 16-5).

Fig. 16-3. Hughes Airwest DC-3C, N56598, formerly C-47A-85-DL, 43-15512, is actually a room of the Oregon Museum of Science & Industry. A brick passageway leads from the main museum building to the airplane. Note that the tail has been raised so that the cabin floor is level. (photo by Peter M. Bowers, September 1985)

Fig. 16-4. The DC-3-362, donated to the California Museum of Science and Industry by the Union Oil Company, was towed on its own wheels 28 miles from its last airport to the museum site. (photo by Robert Beechler)

Fig. 16-5. Since Australia no longer had clearance to fly the controlled air corridors into Berlin, the Dakota IV that it donated to the Berlin Museum had to be given an official RAF serial number for its last flight. (courtesy Arthur Pearcy)

AIRPORT/AIRBASE DISPLAYS

Most of the non-flying display DC-3s are to be found on established civil airports or military air bases, with a few in parks or other public areas. These are often called "Gate Guardians" after the practice of setting up smaller fighter-type airplanes near the gates of military bases.

Unfortunately, many of these, once parked, are sadly neglected. They become roosts for pigeons and other birds, the tires go flat if the axles are not supported, the finish deteriorates, and weeds grow up around the landing gear if the plane is not parked on concrete (Figs. 16-6 and 16-7). They become eyesores, not the historic monuments that they were intended to be.

The opposite situation prevails at some Air Force and Naval Air Bases, where a portion of the flight line or a nearby open area is set aside for the display of aircraft belonging to an official Base Museum or Historical Office (Fig. 16-8). Manpower, either duty or volunteer, is available to keep the display aircraft presentable.

An example is the TC-47B/D-25-DK 44-76502 displayed with other museum aircraft at McChord Air Force Base, Tacoma, Washington. This is an example of an airplane that did not see WWII action being painted as one that did. The markings are those of a 12th Air Force C-47-DL, 41-18456, that served in Italy, was loaned out for service in the China-Burma-India Theatre, and also participated in the northern Europe invasions. The markings are as authentic as conscientious research can make them, but the Army serial number on the tail is that of the actual TC-47B (Fig. 16-9).

Although built as a TC-47B, records show that this C-47 was loaned to the French Air Force after World War II and saw action in Indochina. After that, it served in the South Vietnamese Air Force. Upon return to the U.S., still in VNAF markings and camouflage, it became the property of the USAF Museum and was put in long-term storage at Davis-Monthan AFB at Tuscon, Arizona. When it was loaned to McChord AFB in 1985 for the new museum there, it was no longer airworthy. It was airlifted to McChord in a giant USAF C-5A transport. It has been restored to the point where it could be flown again, but will remain grounded because of restrictions imposed by the USAF museum on loaned property.

Before the TC-47 was airlifted to McChord Field (Fig. 16-10) a team of volunteer workers travelled to Davis-Monthan to start work on it. As an example of a change of procedure dictated by current environmental considerations and avoidance of pollution, the old paint had to be removed the hard way—by sandpaper. There were no drainage facilities where the plane was parked so the old method of removing the paint with many gallons of liquid cleaner could not be followed.

More in keeping with the "Gate Guardian" con-

Fig. 16-6. This former C-47 in non-regulation blue and white colors is displayed adjacent to the Interstate Highway running past the airport at Bellingham, Washington. The plane is a shell, with no engines and no glass in the windows; sheet fiberglass replaces some of the tail fabric. (photo by Peter M. Bowers, September 1985)

Fig. 16-7. Closeup of the Bellingham C-47, showing the plywood plugs in the cowling openings with painted-on engine pushrods. The propellers are supported by iron pipes. Note the empty exhaust pipe channels. (photo by Peter M. Bowers, September 1985)

Fig. 16-8. C-47A-30-DK, 43-48098, on display near the flight line at Offut Air Force Base, Omaha, Nebraska. The use of Normandy invasion stripes is a popular way of dressing up otherwise dull camouflaged C-47s. Marking oddities are the undersize fuselage star and the use of the post-1953 0-prefix for an airplane more than 10 years old on one painted to represent the specific period of June 1944. (photo by Jack Binder)

Fig. 16-9. TC-47B-25-DT, 44-76502, in a park area of McChord Air Force Base, Tacoma, Washington. The markings and reduced-area invasion stripes were obtained from photos of the C-47-DL that carried them; the only unauthentic detail is the use of the airplane's own serial number. (photo by Peter M. Bowers, September, 1985)

cept is the mounting of the complete airplane on a pylon or other structure that puts it above the ground with its landing gear retracted in an attitude of flight (Fig. 16-11). One very practical application of pylon mounting is DC-3C CF-CPY, formerly C-47-DL 41-18540. This was donated by Canadian Pacific Airlines to the city of Whitehorse, Yukon Territory, in 1979, and was set up on a swivel post so it could swing with the wind to serve as the wind tee for the airport (Fig. 16-12).

FLYING MUSEUM PIECES

In contrast to the static museum and airport exhibits, there is another category of display aircraft—the flying museum piece. Many DC-3s are to be found in this category today. Since a DC-3 is too much airplane for an individual to maintain and operate as a hobby, most of those operating as flying museum pieces are owned by established museums or groups of associated individuals who form nonprofit corporations for tax relief, liability

Fig. 16-10. The last flight of the McChord A.F.B. Museum TC-47 was inside a giant Lockheed C-5A "Galaxy" transport. Note that the fuselage has been removed from the center section and that the original 1942 primer paint is now revealed where the wing root fillet has been removed.

Fig. 16-11. A good way to display airplanes is on posts well above the reach of vandals. This is former Dakota IV, KN241, now P2-ANQ of Air Niugini, on display at Port Morseby, Papua-New Guinea. (courtesy Gordon S. Williams)

Fig. 16-12. Former C-47-DL, 41-18540, is a non-flying display item that still serves a useful purpose. As Canadian Pacific Airlines' CF-CPY, it was donated to the city of Whitehorse, Yukon Territory, and was mounted on a free-swivelling post to serve as the wind tee at the airport. (photo by Gordon S. Williams)

insurance, etc. Some function as chapters of the Warbirds of America organization, which is concerned primarily with the preservation and flying of World War II military aircraft. A separate and world-famous organization is the Confederate Air Force (CAF) headquartered at Harlingen, Texas, with affiliated chapters throughout the United States and Canada. In addition to mounting a massive annual air show at Harlingen, the CAF flies some of its aircraft, including C-47s in Normandy invasion markings, to major airshows elsewhere (Fig. 16-13).

DC-3 MISCELLANY

Other DC-3s that are not specifically museum pieces can be found throughout the world, either in whole or in part, serving all sorts of miscellaneous purposes from lunchrooms to hen-coops and even human residences. One oddity worthy of mention is the fuselage of DC-3C/C-47A-20-DK N142A/42-92933, which was converted to a motor home by Mr. "Smoky" Roland of Cardiff-on-the-Sea, California (Fig. 16-14). Shortened at the tail to comply with California highway requirements, this was mounted on a Chevrolet truck chassis and powered with an engine from a Lincoln automobile. Although roomy and comfortable, the rolling DC-3 was uneconomical, getting only 7.75 miles per gallon of fuel.

Other oddities occur unexpectedly. Nature provided a temporary pedestal mount for one USAF C-47, unfortunately far from public view. The belly-landed plane was abandoned at an ice station in the Arctic Ocean. Over a period of years, the adjacent snow was blown away. However, the snow directly beneath the plane was compacted by its weight.

Fig. 16-13. Flying museum pieces of the Confederate Air Force in a fly-by at a 1977 air show. "Z" is a 1939 DC-3-201B still carrying its original registration of NC21729. "N" is former C-47A-20-DK, 42-92999, displaying tail number 42-100588. Note different applications of invasion stripes. (photo by Frederick A. Johnsen)

Fig. 16-14. The shortened fuselage of former C-47A-20-DK, 42-92933, later DC-3C, N142A, was mounted on a truck chassis and fitted out as a motor home by Mr. "Smoky" Roland. (courtesy of Arthur Pearcy)

The higher density of this compressed snow resisted the wind and formed an ice pedestal that supported the nearly intact C-47.

AIRBORNE AD INFINITUM

While some of the museum DC-3s can be expected to survive for many years, even centuries, into the future, one organization is taking steps to ensure that one DC-3 will be flying far into the 21st century.

In a move that reflects great confidence in future world conditions as well as a desire to perpetuate the memory of the DC-3, the Dutch Dakota Association, one of several DC-3 aficionado groups throughout the world, is "pickling" a DC-3 for future flights.

The Association bought a former Finnish Air Force C-47 and is placing it in a weatherproof and fireproof hangar until the year 2010, the 75th anniversary of the DC-3. It will then be reassembled and flown, after which it will be returned to storage until 2035, the 100th anniversary. Hopefully, this process will be repeated for every 25 years, or as long as the famous plane will fly.

Considering that some centuries-old machinery is operable today for display purposes, there is no reason why the Dutch plan should not succeed. Certainly the structure can remain airworthy, and only such components as tires, fabric, and seals, which deteriorate with time regardless of use, will need to be replaced.

Appendix A

Specifications and Performance: DC-1, DC-2, DC-3

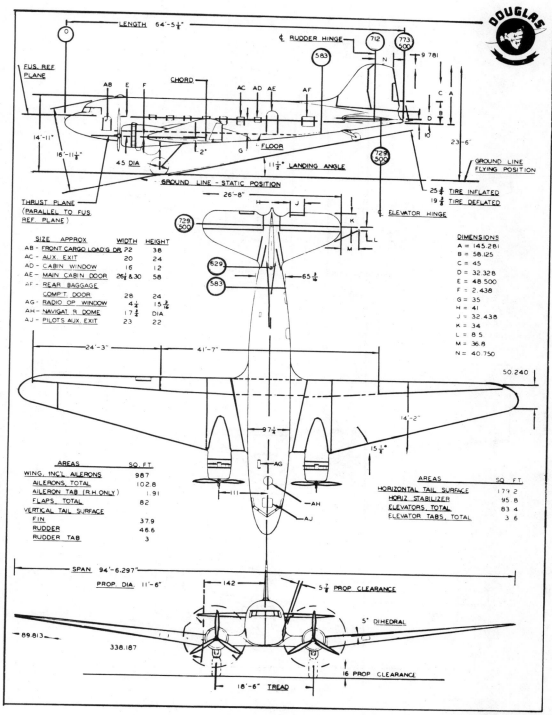

LENGTH 64'-5⅛"

DOUGLAS

℄ RUDDER HINGE

712   773
       500

583

9 781

FUS. REF
PLANE

CHORD

O

AB E F

AC AD AE   AF

N

C A
B
D

14'-11"

16'-11⅛"

45 DIA

2'   G   FLOOR

11½° LANDING ANGLE

729
500

23'-6"

GROUND LINE
FLYING POSITION

THRUST PLANE
(PARALLEL TO FUS.
REF. PLANE)

GROUND LINE - STATIC POSITION

26'-8"

H   J

K

L

M

729
500

℄ ELEVATOR HINGE

25⅞ TIRE INFLATED
19⅞ TIRE DEFLATED

SIZE APPROX	WIDTH	HEIGHT
AB - FRONT CARGO LOAD'G DR	72	38
AC - AUX. EXIT	20	24
AD - CABIN WINDOW	16	12
AE - MAIN CABIN DOOR	26¼ & 30	58
AF - REAR BAGGAGE		
COMP'T. DOOR	28	24
AG - RADIO OP. WINDOW	4¼	15 3/16
AH - NAVIGAT. R. DOME	17¼	DIA
AJ - PILOTS AUX. EXIT	23	22

629

583

65 3/16

DIMENSIONS

A = 145.281
B = 58.125
C = 45
D = 32.328
E = 48.500
F = 2.438
G = 35
H = 41
J = 32.438
K = 34
L = 8.5
M = 36.8
N = 40.750

24'-3"

41'-7"

50.240

14'-2"

9 7¼

15 ½°

AREAS	SQ. FT.
WING, INC'L. AILERONS	987
AILERONS, TOTAL	102.8
AILERON TAB (R.H. ONLY)	1.91
FLAPS, TOTAL	82
VERTICAL TAIL SURFACE	
FIN	37.9
RUDDER	46.6
RUDDER TAB	3

AG

AH

AJ

AREAS	SQ. FT.
HORIZONTAL TAIL SURFACE	179.2
HORIZ. STABILIZER	95.8
ELEVATORS, TOTAL	83.4
ELEVATOR TABS, TOTAL	3.6

SPAN 94'-6.297"

PROP. DIA. 11'-6"

142

5⅞ PROP CLEARANCE

5° DIHEDRAL

89.813

338.187

16 PROP CLEARANCE

18'-6" TREAD

PREPARED BY PRODUCTION ILLUSTRATION - F. KELLOGG -12-15-43

MODEL C-53

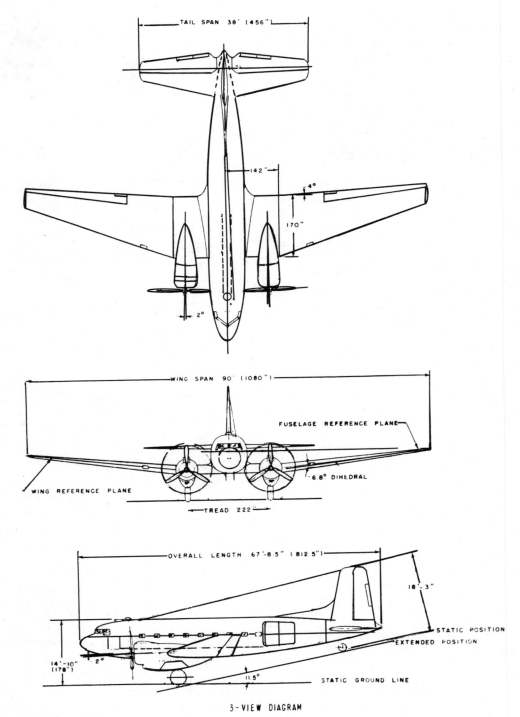

TAIL SPAN 38' (456")

142"

4°

170"

2°

WING SPAN 90' (1080")

FUSELAGE REFERENCE PLANE

6.8° DIHEDRAL

WING REFERENCE PLANE

TREAD 222"

OVERALL LENGTH 67'-8.5" (812.5")

18'-3"

STATIC POSITION

EXTENDED POSITION

14'-10"
(178")

2°

11.5°

STATIC GROUND LINE

3-VIEW DIAGRAM

SUPER DC-3

Table A-1.

	DC-1	DC-2	DST	DC-3A	C-47A	C-47B	DC-3S
Powerplant (Takeoff hp)	Wright SGR-1820-F3 "Cyclone" 710	Wright SGR-1820-3 "Cyclone" 710	Wright SGR-1820-G2 "Cyclone" 1000	Pratt & Whitney SIC3-G "Twin Wasp" 1050	Pratt & Whitney R-1830-92 1200	Pratt & Whitney R-1830-90C 1200	Wright R-1820-694E "Cyclone" 1475
Accommodation	2 crew 12 passengers	3 crew 14 passengers	3 crew 14 passengers	3 crew 21 passengers	2 crew variable	2 crew variable	3 crew 30-38 passengers
Wing Span (ft-in)	85-0	85-0	95-0	95-0	95-6	95-6	90-0
Wing Area (sq ft)	942	939	987	987	987	987	969
Length (ft-in)	60-0	61-11 3/4	64-5 1/2	64-5 1/2	63-9	63-9	67-9
Empty Weight (lb)	11,780	12,408	16,060	16,865	17,865	18,135	19,537
Gross Weight (lb)	17,500	18,560	24,000	25,200	26,000	26,000	31,000
Wing Loading (lb/sq ft)	18.6	19.8	24.3	25.5	26.3	26.3	32.0
Power Loading (lb/hp)	12.3	12.2	12.0	10.5	10.8	10.8	10.5
Maximum Speed (mph)	210	210 @ 8000 ft	212 @ 6800 ft	230 @ 8500 ft	230 @ 8000 ft	224 @ 10,000 ft	270 @ 5900 ft
Cruising Speed (mph)	190 @ 8000 ft	190 @ 8000 ft	192	207	160	160	251
Initial Rate of Climb (ft/min)	1050	1000	850	1130	10,000 ft in 9.6 min.	10,000 ft in 9.5 min.	1300
Service Ceiling (ft)	23,000	22,450	20,800	23,000	24,000	26,400	—
Normal range (Statute Mi)	1000	1000	1000+	2125	1600	1600	—
Maximum Range (Statute Mi)	—	—	—	—	3800	3600	2500

Appendix B

DC-3 Production by Douglas

Civil Orders (1)

Model	Quantity	Plant
DST	21	Santa Monica
DST-A	19	Santa Monica
DC-3	361 (2)	Santa Monica
DC-3A	170 (2)	Santa Monica
DC-3B	10	Santa Monica
DC-3D	28	Oklahoma City
Total	609	

Military Orders

C-41	1	Santa Monica
C-41A	1	Santa Monica
C-47	965	Long Beach
C-47A	2954	Long Beach
C-47A	2300	Oklahoma City
C-47B	300	Long Beach
C-47B	3064	Oklahoma City
C-53	219	Santa Monica
C-53D	159	Santa Monica
C-117A	17	Oklahoma City
R4D-1	66	Long Beach
Total	10,046	

(1) These figures represent civil aircraft ordered, not all of which were delivered to the original customers. They include 149 civil orders requisitioned by the military while still in the factory, some of which were completed with major interior changes for military operations.

(2) Adjusted figures, including military requisitions in the factory and some aircraft ordered as DC-3 but completed as DC-3A following engine change for the military or a different customer.

DC-3 Production by Douglas Plant

Santa Monica	961
Long Beach	4285
Oklahoma City	5409
Total	10,655

Appendix C

Douglas DST/DC-3 Approved Type Certificates, Designations, and Customers

This appendix lists all civil DSTs and DC-3s in sequence of their original Approved Type Certificate (ATC) issuances. The airplanes are then listed under the appropriate ATC in order of their factory-assigned dash numbers, quantities built, and original purchaser regardless of actual sequence of procurement. The numbers listed under Quantity do not necessarily represent solid production runs with consecutive C/Ns, or even procurement on the same contract. For example, the 12 DC-3A-197s built for United Air Lines under ATC A-619 were delivered in three blocks—five, five, and two airplanes each. Other DC-3s and DSTs with different dash numbers and ATCs were built in between United's DC-3A-197s.

The military variants of the DC-3 all had DC-3-numbers, which appear in the appropriate text. Following postwar modification, C-47s and R4Ds were designated DC-3C under ATC A-669 while C-53s reverted to DC-3A. The C-117s completed as DC-3D without dash number were also certificated under ATC A-669. The R4D-8s redesignated C-117D were licensed under ATC 6A-2 as DC-3S, again without dash number.

The FAA certificated DC-3s by the Douglas-assigned designations of DC-3, DC-3A, etc., plus the model of engine installed. As engines were improved, or later series installed, the ATC was amended to allow the use of the new or upgraded engine. Some of the changes resulting in new engine designations were quite minor, as Pratt & Whitney R-1830-SCG and SC3G Twin Wasps becoming S1CG and S1C3G, respectively, when the ignition timing was changed from 20 to 25 degrees before TDC for operation on 90-octane fuel instead of the original 80-octane.

DC-3s and DSTs drafted by the U.S. Army after they were in airline service are indicated in the Remarks column by their Army designations and (A). Those drafted in the factory before delivery to the airlines are indicated by (F). Aircraft fitted with right-hand doors are identified by RHD.

For brevity, most airline names in the Customer column have been abbreviated. The abbreviations used are spelled out on the following pages:

AA	American Airlines, Inc.
ABA	AB Aerotransport (Sweden)
ANA	Australian National Airways, Pty.
CAL	Continental Air Lines, Inc.
CC	Canadian Colonial Airways, Inc. (U.S.A.)
CLS	Ceskoslovenska Latecka Spolecnost (Czechoslovakia)
CNAC	China National Aviation Corp.
C&S	Chicago & Southern Airlines, Inc.
EAL	Eastern Air Lines, Inc.
CAA	Civil Aeronautics Authority (then)
IIA	Inter Island Airlines (Hawaii)
KLM	Koninklijke Luchtvaart Maatschappi N.v. (Holland)
LARES	Linile Aeriene Romane Explotate cu Statul (Romania)
NEA	Northeast Airlines, Inc.
NWA	Northwest Airlines, Inc.
PAA	Pan American Airways, Inc.
PANAGRA	Pan American Grace Airways, Inc.
PCA	Pennsylvania Central Airlines Corp.
TWA	Trans World Airlines, Inc.
UAL	United Air Lines, Inc.
WAL	Western Air Lines (then Western Air Express)

ATC A-607—DST-G2 (1)

Power and Weight Approvals:

Wright GR-1820	-G2	1000 hp	24,000 lb.	May 21, 1936
	-G102	1100 hp	25,000 lb.	Sep. 24, 1937
	-G103	1100 hp	24,000 lb.	Feb. 25, 1938
	-G2E	1000 hp	24,000 lb.	Mar. 1, 1939
	-202A	1200 hp	25,000 lb.	May 31, 1940

DST Dash No.	Quantity	Customer	Remarks
-144	8	AA (2)	RHD, all to C-49E (A)
-217	1	AA	RHD, to C-49E (A)
-217A	2	AA	RHD, all to C-49E (A)
-217B	2	AA	RHD, all to C-49E (A)
-217C	2	AA	RHD, all to C-49E (A)
-318	3	EAL	RHD, 2 to C-49F (A)
-318A	2	EAL	RHD, 1 to C-49F (A)
-406	1	EAL	RHD, to C-49F (A)
	Total 21		

(1) All eligible for operation under ATC A-618 when converted to dayplanes.
(2) Identified and advertised as "Flagship Skysleeper."

ATC A-618—DC-3-G2

Power and Weight Approvals:

Wright GR-1820	-G2 "Cyclone"	1000 hp	24,000 lb.	Aug. 27, 1936
	-G102	1100 hp	25,200 lb.	Sep. 20, 1937
	-G103	1000 hp	24,000 lb.	Nov. 4, 1937
	-102A	1100 hp	25,200 lb.	Mar. 1, 1939
	-G2E	1000 hp	24,000 lb.	Mar. 1, 1939
	-G103A	1000 hp	24,000 lb.	Aug. 1, 1939
	-G202A	1200 hp	25,200 lb.	May 31, 1940

DC-3 Dash No.	Quantity	Customer	Remarks
-178	17	AA (1)	RHD
-194	1	KLM	RHD
-194B	15	KLM	RHD
-194C	3	KLM	RHD
-194E	1	KLM	RHD
-194F	3	KLM	RHD
-194G	1	KLM	RHD
-194H	1	KLM (2)	RHD
-196	1	Russia	RHD
-196A	11	Russia	
-196B	6	Russia	
-201	10	EAL	4 to C-49D (F)
			1 to C-49G (A)
-201A	2	EAL	
-201B	3	EAL	
-201C	3	EAL	
-201D	6	EAL	1 to C-49G (A)
-201E	5	EAL	
-201F	5	EAL	3 to C-49B (F)
-201G	4	EAL	4 to C-49D (A)
-208	4	AA	RHD
-208A	5	AA	RHD
-209	5	TWA	
-209A	4	TWA	
-209B	3	TWA	
-216	2	Swissair	RHD
-220	1	CLS	RHD
-220A	2	CLS	RHD
-220B	1	CLS	
-227	3	Russia	RHD
	2	LARES	RHD
-227A	1	Swissair	
-227B	2	SABENA	
-228	7	PAA	

DC-3 Dash No.	Quantity	Customer	Remarks
-228A	1	PAA	
-228B	1	CNAC (3)	
-229	2	PANAGRA (4)	
-232	2	ANA	
-232A	3	ANA	
-237C	4	Japan	
-260	6	Japan	
-268	1	Swissair	
	1	ABA	
-268B	1	Aer Lingus (Ireland)	
-268C	1	Aer Lingus	
-270	2	CC	RHD
-270A	2	CC	RHD
-270B	3	CC	RHD, 1 to C-49E (F) 2 to C-49H (F)
-270C	1	CC	RHD, to C-51 (F)
-276	1	Swissair	
-277	5	AA	RHD
-277A	2	AA	RHD, 1 to C-49H (F)
-277B	18	AA	RHD, 3 to C-49H (F)
-277C	10	AA	RHD
-277D	6	AA	RHD, 2 to C-49H (F) 4 to C-50 (F)
-279	1	PANAGRA	
-294	1	Air France	
-294A	1	CNAC (via Fokker)	
-313	10	PCA	1 to C-49H (F)
-313A	4	PCA	1 to C-49C (F)
-313B	4	PCA	2 to C-49E 1 to C-50C 1 to C-50D
-313C	1	PCA	To C-49H (F)
-313D	3	PCA	1 to C-49E (F) 1 to C-49F (F)
-314	4	Braniff	3 to C-49H (F)
-314A	4	Braniff	
-314B	3	Braniff	1 to C-49H (F)
-322	4	C&S	RHD
-322A	1	C&S	RHD, to C-49F (F)
-322B	1	C&S	RHD, to C-49D (F)
-357	5	Delta	1 to C-49D (F)
-357A	2	Delta	1 to C-49C (F)
-362	10	TWA	1 to C-49F (F)

226

DC-3 Dash No.	Quantity	Customer	Remarks
-384	5	TWA	All to C-49 (F)
-385	2	Delta	1 to C-49A (F)
-386	2	Delta	Both to C-49C (F)
-388	2	EAL	Both to R4D-2 (F)
-389	5	EAL	All to C-49D (F)
-392	2	PCA	Both to C-50D (F)
-396	4	AA	RHD, all to C-50 (F)
-397	3	Braniff	All to C-50B (F)
-401	2	AA	Both to C-50A (F)
-454	34	Mixed	All to C-49J (F)
-455	23	Mixed	1 to C-49J (F)
			22 to C-49K (F)

Total 357(5)

(1) Identified and advertised as "Flagship."
(2) Not taken by KLM; to UAL then C-48C (A).
(3) 45 percent owned by Pan Am.
(4) 50 percent owned by Pan Am.
(5) Totals for this ATC, including military models drafted from the factory before being received by the airline, are now off by a few due to contradictions between different reference documents and contradictions within the documents themselves, plus the fact that a few taken by the military were not given DC-3 or DC-3A dash numbers by Douglas.

ATC A-619—DC-3A-SB3G (1)

Power and Weight Approvals:

Pratt & Whitney "Twin Wasp" R-1830	-SB3G	1000 hp	24,000 lb.	Nov. 28, 1936
	-SBG	1000 hp	24,000 lb.	Jul. 2, 1937

DC-3A Dash No.	Quantity	Customer	Remarks
-191	10	UAL (2)	RHD, 1 to C-48C (A)
-197	12	UAL (2)	RHD

Total 22

(1) All eligible for operation under ATC A-669 with appropriate engine modifications.
(2) Identified and advertised as "Mainliners."

ATC A-635—DC-3B-G102 (1)

Power and Weight Approvals:

Wright GR-1820	-G102	1100 hp	25,200 lb.	May 3, 1937
	-G202A	1200 hp	25,200 lb.	Mar. 31, 1941

DC-3B Dash No.	Quantity	Customer	Remarks
-202	8	TWA (2)	3 to C-84 (A)
			1 to C-49D (A)
			1 to C-49E (A)
			2 to C-49F (A)
-202A	2	TWA (2)	1 to C-84 (A)
			1 to C-49F (A)
	Total 10		

(1) All eligible for operation under ATC A-618 when converted to dayplanes.
(2) Identified and advertised as "Skysleeper."

ATC A-647—DST-A-SBG (1)

Power and Weight Approvals:

Pratt & Whitney R-1830	-SBG	1000 hp	24,000 lb.	Jun. 30, 1936
	-SB3G	1000 hp	24,000 lb.	Jun. 30, 1936

DST-A Dash No.	Quantity	Customer	Remarks
-207	8	UAL (2)	RHD, 6 to C-48B (A)
			1 to C-48C (A)
	2	WAL (2,3)	RHD, All to C-48B (A)
	Total 10		

(1) All eligible for operation under ATC-671 with appropriate engine modifications.
(2) Identified and advertised as "Mainliners."
(3) WAL was a subsidiary of UAL at this time.

ATC A-669—DC-3A-S1CG (1)

Power and Weight Approvals:
Pratt & Whitney R-1830

Twin Wasp

-S1CG	1200 hp	25,200 lb.	Oct. 31, 1937
-S1C3G	1200 hp	25,200 lb.	May 1, 1939
-SCG	1050 hp	25,200 lb.	May 1, 1939
-SC3G	1050 hp	25,000 lb.	Feb. 9, 1940
-S4CG	1200 hp	25,000 lb.	Feb. 18, 1942

DC-3A Dash No.	*Quantity*	*Customer*	*Remarks*
-191	10	UAL	RHD
-191B (2)	1	UAL	RHD
-197	12	UAL	RHD
-197B	8	UAL	RHD
-197C	5	UAL	RHD
-197D	6	UAL	RHD, One to C-48 (F)
	2	WAL	RHD, One to C-52
-197E	3	UAL	RHD, Two to C-52B (F)
-214	3	ABA	RHD
-228C	10	PAA	
-228D	8	PAA	
-228F	6	PAA	
-237B	5	Japan	RHD
-237D	3	Japan	
-269	6	NWA	
-269A	1	NWA	
-269B	4	NWA	
-269C	2	NWA	One to C-48C (F)
-279A	3	PANAGRA	
-279B	2	PANAGRA	
-313A	2	PCA	
-343	1	WAL	RHD
-343A	1	WAL	RHD
-343B	2	WAL	RHD
-345	1	U.S. Gov't	To PAA with no military desig.
-348	1	FAA	To C-52D then C-48C
-363	1	Swiftflite	To C-48C (F)
-367	3	NEA	Two to "no serial" C-53 (F)
-368	3	UAL	All to C-48A (F)
-375	3	IIA	
-377	1	UAL	To C-48F (F)
-393	1	PANAGRA	To C-52 (F)
-394	1	WAL	To C-52A (F)
-395	2	UAL	To C-52B (F)
-398	1	WAL	To C-52 (F)
-399	1	PANAGRA	RHD

DC-3A Dash No.	Quantity	Customer	Remarks
-402	1	CAL	To C-52C (F)
-408	1	Douglas	To C-53 42-36600
-414	14	Misc.	Seven to C-48C, Two to C-68, One to PANAGRA, four from U.S. Gov't to PAA.
-414A	4	U.S. Gov't	To PAA without military desig.
-438	1	U.S. Gov't	To PAA without military desig.
-453	17	UAL, NWA	All to C-53C, R4D-3 (F)
-447	12	PAA	All to R4D-4 (F)
Total	165		

(1) Includes postwar DC-3C and DC-3D, plus C-53s operating as DC-3A.
(2) Also reported as -191A.

ATC A-671—DST-A-S1CG (1)

Power and Weight Approvals:
Pratt & Whitney R-1830

-S1CG	1200 hp	25,200 lb.	Mar. 26, 1938
-S1C3G	1200 hp	25,200 lb.	May 1, 1939
-SCG	1050 hp	25,200 lb.	May 1, 1939
-S3CG	1050 hp	25,200 lb.	Feb. 9, 1940
-S4C4G	1200 hp	25,200 lb.	Feb. 18, 1942

DST-A Dash No.	Quantity	Customer	Remarks
-207A	2	UAL (2)	RHD, 1 to C-48B (A)
-207B	2	UAL (2)	RHD, all to C-48B (A)
-207C	2	UAL (2)	RHD, all to C-48B (A)
-207D	3	UAL (2)	RHD, 2 to C-48D (A) 1 to C-48C (A)
Total	9		

(1) All eligible for operation under ATC A-671 with appropriate engine modifications.

Appendix D

The American DC-3 Fleet, 1985

This appendix groups the 612 DC-3s on the 1984 U.S. Civil Register (published March 30, 1985) by the 33 separate designations under which they appear. Note the extensive departure from the established practice of identification based on the original ATC designation.

The 102 listed as plain DC-3s comprise a broad mix of original DC-3s, DC-3As, and C-53s, plus C-47s that should properly be identified as DC-3Cs. Some DC-3s and DC-3As appear with their original ATC designations that use civil engine designations, but the DC-3Cs show a variety of engine designations as well as plain DC-3C. In some cases the engine designation that is part of the DC-3 designation reflects the civil designation of the engine, as DC-3C-S4C4G, but in others it uses the military designation, as DC-3A-1830-94 and DC-3C-R-1830-90C.

A really major departure is the use of former military designations instead of the standard civil DC-3 designations. Noteworthy is the fact that some surplus Navy C-117Ds are listed as R4D-8 even though that designation was replaced by C-117D some 15 years before the first C-117Ds became surplus. Some surplus C-117Ds appear as DC-3S while others are identified as "Super DC-3." None of the three turboprop conversions registered in 1985 appears on the register with a turbine designation.

DSTs and DC-3Bs have disappeared from the register as such, and no C-53s appear under that designation.

Designation	Quantity	Designation	Quantity
DC-3	102	DC-3D-R1830-90C	1
DC-3-G102	1	DC-3S	3
DC-3-G102A	5	Super DC-3	4
DC-3-G202A	34	C-47	62

Designation	Quantity	Designation	Quantity
DC-3-R1830-90D	1	C-47A	19
DC-3A	79	C-47B	5
DC-3A-SC3G	2	TX Turbo Jet C-47B (3)	1
DC-3A-S1C3G	20	C-47D	6
DC-3A-S4C4G	10	VC-47D	4
DC-3A-1830-94 (1)	2	C-47H	1
DC-3C	138	C-47J	6
DC-3C-S1C3G	47	R4D-6	1
DC-3C-S4C4G	9	R4D-8	8
DC-3C-R1830-90C	2	C-117A	1
DC-3C-R1830-94	28	C-117B	2
DC-3C-R (2)	1	C-117D	9
		Dakota 4	2

(1) As registered, without the R preceding 1830.
(2) As registered, no engine displacement following R.

(3) Not a turbojet conversion; named for Texas Turbo Jet, Inc., an owner.

Appendix E

Military Colors and Markings for DC-3

The twin subjects of military aircraft colors and markings are enormously complex, and are the subject of many specialized books. Only highlights of those applying to U.S. and British DCs will be covered here. Comments on specific applications will be found in appropriate photo captions throughout this book. Details of serial and "buzz" numbers will be found in Chapters 6, 9, and 14.

Service Designation

Until May 15, 1942, all U.S. Army DCs had **U.S. ARMY** applied to the underside of the wings in 24-inch square figures, **U.S.** beneath the right wing and **ARMY** under the left. The letters were not painted out immediately after May 15, but were deleted when convenient—if at all.

After formation of the U.S. Air Force in September 1947, the legend **U.S. AIR FORCE** and sometimes **UNITED STATES AIR FORCE** was painted above the window line of C-47s and C-117s. By the early 1950s this was standardized for C-47s and C-117s as **U.S. AIR**

FORCE in 12-inch figures centered on the nose. C-47s used by the National Guard and the Air National Guard after September 1947 carried a great variety of organizational applications, some spelling out the name of the state and Air National Guard in full and others using only abbreviations. In early postwar applications, the star insignia was not used on the side of the fuselage. In most cases, the letters **ANG** appeared above the serial number on the fin.

C-47s of the U.S. Army after 1963 were marked very inconsistently, often merely substituting the word **ARMY** for the **AIR FORCE** or **NAVY** on the existing marking of the transferred C-47. Sometimes the word **ARMY** was used along on the fuselage and sometimes in conjunction with the name of the particular Army organization, as **LEXINGTON BLUE GRASS ARMY DEPOT**. By 1969 the service designation was standardized at **U.S. ARMY** under the left wing and above the right wing.

Until the adoption of camouflage, Navy aircraft

carried the words **U.S. NAVY** in large letters on each side of the rear fuselage. With camouflage and past the end of World War II, this was reduced to the single word **NAVY** in one-inch figures on the vertical fin just above the serial number. Some NMF R4Ds enlarged this lettering to three inches. In the late 1940s the **NAVY** lettering, along with the airplane model and serial number, was relocated in small figures to the lower rear fuselage just ahead of the horizontal tail.

In February 1950, the word **NAVY** was removed from beneath the tail and applied to the fuselage and the underside of the left wing. For transports such as the R4D/C-47, the service name **UNITED STATES NAVY** or **UNITED STATES MARINES** was spelled out in full in letters at least 12 inches high above the cabin windows.

NATIONAL MARKINGS

The national insignia for military aircraft, called "star-in-circle" by the U.S. and "roundels" by Britain, varied greatly during the service lives of the DCs. It was possible for some early U.S. Army C-47s that remained in service past January 1947, to have carried *five* different forms of the U.S. star. Britain had similar variations of its own roundels.

U.S. National Markings

Star-in-Circle—The U.S. insignia in use at the time the DCs entered service was a white five-pointed star centered on a blue disc and containing a red center disc (Fig. E-1A). This was applied to the upper and lower surfaces of both wings only until camouflage was adopted for Army and Navy transports early in 1941. It was then applied to both sides of the rear fuselage and the marking was removed from the upper right and lower left wingtips. This application was for camouflaged aircraft only into early 1943. The U.S. Navy reapplied the stars

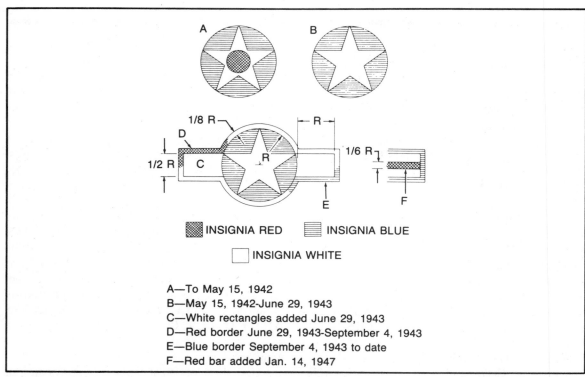

A—To May 15, 1942
B—May 15, 1942-June 29, 1943
C—White rectangles added June 29, 1943
D—Red border June 29, 1943-September 4, 1943
E—Blue border September 4, 1943 to date
F—Red bar added Jan. 14, 1947

Fig. E-1. Progressive changes to U.S. star insignia, 1930s to date.

Fig. E-2. C-47A-45-DL, 42-24119, displays the white rectangles that were added to the U.S. star insignia in June 1943, and the short-lived red border that was replaced by blue in September. (Douglas photo)

to both wings in January 1942, but reverted to the unbalanced form in February 1943, when one star on each wing and one on each side of the fuselage was standardized for all aircraft of both services.

On May 15, 1942, the red center of the star was removed because of its similarity to the Japanese "meatball" (hinomuru) marking (Fig. E-1B). On June 29, 1943, the marking was modified to increase its visibility by adding a white rectangle to each side (Fig. E-1C) and surrounding the whole device with a red border (Fig. E-1D). Since a brief glimpse of red in a combat situation could still be mistaken for a Japanese marking, the red border was changed to blue on September 4, 1943, this basic shape remains in use today* (Fig. E-1E). The final change was made on January 14, 1947, when a red bar was added to the center of each rectangle (Fig. E-1F). It would have made much more sense to restore the red border; a blue border around a blue circle has served only to confuse artists, model builders, and restorers of antique airplanes since its initial application. Since the addition of the bars, the U.S. national marking is generally referred to as "star and bar" instead of "star-in-circle" (Fig. E-2).

The stars for U.S. Army/Air Force and U.S.

Navy DCs remained fairly constant in size and location from WWII to their retirement except for a reduction to 15-inch basic circles in USAF C-47s and other camouflaged types used during the Vietnam war and subsequent years.

Rudder stripes—The standard U.S. Army tail marking from November 1926 to May 18, 1942, was one vertical blue stripe one-third the maximum chord of the rudder, located adjacent to the hinge line, and thirteen alternating horizontal red and white stripes in the style of the American flag (Fig. E-3A). Rudder stripes were deleted from camouflaged Army planes early in 1941 and the stripes were deleted from all Army planes on May 15, 1942.

The Navy had made decreasing use of its own arrangement of three vertical red, white, and blue rudder stripes, with the red at the trailing edge, from the late 1920s. They were entirely gone by 1940, and only the two Marine Corps R2D-1s used them—and then only briefly—but all four Marine R3D-2s were delivered with them.

On January 5, 1942, the U.S. Navy added 13 red and white rudder stripes to camouflaged aircraft only, but without the vertical blue stripe of the Army marking (Fig. E-3B). These stripes were deleted May 15, 1942, along with the red centers of the stars.

British National Markings

As did the U.S., Britain had numerous changes

---

*While the basic form continues, the marking is often applied today in only shades of gray or black for lower visible-light and infrared visibility.

of National markings during WWII and afterward. Only those pertinent to DC-2Ks and "Dakotas" will be covered here.

Roundels—The prewar British Roundels were blue, white, and red concentric circles with the blue on the outside (Fig. E-4A). These were officially called Type A. These were carried on the wings and fuselages of Australian DC-2s while they were in NMF. The Dakotas did not generally carry roundels under their wings during WWII.

When camouflage was adopted by England in 1937, a yellow ring equal in thickness to the others was added to the fuselage roundels, which were called Type A1 (Fig. E-4B). By the time the DC-2Ks and DC-3s were acquired, the roundels on the upper wing had been changed to the proportion shown and identified as Type B (Fig. E-4C), which deleted the white. The Australians, Canadians, and other British possessions with their own air forces followed suit.

On June 24, 1943, British and Commonwealth aircraft operating east of 60 degrees of East Longitude (from the western border of India eastward into the Pacific Ocean beyond New Zealand) adopted new two-color roundels generally in the Type B proportion but with a white center to avoid confusion with the Japanese marking (Fig. E-4D). In some cases, the white was toned down to a light blue-gray to reduce visibility.

In July, 1942, the proportions of the Type A1 and B roundels in use were changed to the Type C and C1 shown in Fig E-4E. These changes also applied to aircraft east of Longitude East 90 until June of 1943. The type B roundel remained on upper wing surfaces but the yellow-ringed Type C1 was used on camouflaged fuselages.

The end of WWII saw a final change of roundel proportion, the Type D shown in Fig. E-4E. This was applied to the fuselage and both surfaces of the wing on Dakotas.

In 1946 Canada replaced the British-style roundels with a uniquely Canadian device featuring a red maple leaf in place of the red center. Australia replaced the red center with a red kangeroo in the early 1950s and New Zealand replaced it with a red Kiwi bird.

Fin Flashes—A marking unique to Britain but later adopted by some other nations is the fin flash, a three-color marking used as a replacement for rudder stripes. When adopted before the retreat

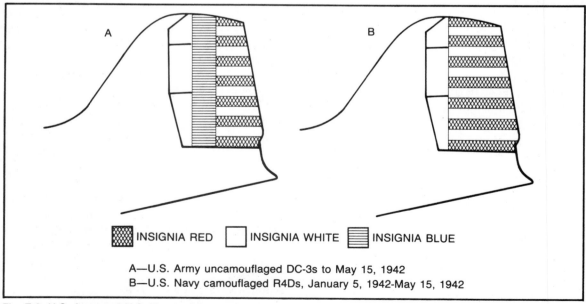

INSIGNIA RED   INSIGNIA WHITE   INSIGNIA BLUE

A—U.S. Army uncamouflaged DC-3s to May 15, 1942
B—U.S. Navy camouflaged R4Ds, January 5, 1942-May 15, 1942

Fig. E-3. U.S. Army and U.S. Navy rudder stripes.

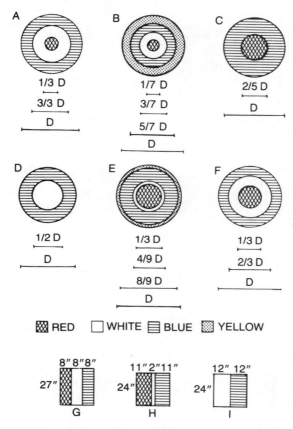

A—Type A roundel used mostly on uncamouflaged aircraft to July, 1942.
B—Yellow ring added to Type A roundel, making Type A1, for camouflaged aircraft, to July, 1942.
C—Upper wing roundel, Type B, on camouflaged aircraft to end of World War II.
D—South East Asia and Pacific Roundel, from June 24, 1943. Size of center varied.
E—New roundel proportions of July, 1942. Type C without border, proportions for bordered Type C1 shown.
F—Postwar-II roundel proportions in use in 1985.
G—Fin flash December 1940-July 1942.
H—Fin flash proportions July 1942 to end of World War II.
I—South East Asia and Pacific fin flash from June 24, 1943, to end of World War II.

Fig. E-4. British roundels and fin flashes.

from France in 1940, the colors covered the entire vertical fin. Proportions were standardized in December 1940 to the size shown in Fig. E-4G, with the red stripe forward. In June 1942, coincidental with the change of roundel proportions, fin flash proportions were changed as shown in Fig. E-4H and remained in use to war's end. Quite a few U.S. Army C-47's in the North African and Normandy invasion used British fin flashes in addition to their standard U.S. markings.

East of 60° Longitude, fin flashes were also modified into equal halves to eliminate the red (Fig. E-4I). After the war, flashes for all British military aircraft reverted to equal widths of red, white, and blue. The RAF retains them to this day, but Canada replaced them with Canadian flags of similar size.

Australia and New Zealand retained standard British postwar fin flashes in spite of their roundel changes.

BASIC COLORING

The overall coloring applied to U.S. and British DCs has also varied greatly over the years, as indicated by photographs throughout this book.

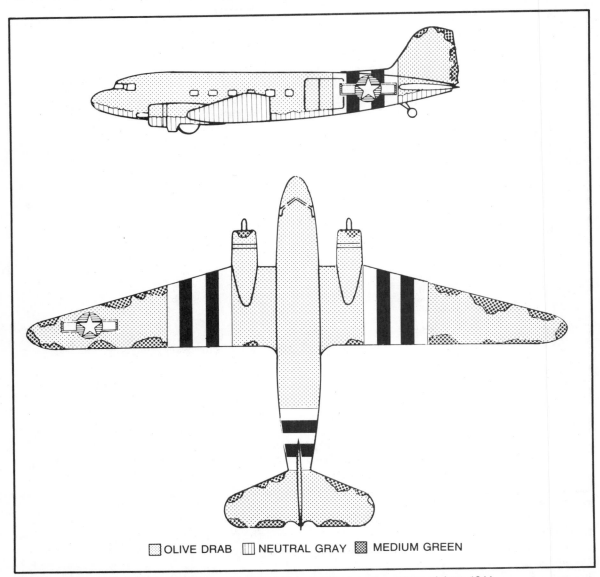

▢ OLIVE DRAB   ▥ NEUTRAL GRAY   ▩ MEDIUM GREEN

Fig. E-5. Standard U.S. Army camouflage with added high-visibility invasion stripes of June 1944.

Fig. E-6. C-47-DL, 41-38576, in non-standard British "sand and spinach" camouflage at Accra, West Africa, in 1942. (courtesy Arthur Pearcy)

U.S. Army/Air Force Coloring

When first adopted, U.S. Army DCs were in natural metal finish (NMF). Aircraft assigned to high-ranking officers were given a high polish. In February 1941, bombers, transports, and other tactical types began to receive the olive drab or gray camouflage already in use by fighters (Fig. E-5).

The OD was specifically identified as Dark Olive Drab, Shade No. 41, and the gray was Neutral Gray, Shade No. 43. Neither color was applied over the black rubber de-icer boots on wing and tail leading edges.

In 1943, the OD camouflage modified for airplanes parked on primarily green terrain. Irregular blotches of Medium Green paint, Shade No. 42, were applied to wing and tail leading and trailing edges to break up the outlines of the airplanes when viewed from above.

This remained standard until late 1943, when Allied air superiority in Europe made camouflage unnecessary. Although from that date on some C-47s and other transports began to be delivered in NMF, most C-47s continued to have camouflage applied at the factory to the end of production. Camouflage was retained on existing C-47s, but was to be removed at major overhaul. Some USAF C-47s retained their now-shabby OD and gray into the late 1940s. During the war, a few C-47s were delivered in special desert camouflage that substituted a tan color called Sand, Shade No. 49, for the OD. This soon faded to a lighter shade that most associated personnel called "pink." Some C-47s carried British "sand and spinach" camouflage instead of the standard Army OD (Fig. E-6). Other temporary

239

Fig. E-7. C-47A-45-DL with black paint applied in the field to undersurfaces and part-way up fuselage sides to reduce visibility during night flights over or near enemy-occupied territory. (Douglas photo)

special coloring was also applied (Fig. E-7).

After World War II natural metal finish became the standard for Army and Navy transport-category aircraft, and wartime camouflage was gone from surviving C-47s by 1950. In the early 1950s USAF and Navy C-47s and R4Ds began to take on the appearance of civil airliners, with bright colors and white fuselage tops. Markings standards for C-47s and C-117s as published by the Air Force are shown in Fig. E-8.

At the time of the Vietnam war—and to date—USAF tactical and strategic aircraft went back into camouflage, with various patterns and colors similar to British WWII practice determined by the theater of operations. The colors for C-47s used in Vietnam are shown in Fig. E-9.

When the U.S. Army operated C-47s from 1963 to 1982, coloring was very inconsistent, often retaining the coloring of the providing organization at the time of transfer. In the 1960s some special

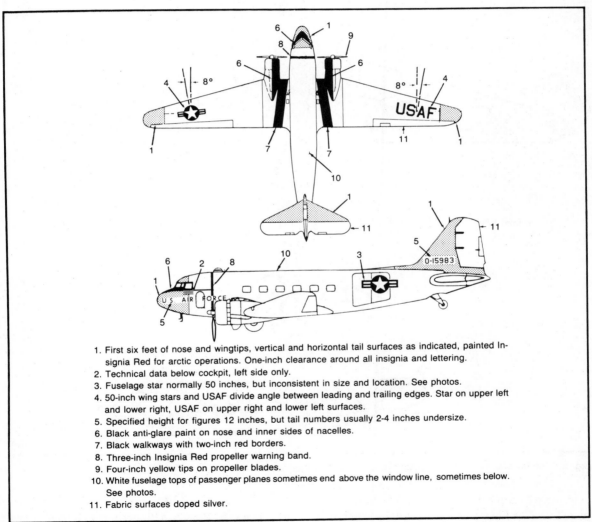

1. First six feet of nose and wingtips, vertical and horizontal tail surfaces as indicated, painted Insignia Red for arctic operations. One-inch clearance around all insignia and lettering.
2. Technical data below cockpit, left side only.
3. Fuselage star normally 50 inches, but inconsistent in size and location. See photos.
4. 50-inch wing stars and USAF divide angle between leading and trailing edges. Star on upper left and lower right, USAF on upper right and lower left surfaces.
5. Specified height for figures 12 inches, but tail numbers usually 2-4 inches undersize.
6. Black anti-glare paint on nose and inner sides of nacelles.
7. Black walkways with two-inch red borders.
8. Three-inch Insignia Red propeller warning band.
9. Four-inch yellow tips on propeller blades.
10. White fuselage tops of passenger planes sometimes end above the window line, sometimes below. See photos.
11. Fabric surfaces doped silver.

Fig. E-8. Markings for natural metal finish C-47s and C-117s as standardized in early 1950s.

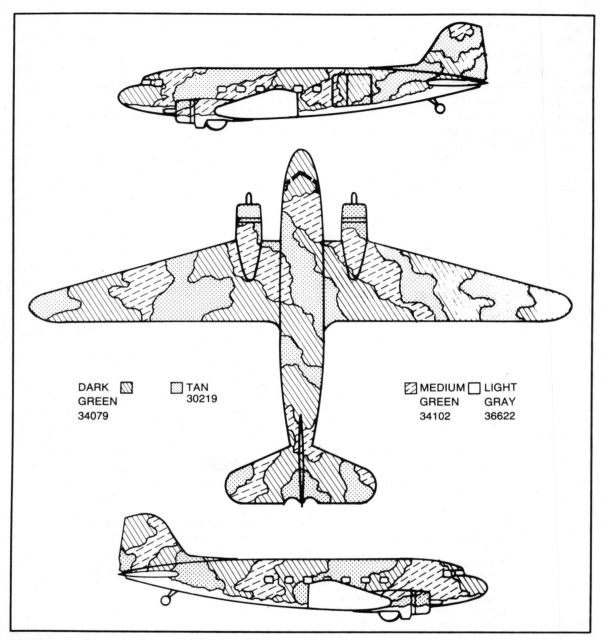

Fig. E-9. Multi-color camouflage applied to C-47s during the Vietnam War.

DARK ⊠
GREEN
34079

□ TAN
30219

⊠ MEDIUM □ LIGHT
GREEN   GRAY
34102   36622

coloring was applied, notably overall white with orange trim (see Figs. 13-5 and 14-20). By 1969 Army coloring for C-47s was standardized at dark glossy brown and white as shown in Fig. E-10.

U.S. Navy Coloring

The U.S. Navy had different camouflage colors than the Army upon adoption in February 1941. By the time the first R4D-1s were delivered in

Fig. E-10. U.S. Army C-47J (ex-Navy 50761) displaying the brown and white coloring standardized in 1968. Upper side of wing is painted as the lower except for U.S. ARMY applied to right wing. Note use of additional antennae and modified cockpit windows. (photo by Robert Esposito)

Fig. E-11. One of the original 66 R4D-1s delivered early in 1942 with contemporary Navy blue-gray camouflage. Note return of the star to upper right wing from January 1942 to February 1943. (USAF photo)

243

February 1942, top and side coloring was a non-specular (dull finish) blue-gray that actually appeared to be a green-gray (Fig. E-11). Undersides were non-specular light gray, with the line of separation as on Army aircraft. However, most Navy R4Ds, being transfers from Army contracts, were delivered in Army colors. A very few that went through Navy overhaul depots after 1943 received the later Navy coloring of dark sea-blue upper surfaces graduated through lighter shades down the sides to white undersides (Fig. E-12).

All Navy R4Ds abandoned camouflage after WWII and some were in service with NMF before V-J Day. Navy R4Ds (by then C-47s and C-117Ds) did not readopt camouflage during the Vietnamese war.

U.S. Special-Purpose Coloring

It became common practice by both the U.S. Army and Navy to apply nonstandard coloring to their C-47s and R4Ds for special purpose. In some cases, this resulted in high-visibility coloring added to major portions of camouflaged airplanes.

Arctic Markings—One of the earliest applied to Army C47s was solid insignia red for upper and lower wing surfaces from the inner end of the ailerons to the wingtip and to the entire tail to a point ahead of the leading edge of the stabilizer (Fig. E-13). From the late 1940s this was reduced to cover only the nose, the outer six feet of the wing (not including ailerons), and the vertical fin and horizontal stabilizer of C-47s.

For Arctic and Antarctic operations, the Navy applied International Orange to the noses, tails, and outer portions of the upper wing surface for increased visibility against snow. Some of the R4Ds used in the initial postwar-II Navy Antarctic were painted overall chrome yellow or International Orange.

Air-Sea Rescue—Rescue markings were used jointly by the Army/Air Force, the Navy, and the U.S. Coast Guard. Details varied over the years, but the basic marking, adopted in 1945, and applied over camouflage or NMF, was the outer six feet of the wings painted chrome yellow and set off by a six-inch black band, and a three-foot yellow band with six-inch black borders around the fuselage just ahead of the tail. On some Army/AF C-47s, the upper surface of the center section was also painted yellow and the color was carried over the top of the adjacent portion of the fuselage.

Fuselage Tops—In the 1950s, both Air Force and Navy C-47s and R4Ds began to adopt the airline practice of painting the top of the fuselage above the windows white to reduce solar heating of the cabin (Fig. E-14). In an opposite move, the Navy painted the upper fuselage of some R4Ds, C-47s, and C-117Ds dark gray, like the camouflage of contemporary patrol planes, to *increase* solar heating of the cabin for Arctic/Antarctic operations.

In the mid-1950s, both the Air Force and the Navy sought to reduce the hazard of mid-air colli-

Fig. E-12. This paratrooper displays a rare application of standard 1943-44 Navy blue-and-white camouflage to an R4D, most of which were delivered in Army OD and gray. (Douglas photo)

Fig. E-13. A C-47A in early postwar-II Arctic markings—insignia red from wingtips to the inner ends of the ailerons and red for entire tail and fuselage aft of the leading edge of the stabilizer. (photo by Logan Coombs)

sion by adding large areas of high-visibility fluorescent "Day-Glo" orange to many non-camouflaged aircraft. For C-47's and R4D's, this was mostly in the form of solid color on the nose to the rear of the cockpit windows, and a six-foot band around the rear fuselage. However, the requirement was not rigid, and some applications were imaginatively adapted to the lines of the airplane much in the manner of civil airliners (Fig. E-15).

The fluorescent coloring was carried for several years but was gradually abandoned because rapid fading and the difficulty to touching up the color made the aircraft unsightly. The "Day-Glo" was replaced by more conventional red-orange in the 1960's and the entire idea was abandoned by 1970.

BRITISH COLORING

Except for Australia's NMF DC-2s, all Com-monwealth DCs were camouflaged upon entering service. The scheme used by various commands differed, in addition to which changes were made from time to time. The variations are too numerous to list here except to say that top and sides were in various patterns of green, gray, earth, and sand, with the undersides a uniform light gray. While some British Dakotas got specific British camouflage schemes in British depots, most were received and operated in U.S. Army OD and gray. Camouflage for Dakotas was abandoned right after WWII.

INVASION MARKINGS

For the North African invasion of November 1942, a broad yellow outline was added to the fuselage stars and sometimes the wing stars of participating U.S. Army and Navy aircraft (Fig. E-16). This was a tactical marking, not a national mark-

Fig. E-14. A C-117C with white-top fuselage and fin photographed in 1955. Stripes around windows, actually projections of the blue border and red bars of the insignia, give a very "airline" appearance. The black under the rear fuselage is anti-corrosion paint to protect the fuselage from discharges from the lavatory. (photo by William T. Larkins)

245

Fig. E-15. A C-47A-90-DL with ingenious application of the required fluorescent "Day-Glo" orange to nose and rear fuselage. In this 1962 photo the U.S. AIR FORCE lettering has been returned to its late 1940's position above the cabin windows. (Photo by Victor D. Seely)

ing change, and remained in declining use until July 1943, when the white rectangles were added.

For the June 6, 1944 invasion of Normandy, all tactical aircraft of the Allied Expeditionary Air Forces (AEAF) were given a unique high-visibility marking that could be distinguished at far greater distances than the various national markings. This consisted of three equal-width bands of white paint and two of black circling the rear fuselage, with similar bands chordwise on both surfaces of the wing. On C-47s and Dakotas, the fuselage bands were 24 inches wide with the rear edge at the leading edge of the horizontal stabilizer; on the wings they were also 24 inches wide, starting at the inner end of the outer wing panels and extending partway onto the inner ends of the ailerons. Some

Fig. E-16. Yellow rings were added to the star marking for the North African invasion of November, 1942. This specially equipped C-47-DL, 41-18527, retained its yellow rings through the invasion of Sicily in July, 1943. Note the British fin flash below the tail serial number. (Photo by Howard Levy)

C-47s and Dakotas carried the stripes right over the rubber de-icer boots on the leading of the wing while others did not.

For subsequent assaults in Europe, notably Southern France and Holland, the upper halves of the fuselage bands and the upper wing bands were painted over, leaving only the bottom marking. By the time of the Rhine crossing in 1945, few C-47s or Dakotas still had underside striping.

An interesting oddity of C-47s painted today with the invasion markings for display purposes is the meticulous care taken in laying out, masking, and painting the stripes. In preparation for the invasion, these were applied hurriedly by hand and the edges were far from being perfect straight lines.

SILVER FABRIC

In spite of any special coloring applied, most uncamouflaged C-47s and R4Ds in postwar service had their fabric-covered movable control surfaces doped silver. The reason for this was that silver faded the least, and did not need touching-up to maintain aircraft appearance. Adding even small amounts of paint to the movable surfaces of high-performance aircraft could throw those surfaces out of balance and induce high-speed flutter problems. This was certainly not a problem for DC-3s, but the use of silver dope was a reflection of prevailing military requirements applying to all aircraft with fabric-covered surfaces.

Appendix F

U.S. Army
Serial Numbers for DC-2 and DC-3

To enable readers to identify any U.S. Army or Air Force DC-2 or DC-3 when the serial number is known, this appendix presents all of the U.S. Army serial numbers assigned in sequence of issue. It should be emphasized that the "tail number" appearing prominently in most photographs does not match the actual serial number. The full serial 41-7708 for a C-53 appears on the tail only as 17708, the first digit of the Fiscal Year being dropped, along with the dash. After 1953, the prefix 0- was added to the tail number to identify airframes over 10 years old and avoid duplication of a 1951 serial number that would also appear as 17708.

Accurate identification from tail numbers is sometimes complicated by the fact that on occasion only the last five digits of the serial appeared on the tail. The revised tail number application on camouflaged aircraft of the Vietnam War period and subsequent also used only five digits.

Serial No.	Airplane	Quantity	
36-1	XC-32	1	
36-70/87	C-33	18	(1)
36-345, 346	YC-34	2	
38-497/501	C-39	3	
38-502	C-41	1	
38-503/535	C-39	33	(2)
40-70	C-41A	1	
41-7681	C-48	1	
41-7682/7684	C-48A	3	
41-7685/7689	C-49	5	
41-7690	C-49A	1	

Serial No.	Airplane	Quantity	
41-7691/7693	C-49B	3	
41-7694	C-49	1	
41-7695	C-50C	1	
41-7696	C-50D	1	
41-7697/7700	C-50	4	
41-7701	C-52C	1	
41-7702	C-51	1	
41-7703/7705	C-50B	3	
41-7706, 7707	C-52B	2	
41-7708	C-52	1	

(1) 36-70 to C-38
(2) 38-503, 513, 528 to C-42.

Serial No.	Airplane	Quantity	
41-7709	C-50D	1	
41-7710, 7711	C-50A	2	
41-7712, 7713	C-50D	2	
41-7714	C-52A	1	
41-7715	C-49C	1	
41-7716/7720	C-49D	5	
41-7721	C-49C	1	
41-7722/7866	C-47-DL	145	
41-18337/18699	C-47-DL	363	(3)
41-19463/19499	C-47-DL	37	
41-20045, 20046	C-53	1	
41-20047/20050	C-53B	4	
41-20051	C-53	1	
41-20052	C-53B	1	
41-20053/20056	C-53	4	
41-20057/20059	C-53B	3	
41-20060/20136	C-53	33	
42-5635/5704	C-47-DL	70	(4)
42-6455/6504	C-53	50	(5)
42-6505	C-52D		(6)
42-14297, 14298	C-68	2	
42-15870/15894	C-53	25	
42-23300/23346	C-47A-1-DL	47	
42-23347/23355	C-47A-5-DL	9	
42-23356/23379	C-47A-10-DL	24	
42-23380/23412	C-47A-15-DL	33	

(3) 41-18496 to XCG-17
(4) 42-5761 to XC-47C
(5) 42-6480 to XC-53A
(6) To C-48C 42-38260

Serial No.	Airplane	Quantity
42-23413/23537	C-47A-20-DL	125

Serial No.	Airplane	Quantity
42-23538/23580	C-47A-25-DL	43
42-23581/23787	C-47A-30-DL	207
42-23788/23962	C-47A-35-DL	175
42-23963/24085	C-47A-40-DL	123
42-24086/24137	C-47A-45-DL	52
42-24138/24321	C-47A-50-DL	184
42-24322/24337	C-47A-55-DL	16
42-24338/24419	C-47A-60-DL	82
42-32786/32923	C-47-DL	138
42-32924/32935	C-47A-DL	12
42-38250, 38251	C-49H	2
42-38252	C-49G	1
42-38253, 38254	C-49H	2
42-38255	C-49G	1
42-38256	C-49D	1
42-38257	C-49H	1
42-38258/38260	C-48C	3 (7)
42-38324/38326	C-48B	3
42-38327	C-48C	1
42-38328/38331	C-49H	4
42-38332/38338	C-48C	7
42-43619/43623	C-49E	5
42-43624	C-49D	1
42-56089/56091	C-48B	3
42-56092/56097	C-49E	6

(7) 42-38260 originally C-52D 42-6505

42-56098/56012	C-48B	5
42-56013/56017	C-49E	5
42-56609/56612	C-48B	4
42-56613	C-49F	1
42-56614, 56615	C-49G	2
42-56616	C-49F	1
42-56617, 56618	C-49E	2
42-56620, 56621	C-49F	2
42-56623	C-49F	1
42-56625/56627	C-49E	3
42-56628	C-49F	1
42-56629	C-48B	1
42-56630/56632	C-49G	3
42-56633	C-49F	1
42-56634	C-49E	1
42-56635	C-49G	1
42-56636, 56637	C-49F	2
42-57154/57156	C-32A	3

Serial No.	Airplane	Quantity	
42-57157	C-84	1	
42-57227, 57228	C-32A	2	
42-57506	C-49H	1	
42-57511/57513	C-84	3	
42-58071/58073	C-32A	3	
42-61095, 61096	C-32A	2	
42-65577/65579	C-32A	3	
42-65580/65582	C-49H	3	
42-65583, 65584	C-49D	2	
42-68687/68689	C-49H	3	
42-68693/68851	C-53D	159	
42-68857, 68858	C-32A	2	
42-68860	C-49D	1	
42-70863	C-32A	1	
42-92024/92091	C-47A-DK	68	
42-92092/92415	C-47A-1-DK	324	
42-92416/92572	C-47A-5-DK	157	
42-92573/92743	C-47A-10-DK	171	(8)
42-92744/92923	C-47A-15-DK	180	
42-92924/93283	C-47A-20-DK	361	(9)
42-93284/93823	C-47A-25-DK	540	
42-100436/100635	C-47A-65-DL	200	
42-100636/100835	C-47A-70-DL	200	
42-100836/101035	C-47A-75-DL	200	
42-107422	C-49H	1	
42-108794/108800	C-47A-DK	7	
42-108801/108836	C-47A-1-DK	36	
42-108837/108854	C-47A-5-DK	18	
42-108855/108873	C-47A-10-DK	19	(10)
42-108874/108893	C-47A-15-DK	20	
42-108894/108933	C-47A-20-DK	40	
42-108934/108993	C-47A-25-DK	60	

(8) 42-92577 to C-47C-10-DK
(9) 42-93159 to C-47B-DK
(10) 42-108868 to C-47C-10-DK

Serial No.	Airplane	Quantity
43-1961/1994	C-49J	34
43-1995/2017	C-49K	23
43-2018/2034	C-53C	17
43-15033/15432	C-47A-80-DL	400
43-15433/15632	C-47A-85-DL	200
43-15633/16132	C-47A-90-DL	500
43-16133/16432	C-47B-1-DL	300
43-30628/30639	C-47-DL	12
43-30640/30761	C-47A-DL	122

Serial No.	Airplane	Quantity	
43-47963/48262	C-47A-30-DK	300	
43-48263/48562	C-47B-1-DK	300	(11)
43-48563/48912	C-47B-5-DK	350	(12)
43-48913/49262	C-47B-10-DK	350	(13)
43-49263/49612	C-47B-15-DK	350	(14)

(11) 43-48379, 48506 to B-2
(12) Four to B-6, three to B-7, one to B-8, five to B-9
(13) 24 to B-11, eight to B-13, one to B-14
(14) 13 to B-16, six to B-18, four to TC-47B-15

Serial No.	Airplane	Quantity	
43-49613/49962	C-47B-20-DK	350	(15)
44-52990, 52991	C-48C	2	
44-52999	C-49D	1	
44-76195/76524	C-47B-25-DK	320	(16)
44-76525/76854	C-47B-30-DK	330	(17)
44-76855/77184	C-47B-35-DK	330	(18)
44-77185/77294	C-47B-40-DK	110	
44-83226, 83227	C-32A	2	
44-83228, 83229	C-49H	2	
45-876/1055	C-47B-45-DK	180	
45-1056/1139	C-47B-50-DK	84	
45-2545/2561	C-117A-1-DK	17	(19)
49-2612/2641	C-47-DL	30	(20)
51-3817	YC-47F-DO	1	
66-8836	C-47H	1	(21)

(15) 17 to B-23, 12 to TC-47B-20
(16) Seven to B-27, 16 to B-28, 39 to TC-47B-25
(17) 51 to TC-47B-30
(18) 23 to TC-47B-35
(19) 45-2549 to C-117A-5

(20) Former C-47 and C-47A refurbished for MDAP transfer to Greece.
(21) Civil-registered DC-3 from U.S. Department of Immigration and Naturalization.

Appendix G

U.S. Navy

Serial Numbers for DC-2 and DC-3

This appendix presents all of the U.S. Navy serial numbers (BuNos) assigned to DC-2 and DC-3 aircraft in sequence of assignment in three separate Navy serial number series. See Chapter 14 for designation changes of 1962.

1st Series

Serial No.	Aircraft	Quantity	
9620/9622	R2D-1	3	
9993, 9994	R2D-1	2	

2nd Series

3131/3143	R4D-1	13	(1)
4692/4706	R4D-1	15	(1)
4707, 4708	R4D-2	2	

3rd Series

01648, 01649	R4D-1	2	(1)
01977/01990	R4D-1	14	(1)

Serial No.	Aircraft	Quantity	
05051/05072	R4D-1	22	(1)
05073/05084	R4D-3	12	
06992/06999	R4D-3	8	
07000/07003	R4D-4	4	
12393/12404	R4D-1	12	
12405/12446	R4D-5	42	
17092/17248	R4D-5	157	
17249/17291	R4D-6	43	
30147	R4D-1	1	
33615/33621	R4D-4R	7	
33815/33820	R4D-4	6	
37660/37680	R4D-1	21	
39057/39095	R4D-5	39	
39096/39098	R4D-6	3	
39099	R4D-7	1	
39100	R4D-6	1	
39101/39108	R4D-7	8	
39109	R4D-6	1	
39110/39136	R4D-7	27	
50740/50839	R4D-6	100	
91104	R4D-1	1	(2)
99824/99857	R4D-7	34	
99099	DC-3A	1	(3)
150187/150190	R4D-6	4	(4)

(1) These are the only R4D's built on U.S. Navy contracts.
(2) Ex-RAF FD797.
(3) Operated under civil designation as with some other civil acquisitions.
(4) From USAF in 1961.

Index